The Brothers and Sisters Learn to Write

POPULAR LITERACIES IN CHILDHOOD AND SCHOOL CULTURES

Anne Haas Dyson

TEACHERS
COLLEGE
PRESS

Teachers College, Columbia University
New York and London

For David George Haas, my brother,
and all who bring music and art to children

Published by Teachers College Press, 1234 Amsterdam Avenue, New York, NY 10027

Library of Congress Cataloging-in-Publication Data

Dyson, Anne Haas.
    The brothers and sisters learn to write : popular literacies in childhood and school cultures / Anne Haas Dyson.
      p.   cm. — (Language and literacy series)
    Includes bibliographical references and index.
    ISBN 0-8077-4281-3 (cloth : alk. paper) — ISBN 0-8077-4280-5 (pbk. : alk. paper)
    1. Children—Language. 2. Educational sociology—United States. 3. Popular culture—United States. 4. Semiotics. 5. Literacy. I. Title. II. Language and literacy series (New York, N.Y.)

LB1139.L3 D97   2003
302.2'244—dc21   2002073565

ISBN 0-8077-4280-5 (paper)
ISBN 0-8077-4281-3 (cloth)

Printed on acid-free paper
Manufactured in the United States of America

10   09   08   07   06   05   04   03   8   7   6   5   4   3   2   1

LANGUAGE AND LITERACY SERIES

Dorothy S. Strickland and Celia Genishi, SERIES EDITORS

ADVISORY BOARD: RICHARD ALLINGTON, DONNA ALVERMANN, KATHRYN AU,
EDWARD CHITTENDEN, BERNICE CULLINAN, COLETTE DAIUTE, ANNE HAAS DYSON,
CAROLE EDELSKY, JANET EMIG, SHIRLEY BRICE HEATH, CONNIE JUEL, SUSAN LYTLE

(Continued)

Contents

Acknowledgments

"Wow. I can't believe I did all this in the first grade." Fifth-grader Wenona*
and I sat together in a corner of the school cafeteria, a full hour before the
children would begin jogging, dancing, and dragging in for lunch. As the
kitchen crew bustled in the background, we looked over a file folder filled
with samples of her first-grade writing. Wenona was taken aback by the
sheer volume of her effort. "WOO-ee" is a good summary of her response.

More than a few months have passed. I am sitting in my apartment,
contemplating my "book" file. Woo-ee. Wenona and her close friends, the
self-named "brothers and sisters," drew on all manner of textual and media
material as they played and worked together in the first grade. Somehow
I have managed to untangle those threads and, then, reweave them into
my own account of their adventures in school literacy.

In truth, of course, *I* did not manage to do anything. Here I name some
of the people who helped. To begin (literally), Carol Tateshi of the Bay
Area Writing Project sent me to Rita, the classroom teacher under whose
masterful guidance the brothers and sisters flourished. Those good-hearted
children allowed me to sit beside them and, in Wenona's words, to "speak
to [them] when you—ever you need to." I needed to quite a lot. The
children's parents graciously granted me permission to observe their children and even allowed me precious evening hours for talk about their
children and the project.

In the classroom and out, I was assisted in all aspects of this study by
Soyoung Lee, a superb doctoral student at UC-Berkeley. Soyoung trekked
to the school to photocopy children's work, traveled virtual and actual
highways to track down the sources of lyric fragments, football jersey
numbers, and oddly drawn creatures. She arranged interviews, formatted
tables, and edited chapter draft after chapter draft. Soyoung and I were
assisted at varied times by yet another hardworking media detective, Sheila
Shea. Both Sheila and Soyoung were helped by many kind souls at media
establishments in the Bay Area. Among them were Glorius, receptionist

---

*All children's names are pseudonyms.

at a local radio station, Jaun Bauza and Kara Foster, of Tower Records, Anne Trinca, of Yerba Buena Center for the Arts, and MC (Kevin) Flow.

Our gracious professional media experts, featured in Chapter 8, are provided the security of pseudonyms and buckets of gratitude. Much appreciation as well goes to Yongsik Moon for assorted technical support and good humor. And although we do not know her, we often sing our praises to Leonie, creator of Leonie's Lyrics web site.

The project would not have happened without the support of the Spencer Foundation and the UC-Berkeley Committee on Research. The findings and opinions expressed herein are, of course, my sole responsibility.

As always, I want to thank my most dependable guides and supporters, my family and, as Wenona would say, my fake sister Celia Genishi. An extra nod to my sister Ruthie, for kindly taping movies for me, and a textual hug to those media-savvy people—my sister Mary's and Bill's kids, Evan, Megan, and Liz (who wanted me to put her name in this book).

Prologue

DENISE: See, we like rap-ping, and like, singing songs . . . See, we in a club, kind of like.

VANESSA: See, if you know how to do a bounce, you can get in. But if you don't . . . you can't get in. Cause see, it's called, The Bouncy Club. . . . All we play is Brandy [singer], TLC [singing group], um, a whole lot of stuff. . . . Teenagers.

DENISE: Teen age ers.

. . .

VANESSA: It don't be no rock and roll. (Two 6-year-olds playing way cool teenagers)

One of my favorite *New Yorker* covers shows an auditorium littered with childhood stuff. Slouching over chairs, rollicking down aisles, and slipping off steps are the polka dots, stripes, and primary-colored solids of children's abandoned apparel. The owners of this motley mess are bunched together near the stage door, where a stately woman in glasses whispers, "Shhh!" Between the curtains, in perfect linear order, little pink tutus emerge as tidied up children travel on their tippy toes across the stage, itself an idyllic pastoral scene. The meaning of this illustration lies in its juxtaposition of childhood liveliness and framed linear order. In that juxtaposition inhere the grand theoretical issues and the intense political conversations that undergird the child dramas of this book.

The book is, at its core, about childhood literacy development, a topic now dominating political as well as pedagogical discussions. These discussions usually have little to do with the complex gestalts of contemporary childhoods. Rather, in their most positive form, they build on an uplifting tale of progress: Orderly children progress smoothly from a book-filled childhood, to sold-out achievement test performances, to eventual stately marches across graduation stages. The children's unidirectional march is undeterred by the distractions of the popular media and buoyed by the applause of a grateful nation, its faith in the future secured.

1

But I am not interested in romanticized children proceeding through staged performances. I have some bouncy ones to contend with herein. To be sure, these children (especially Denise and Vanessa) might have been more than eager to experience the possibilities of ballet. But, like children the world over, they appropriated available symbolic, textual, and cultural resources to fashion a childhood. The dialogue about the dance club that opens this prologue was partially woven from the textual threads of *Soul Train* (Cornelius, 1970), a television show that Denise and Vanessa had watched the night before, and of *The Night I Followed the Dog* (Laden, 1994), a classroom library book they had just reread about a night club for dogs.

In this book's portrayal of literacy development, I do not leave the tangled threads of children's textual lives out of my viewing frame. Rather, I concentrate on children's cultural productions on and just off stage in their urban primary school. I pose the basic developmental question about the nature of change over time in children's written language use, but I do so against the fabric of a particular childhood. Denise and her friends wove that fabric from textual threads they gathered from media forms of many kinds, among them television, videos, and that common traveling companion, the radio. What do the textual processes and practices through which children construct a childhood have to do with school literacy learning? Or, to rephrase that question, through what means do young children, contemporary kids in media-saturated times, appropriate written language into an already richly productive repertoire?

Herein, the answer is presented in child dramas, whose energizing mechanism seems more akin to hip-hop sampling than stately marches or tippy-toe promenades. The featured children stretch, reorganize, and rearticulate their textual resources (and appropriate new ones) on their travels into school literacy. The key to successful journeys is not a particular kind of childhood but particularized childhood qualities—an openness to appealing symbols, and a tendency to flexibly and, often, playfully, adapt resources to changing conditions.

Another image comes to mind, this one from a favorite movie, *The Buena Vista Social Club* (Cooder & Wenders, 1999), about elders with young hearts—still living but heretofore forgotten musical masters of Cuban orchestral and dance music. In one scene, little girls in leotards leap, pirouette, and do deep knee bends as the fingers of pianist Ruben Gonzales dance on the keys. The children seem both disciplined and joyful, as they experience some of the aesthetic possibilities of the body's musical movement. Soon, the small dancers are crowded around the piano, doing knee bends to Gonzales's beat. The children are in synch, grinning and bending. Then a syncopated bounce pops up in the music. In response, the children's hips cannot resist swaying. Their knees straighten, but their elbows bend and bounce with the beat.

There is pleasure and power in learning to craft movement, sound, and, yes, written words. But it's the breadth of the symbolic repertoire, the sense of competent agency, and the social sophistication to shift one's actions to suit local conditions, that allow children to become full participants in their presents and in their travels into their futures. And so, now that I have woven my own textual threads from audiotapes, pictures, and film, threads invoking the possibilities of rap, ballet, and Latin dance music, it is time to formally introduce the project in which I met the bouncy textual weavers featured herein: Denise, Vanessa, and their close friends, who called themselves "the brothers and the sisters."

1

School Literacy: The View from Inside a Child Culture

DENISE: Hey Vanessa!
VANESSA: Yeah?
DENISE: Are you ready?
VANESSA: For what?
DENISE: To jig!
VANESSA: Jig what?
DENISE: a low!
VANESSA: Well my hands up high, my feet down low, and this the way I jig-a-low.
DENISE: Her hands up high, her feet down low, and this the way she jig-a-low.

Vanessa and Denise, the two bouncy 6-year-olds mentioned in the Prologue, had their ears wide open to the voice-filled landscape of their everyday lives. And within that landscape, they found textual toys—symbolic materials useful for play—in the words of radio deejays and singing stars, TV advertisers and movie characters, churchgoers, teachers, "teen-age-ers," and, even, other kids (who were the source of that jig-a-low "stomping game").

Although the particularities of childhoods vary across historical time and cultural space, children all over the globe, like Denise and Vanessa, borrow voices from close-at-hand people, and also from close-at-hand technology, including television, videos, and radios. They build local child cultures by appropriating—by taking over for their own purposes—textual material from any available cultural repositories (Dyson, 1993, 1997; Stephens, 1995; Whiting & Whiting, 1975). In this "scaveng[ing] of form and theme," young children, as well as older youth (Goldman, 1998, p. 143; Willis, 1990), include in their cultural material longstanding childhood traditions as well as the more ephemeral content and genres of popular media. Through an eclectic mix of appealing symbolic stuff, children produce their cultural practices and, thereby, their friendships, expressive practices, and imaginative worlds (Dyson, 1993, 1997; Marsh, 1999; Sutton-Smith, Mechling, Johnson, & McMahon, 1995).

In this book, I feature a local version of this global phenomenon at the turn of the 21st century: the childhood symbols and practices of Denise, Vanessa, and a small circle of friends. Careful observation of the children in action reveals textual threads that lead back to their social lives as family members, church goers, friends, students and, more particularly, as sports fans, radio listeners, and video watchers—as active participants in the popular forms of symbol use (in the popular literacies) of their daily lives.

But I have more in mind here than portraying the cultural sources of the children's playful practices. Denise and her friends were constructing their shared childhoods in school. And schools have their own agendas for little children, which involve learning written language. What could all this childhood stuff—the chanting, stomping, and bouncing, the interest in radio stars, teenagers, and (soon-to-appear) football players and animated gorillas—possibly have to do with educational standards and literacy learning?

Educational research, and literacy research in particular, tends to look outward at children's lives from inside the world of official school practices (Clay, 1998). From this vantage point, educators are allowed only a narrow window through which to peer. Thus, children's cultural worlds as children—and the breadth of their textual experience, the depth of their social and symbolic adaptability—disappear. The spotlight rests on those experiences and resources that reflect back comfortable, tidy images of children on the literacy path (e.g., experiences with books, knowledge of letter sounds). Learning to manipulate written symbols thus becomes a fragile gift for the textually tidy and a reward for proper childhoods—those centered around school-valued practices (Snow, Burns, & Griffin, 1998).

Herein, I hope to turn this view inside out, as I look from inside a particular child culture out toward school demands. In this way, I aim to provide conceptual substance for a different theoretical view of written language development, one that normalizes variations in (as well as broadens conceptions of) children's literacy resources and learning pathways. In this view, it is not the presence of singular bits of written language experiences that are developmentally critical (as valuable as those experiences may be) but the complex gestalts of children's cultural resources. Those resources evidence children's powers of adaptation and improvisation; and it is children's exploitation of these cross-cultural childhood strengths (Stephens, 1995; Sutton-Smith, 1997) and their ways of stretching, reconfiguring, and rearticulating their resources, that are key to literacy learning in contemporary times.

This view does not in any way diminish the importance of the official school curriculum, but it does disrupt an imagined singular developmental path to school success. Into children's symbolic repertoires of sounds and images come the school's officially sponsored written texts and required writing times. Since written texts figure differently into children's social and cultural lives outside of school (e.g., Heath, 1983; Purcell-Gates, 1995; Walker-Moffat, 1995), as do varied kinds of media texts (e.g., radio songs, playground rhymes, film stories, televised sports reports [Dyson, 1997]), children have varied textual landscapes against which to interpret the school's efforts to teach them written language. And against their existent landscapes, children orchestrate their resources to try to make sense of, and through, this newly foregrounded medium.

The sort of developmental vision I aim for seems captured in the comments of Bess Hawes, a colleague of the late folk artist Bessie Jones. As Hawes documented, Jones led workshops for contemporary Californians on the play songs of her childhood at the turn of the last century in a southern Black rural community. In the workshops, Jones and her colleagues, members of the Georgia Sea Island Singers—most of them middle-aged or older, would move, clap, and sing "the vitality of childhood traditions" (Jones & Hawes, 1972, p. xvi). In so doing, these grown-ups embodied

> the principle of antiphony: the constant and continuous interplay of fantasy and reality. . . . They answer each other—the child and the grownup, the hands and the feet, the group voice and the solo voice, the words and the action, the dream world and the real world, in a continual and mutually supportive conversation. . . . And it is out of this mixture, the interweaving of the solid and day-to-day and the fantastic and poetic that the meaning, so important to Mrs. Jones, emerges. (p. 190)

This is how meaning will be constructed herein as well. Denise and her friends used the symbolic stuff of their everyday lives to compose "the fantastic and poetic" texts that regulated their lives together. Rita, their teacher, offered the children access to written language as a symbolic medium used in varied ways. In response, children drew from their everyday textual materials and familiar forms of agency—of engaging in meaningful action—to construct a functional understanding of the written medium for their lives as children *and* as students. In this book, I follow the textual threads as the children weave their resources, and thus themselves, around and then into the very fabric of classroom literacy practices.

These are my aims, then: to document the nature of a shared childhood and the textual toys it entailed; to use the vantage point of that childhood to articulate a developmental vision that moves beyond the textually tidy developmental path. This is no easy task, since that linearity has persisted even as theoretical explanations for literacy development have multiplied (Dyson, 1999). There is the linearity of behavioristic lists of singular skills, of developmental "stages" predicting carefully sequenced behaviors, and even of apprenticeship models tracing singular textual practices (e.g., "story writing," "science reporting"), inattentive to children's complex juxtapositions, blends, and differentiations of practices from an array of sources. Thus, before proceeding, I am going to summon the children to help me clarify my intentions.

Below, I briefly slip into the children's world, just as I did in 1996 when this project formally began. Then, I use the remainder of this introductory chapter, first, to explain the project's guiding concepts; second, to describe the basics of its methodology (including its site); and finally, to orient readers to the flow—or perhaps, the bounce—of chapters to come.

SLIPPING INTO A CHILD CULTURE

When I first visited Rita's first-grade classroom in the East San Francisco Bay, I paid attention to children's actions within the official school world. As someone interested in written language development, I watched as the familiar scenes of children's productions formed on their pages—names of family members and friends, pictures of dressed-to-impress girls, and energetic power swirls that obscured the figures behind the action.

But squatting alongside a table of lively children, I was drawn into child talk that was both intriguing and confusing. Denise and Vanessa were at this table, as were Marcel, Wenona, Noah, and Lakeisha. On that day and in those to come, I heard talk about what "mama said" the children should or would do after school, comments on necessary out-of-state trips for hockey games and football practice (Texas and Minnesota were favorite destinations of these California-based children). Apparently, or so I thought, the children rode the bus to the same day care center after school, where "Coach Bombay" was waiting for them. In addition to the talk, there was much intermittent singing—songs I did not know at all, but oh so quickly, one child's voice was joined by the others. Sprinkled throughout the interaction were references to each other as "sister" and "brother," and one confusing discussion in which Denise relented and referred to Wenona and Lakeisha as "stepsisters" instead of "sisters" to appease a seemingly affronted Vanessa.

Initially I looked for the explanation of these conversations in the literal world I assumed the children shared beyond the school. Through phone calls, trips to the children's neighborhood, and talks with their teacher Rita (and, eventually, parents), I learned what now seems obvious: there was no common mama, no common day care, and no actual Coach Bombay (whose roots were cinematic—based on the movie *D2: The Mighty Ducks* [Avnet, Claybourne, Kerner, & Weisman, 1994]). The family relationship among the children had been forged in, not outside of, school. (Some of you, dear readers, may be as confused as I initially was with all this talk of popular sports, music, and entertainment. The glossary provides brief explanations of these aspects of contemporary U.S. culture.)

So then I began to look differently, delving into the particularities of the worlds of words the children composed together. The textual threads of these words were not primarily in shared literal experiences, but in shared symbolic and textual ones. The children did not live in the same household (or even the same block), but they did share a common sociocultural landscape. They had, for example, a favorite radio station and saw many of the same videos; they referenced the same sports teams, and most watched the same televised sports shows; and they were all comfortable with a religious discourse and the promise of a heavenly reward. Their cultural landscape offered diverse symbolic material for child appropriation and recontextualization—that is, for reuse in their own conversations, stories, and play.

To illustrate, I bring into my frame, once again, Denise and Vanessa, intensely involved in talk. (See Appendix A for the transcription conventions I used.)

> DENISE: If Aaliyah [the singer] was my cousin . . . I'll bring her to
> school one day.
> VANESSA: But that's not your cousin.
> DENISE: I said i̲f̲.
> VANESSA: You would be rich, Denise. You would be—
> Candy fulla your pocket.
> Can't even eat it all, in your pocket.
> OH:: Rolled up in your shirt and all up mixed up in—
> DENISE: And what if they didn't give me none of their money?
> VANESSA: PHEW! Then I would be calling the police. . . .

Denise and Vanessa were sitting side by side doing a class assignment. Around and in between, they had been recalling their cousins for each other, reciting their names as fast as they could to impress each other with their memories and the numerical size of their relations. One of Denise's cousins shared a name with a popular (and recently deceased) R & B singer, Aaliyah. And if that Aaliyah was really her cousin, she'd bring her to school, show her off to her fake family, her circle of close friends, especially her "best fake sister," Vanessa.

The girls' conversation was quick-paced and intricately woven, consisting of varied turns and adaptive readjustments. It moved from a fanciful narrative by Denise, to a critical response from Vanessa, countered by Denise's metalinguistic attention to a key word ("I said *if*"). Then came Vanessa's poetic turn, with its repetitive but crescendoing structure and vivid images and, finally, after Denise's narrative disruption, Vanessa's quick about-face: from joyous poetry to a hard-edged narrative, in which the police were called to complain about a cousin not exercising family love and sharing the wealth.

This verbal dancing was supported by the children's sociocultural common ground. Denise and Vanessa were, for example, both small children; for them, visions of wealth translated into tiny, affordable treasures—pockets full of candy—associated with children's cultural sensibilities and socioeconomic possibilities. They were also participants in an African American community, with extended families of aunties and cousins that stretched beyond small nuclear ones. And they were young girls for whom glamorous futures seemed vividly displayed in the lives of singers (cf., Walkerdine, 1997); they pretended to be star singers heard on the radio and recalled with ease the names of many African American singers and, moreover, could playfully participate in their textual practices (e.g., the mood, rhythm, and melodic features of raps versus "love songs," for example). Moreover, they knew something of the ideologies associated with stardom, including wealth, although that wealth was expressed, to circle back now, in childhood terms: "Can't even eat it all, in your pocket." Against this complex cultural landscape, Denise and Vanessa were discursively adaptive, lively, and competent. In a similar way, so were all the brothers and sisters.

If I back up now from the closely framed playing children, I can locate them in their classroom and in relationship with the official school world. The school was, afer all, central to the formation of this childhood culture. School brought the children together and provided a site in which they marked both their specialness and their connections to others. If Aaliyah was really her cousin, Denise would bring her to school, no doubt to show her off to her fake family. Noah said he would bring to school the "little tiny baby gorilla" his mother promised him (a gorilla that seemed akin to a favorite video game character, Donkey Kong [Stamper, 1986]). And Marcel shared with the whole class his adventures in the football playoffs.

Imagine, now, these children, skillful manipulators of symbolic material and of each other as well, looking out at the horizon of school literacy tasks. New horizons, as Bakhtin (1981, p. 282) noted, always introduce "new elements into the discourse"—new words, new topics, new genre forms and, of course, in school, a newly foregrounded medium, written language. But those new elements mingle with the old, and so it was with the children. Their responses to literacy events, especially those allowing them room for discretion, for choice, were shaped not only by official curricular purposes, relationships, and textual information, but also by unofficial child relationships and by their use of cultural materials that figured into their lives as children.

And so the children ventured outward, expanding their social circles, informed by understood forms of agency and familiar communicative practices, often making use of their familiar textual toys. These toys were useful, in part because they provided conceptual content, functional genres, models of textual structures and elements, and a pool of potential characters, plots, and themes. At the same time, playing with those old toys in new practices could be disruptive, and thus give children and their teacher much material for reflection on symbolic conventions, social expectations, and ideological values. For example, the visual adventures of which Noah was so fond did not so easily translate into the syntax of written narratives (e.g., a written "I saw a dinosaur" just doesn't have the dramatic action of a drawn toothy creature about to devour a toothpick human [inspired by the movie *Jurassic Park* (Kennedy, Molen, & Spielberg, 1993)]). The radio songs the children sang were, they knew, "too fast" for 6-year-olds (and for their teacher). And reporting brother-and-sister games outside the social circle of close friends required new kinds of textual negotiations (e.g., some kind of acknowledgment that experiences are "fake" and not "real"—a "once upon a time" opening, perhaps).

It is the processes of transporting and transforming material across symbolic and social borders—and the interplay of childhoods and school agendas they entail—that are at the heart of the developmental vision I aim to illuminate herein. These recontextualization processes mess up the singular developmental pathway. There can be no such pathway because children are negotiating their ways into varied school literacy practices and, moreover, they are doing so by making use of diverse symbolic and communicative experiences.

Before I ever began this project, I, like many other educators, already knew that children build *from* what they know, as the cliché goes. But I didn't know how they build *with* what they know, the processes through which childhood practices interconnect with official school ones. And that is what *I* gradually learned, when, as researcher, writer, and the children's "fake mama," I followed the intertextual threads of children's communicative practices as they entered into school literacy. In the next two sections of this chapter, I explain my key conceptual and methodological tools.

CONCEPTUAL TOOLS FOR TRACING
THE THREADS OF CHILD LITERACY

In tracing the intertextual threads of children's composing practices, I am offering a "developmental" view; that is, a view of children changing over time in their ways of using written language. But "development" is a problematic concept, carrying with it "contextual overtones" incompatible with my own (Bakhtin, 1981, p. 293).

My use of the term is consistent with current sociocultural approaches to development (e.g., Miller & Goodnow, 1995; Rogoff, 1990; Watson-Gegeo, 1992). In these approaches, development is a process, not a series of stages nor a set of sequentially learned skills. This process is enacted as children participate in, and thereby enact interpretations of, the recurrent social activities of their daily lives. These activities are mediated by—revealed and accomplished through—socially organized and symbolically mediated actions, especially ways of talking (Vygotsky, 1987). Although adults offer assistance of varied types (arranging the environment, modeling, guiding, informing), children themselves are also actively making sense of these activities, developing frameworks for action (Bruner & Haste, 1987).

Children, then, contextualize their behavior in some kind of activity frame and, over time, they recontextualize what they regard as relevant ways of participating from one situated event to the next. Over time, children's interpretations (their sense of activities' functional possibilities) change, as do the social roles or responsibilities they assume and the means (skills and concepts) they control. They therefore come to share in the "normative expectations and . . . meanings or significances" of events shared by a social group of people; that is, these events become differentiated cultural practices (Barton, 1994; Miller & Goodnow, 1995, p. 9).

This general approach of studying "person-participating in-a-practice" is the one I adopt herein (Miller & Goodnow, 1995, p. 8). I attend to changes in how children participate in official school events in which written language is used (i.e., in literacy events). I analyze how children make those events meaningful (i.e., how those events are associated with cultural knowledge, social relations, and shared experiential history). But my specific approach is informed by Bakhtin's dialogic theory (1981, 1986), another key conceptual tool.

As I elaborate in the subsections to follow, dialogic theory situates children not simply within a particular studied practice, but on a landscape of interrelated voices. These voices enact the varied communicative practices that constitute children's worlds (Hanks, 1996), and these practices involve varied symbol systems (e.g., written language, drawing, music) and material technologies (e.g., video, radio, animation). Situating children on a landscape of voices allows me to portray how they maneuver through social space, rather than only how they participate in a recurrent practice over temporal time. Of particular interest in this project is children's maneuvering as they participate in both the social world of the brothers and sisters and that of the official classroom.

Moreover, a view of practices as kinds of voices allows me to articulate more precisely the kind of participation process that matters in this study of writing development. I am interested in changes in how children make use of the landscape of voices that surround them. That is, I am interested in recontextualization processes—the processes of differentiating, appropriating from, translating across, and reframing textual material within communicative practices and their symbolic media (Bauman & Briggs, 1990). As researcher, I aimed to follow the textual threads as children entered into school literacy practices, blending and differentiating communicative practices and the resources they entailed, not all of which originated in the official classroom world.

Maneuvering on a Landscape of Voices

The usual ways of understanding development have much in common with ancient Greek adventure stories, at least as the latter are explained by Bakhtin (1981). In his view, those ancient stories happen in an abstract space, separate from the local substance of daily life. Written language development, reduced to a list of skills, or a sequence of stages, has similar connotations. For this reason, the word "development" can imply an interest in the universal child, who usually reduces to a mythic middle class one developing "normally" (Dyson, 1995, 1999; Kessen, 1979; Steedman, 1992).

In his history of the novel, Bakhtin (1981) examines literary works in which heroes' movement through a story became a movement through the time and spaces of their everyday lives. Indeed, in the contemporary novel, heroes are not located on a singular pathway but on a complex landscape. That landscape organizes social space and, as is befitting a novel, it does so through organizing voices themselves. Those voices index social scenes through the use of certain kinds of dialogues or genres (e.g., when characters engage in jokes, sermons, raps, operas), and they also index larger societal categories through the use of certain language varieties (e.g., when characters use registers, dialects, and even diverse languages, all of which may index class, gender, ethnicity, age, profession).

Although organized, this landscape of voices is dynamic, not static. Characters in novels, like their authors—and like small children—move through time and space by appropriating for themselves available words and genres. They are not joining a chorus of like voices but, rather, entering into dialogues with many other speakers, both present and long since gone. Speakers (or writers) dialogue with the past because, over time, speakers have enacted particular social situations in similar ways; thus, their utterances acquire certain shared features and, thereby, the "flavor of a given genre," with characteristic forms, themes, and evaluative slants (Bakhtin, 1981, p. 289). New speakers must use words that sound socially appropriate, or no one may attend and respond.

But speakers must also give the expected words their own accent, infuse them with their own intention as they reach out to particular other(s) in the current social scene. This relationship between self and social landscape, between individual intention and available textual materials, will be evident in the child dramas to come. As the children move through the time span of their school year, they will not be moving along a linear pathway but negotiating an expanding social landscape as they encounter new genres (or communicative practices [Hanks, 1996]), with a newly foregrounded symbolic medium and new social expectations, challenges, and possibilities.

Borrowing and Revoicing as Developmental Processes

Young children first borrow and revoice words as they learn to participate in the routine activities, or practices, of their everyday lives (e.g., dressing, eating, and playing early games like "peek-a-boo"). These practices "come packed with values about what is natural, mature, morally right, or aesthetically pleasing" (Miller & Goodnow, 1995, p. 6). Thus, children's subjectivities (their senses of themselves and their own possibilities for action) develop along with their symbolic resources and cognitive capacities (Bruner, 1990).

Children's articulation of possible selves is audible and visible in their early storytelling and play: They literally appropriate and recontextualize voices (i.e., "speaking personalit[ies]" [Bakhtin, 1981, p. 434]). Research on family conversation (e.g., Dore, 1989; Nelson, 1996), family stories (Miller & Mehler, 1994), children's responses to books (e.g., Miller, Hoogstra, Mintz, Fung, & Williams, 1993; Wolf & Heath, 1992), and their dramatic play (e.g., Garvey, 1990) all illustrate children's attentiveness to plot lines and character voices that are aesthetically marked and affectively charged and, also, ones that allow them powerful and/or appealing positions (like those way cool teenagers mentioned in the Prologue).

As Nelson (1996) emphasizes, interwoven in children's story and play are complex discourses of "time, space, geography, religion, gender roles, biology, and the natural world" (Nelson, 1996, p. 218)—and, I would add, texts themselves. Recall, for example, the discourses (i.e., the systems of categories, terms, and statements [Williams, 1983]) about music, wealth, and family relations, not to mention the discursive skill, embedded in Denise and Vanessa's Aaliyah play. The role of school, then, is to provide cultural symbolic forms, including written language and disciplinary taxonomies and genres, that help children gain distance from, differentiate, and recontextualize their everyday experiences within the academic discourses and practices of school (a view based on Vygotsky, 1962).

However, these recontextualization processes are not likely to unfold as Nelson anticipates; that is, in "a seamless weaving together" as a child's "experience-based constructions," learned through daily interactions, "gradually incorpora[te] the potential of social and cultural forms" learned in school (Nelson, 1996, p. 352). Nelson may so imagine this process because, like the literature upon which she draws, she refers only to children borrowing cultural material from adult conversation and children's literature. Her vision of borrowed material is completely compatible with the "selective tradition" (Williams, 1965, p. 66)—the cultural materials traditionally valued in school.

But children's initial school efforts are not confined by the traditions of school, which, after all, must be learned (Dyson, 1993, 1997). Children make their own choices from available meanings and practices and, as already noted, these choices include the textual toys they bring to school from the popular media. These textual appropriations invoke social involvements often considered quite alien to the goals of school. Indeed, expressing a disdain for popular texts is a way of marking socioeconomic "distinction" on the societal landscape (Bourdieu, 1984). In early childhood classrooms, teachers themselves may disdain such knowledge and bemoan the homes that allow children such pleasures (Seiter, 1998). Although there is reason for concern about the media images available to children, including human omissions and stereotypes (existent as well in children's print media [Harris, 1992; Sims, 1982]), there is no denying the popular media's pervasiveness in contemporary societies, nor in contemporary childhoods, much less the increasingly multimodal nature of literacy practices themselves (Fisherkeller, 2002; Marsh & Millard, 2000; New London Group, 1996).

This pervasiveness, combined with the media's usual absence in official school contexts, contributes to the lack of seamlessness children may experience. Like all learners, children must use *familiar frames of reference* (i.e., familiar practices) to make sense of new content, discursive forms, and symbolic tools. At the same time, *new frames or practices* allow them vantage points for critical reflection on both old and new content, forms, and tools. Through the reframing of textual material across symbolic media (e.g., audiovisual sources and printed pages), social activities (e.g., playing video games and writing stories), and ideologies (e.g., different values governing how time is spent at home and at school), seams may be exposed.

These exposed seams—of symbolic conventions, social expectations, and ideologies—are not necessarily negative. Quite the contrary. Such seams may become material for deliberate reflection on, for example, the functional nature of drawing relative to writing, the expectations for storytelling in official contexts relative to peer or home contexts, the pleasures condoned by teachers relative to diverse significant others. Through borrowing and revoicing voices from their landscape of possibilities, children may learn about the symbolic, social, and ideological "options, limits, and blends" of practices (Miller & Goodnow, 1995, p. 12), which is what literacy development entails.

Tracing the Trajectories of Communicative Practices

So now I have discussed Bakhtin's *landscape of voices*. Given this landscape, a child who writes a cartoon-inspired story, a rhythmic rap, a version of a movie or a (fake) professional football report is not just producing a text in the current social scene, but positioning themselves on the societal landscape; in so doing, that child is orchestrating cultural material embedded in textual practices that have seldom received positive press in early schooling. In *recontextualizing*—borrowing and revoicing—this material in school contexts, children reorganize and rearticulate their resources and, in the process, they may differentiate and expand their knowledge about symbolic systems, social practices, and the ideologically complex world. In this view of development, the children do not move in step along a narrow literacy path but, at least ideally, more deliberately maneuver on an expanding landscape.

These notions, following each other in the succession of printed lines of this book, did not arrive in any such order. I read (and borrowed) the words of Bakhtin and appealing developmentalists (who used phrases like "cultural practices"). But I also untangled the threads of children's textual productions as they learned to write. In this effort, the children's textual media toys were exceedingly useful, because they were relatively easily identifiable as originating out of school. I could follow the threads of these toys to their nonacademic sources and, at the same time, track their academic fates as the children wound them into varied school-defined practices (e.g., reporting what one has learned, narrating a true story or a fictional one, crafting a poem).

Also useful was Hanks's (1996) concept of evolving communicative practices. In his Bakhtinian-informed work, genres are analyzed as kinds of practices; that is, they are viewed as ways of participating in society's social life, be they short conversational turns (e.g., a greeting) or extended prose (e.g., this book). Moreover, genres are also understood as integral aspects of a group's habitus, of their disposition to perceive and act upon the world in certain ways (after Bourdieu, 1977). Ways of telling stories (through varied media), of passing on and receiving local and national news, of celebrating, communicating, or praying through song can all seem quite natural to cultural insiders. These genres, or communicative practices, are neither rigid types nor formless inventions; they are potential ways people produce meaning, and they are shaped by formal symbol systems, by the existent social constellation, and by strategic improvisation in the interactional moment.

Hanks is not interested in children's textual unruliness or their development in school places. His landscapes are those of present and historical Mayans, whose evolving genres have reflected the sociocultural and power shifts brought about under colonial rule. But he is interested in the ways practices interweave, differentiate and, more generally, evolve over historical time and across social space. He traces these trajectories of practices by following their enactment in particular events. Trajectories become visible as producers orient themselves to particular social constellations by, for instance, adopting particular words or phrases that appeal to, or appease, the powers that be, or by using indexical elements (like personal pronouns or demonstratives) that situate producers among other participants. In these and other ways, language users establish linkages to their "spaces of engagements" (p. 245).

And so it was with Denise and her close friends, as they engaged in their spaces of engagement, often negotiating their way among the social worlds governed by peers and by their teacher. In these worlds, too, communicative practices are subject to sociocultural and power shifts, though more modest in scale than those Hanks studied (and potentially more trivialized, since they are viewed from the perspective of people whose views count little among grown-ups). As will be abundantly evident, the children's initial ways of engaging in school practices were not necessarily characterized by strategic, or deliberate, improvisation, nor did their resulting texts necessarily have a "definite generic skeleton"—a clear genre home (Bakhtin, 1981, pp. 59–60). But, as the children engaged in recontextualization processes, they did link textual practices from different social worlds. Guided by the intricate weaving of their textual toys, I followed children's pathways into school literacy as they juxtaposed, interwove, and sometimes deliberately differentiated kinds of speaking voices or genres.

METHODOLOGICAL TOOLS FOR CONSTRUCTING THE PROJECT DATA SET

First grader Wenona and I are sitting together on a small picnic bench on the north side of the school building. Behind us, through the large glass doors, is the hallway to the cafeteria and, further back, the asphalt of the playground. In front of us the street traffic moves up and down a steep hill under a canopy of trees.

It is my last day at the school and Wenona has told me she wishes she could sing in my microphone. So, with Rita's permission, we have come outside by ourselves and now are sitting—or I am, because Wenona has risen to sing. She throws her head back, and her braids wave in the wind. With her arms outstretched, Wenona improvises a song that has the melody, and certain key phrases, of Whoopi Goldberg's "If You Want to Be Somebody" (from the movie *Sister Act 2* [Steel, Rudin, Iscovich, Mark, & Duke, 1994]) and the spirit of *Sesame Street*'s "People in Your Neighborhood" (Moss, 1970). Following is a brief excerpt:

MM mm:
If you want to go somewhere,
just wake up and pay attention
Oh Oo::

Time or never
to make your dreams come true
Hey hey hey hey

This is the family
And this is where we live
We are sisters and brothers and mothers and cousins and
    friends
Yeah yeah yeah yeah yeah yeah yeah yeah

. . .

This is my life
and this is my neighborhood today
It's pretty out in the world
It's a brand new day ay

Wenona's real family did not live in the school's immediate neighbor-hood. The school was the home of her fake family, and that family arrived every day on big yellow school buses that brought them in from another section of town. The children's arrival on the bus, like the arrival of their cultural references in the school itself, speaks to the challenges that children, teachers, and all citizens face in making connections in a com-plexly divided world. Below, I provide details on the project's site and procedures.

Participants and Site

Wenona, Denise, and the other brothers and sisters attended an elemen-tary school (K-5) officially described as having the "greatest crosstown span" in this East San Francisco Bay district (i.e., the greatest socioeconomic mix). Approximately half the school's children were African American, approximately a third European American, and the rest were of varied Latino and Asian ancestries. Roughly 40% (112 of the 286 children at-tending this small urban site) qualified for free/reduced lunch. (Table B.1 in Appendix B provides pseudonym and demographic information on the 20 first-grade children in Rita's classroom.)

In order to integrate (and fill) the school, which was in a middle-class, primarily European American neighborhood in the northern section of the city, the district bused children from the southwest section of the city, which was primarily African American and working class. (To illustrate these racial and socioeconomic contrasts, Tables B.2 and B.3 in Appendix B contrast two 1990 census tracts serviced by the school, one a northeast tract, the other a southwest tract.) The busing arrangement was rooted in efforts to integrate the schools, which dated from the late 1960s. The dis-trict was the first in the country to attempt integration. The plan, how-ever, did not work as envisioned, because of the flight of more affluent white children to private schools. And so, each morning, two-thirds of Rita's children traveled across town to her classroom.

I learned of Rita through Carol Tateishi, director of the Bay Area Writing Project. Knowing of my interest in children's cultural productions, including their writing and art, Carol had recommended a visit to Rita's first grade. Rita's classroom, she said, allowed much space for such pro-duction, and so it did.

Rita is an experienced teacher, with professional roots in the British primary schools of the 1960s. Rita integrated literacy and the expressive arts throughout her day. During the course of my project, Rita's curricu-lum included both open-ended writing activities (e.g., "writing work-shop," where the children wrote and drew relatively freely, followed by class sharing) and more teacher-directed ones (e.g., assigned tasks in study units, in which children wrote and drew as part of social studies and science learning).

Rita is herself a visual artist and a music lover. She was serious about engaging the children in a careful study of visual artists and in their own thoughtful production of artistic works. She found in children's artwork an interest in vivid colors, recurring patterns, and playful lines; and she introduced her class to adult artists, many of whom also favored strong colors and imaginative abstractions (among the painters she introduced were traditional Mbuti women artists, W. Kandinsky, Georgia O'Keefe, Paul Klee, Jacob Lawrence, and Henri Matisse). In varied ways, through her actions and words, Rita taught the children that artists were people who understood their expressive options, made decisions, and enjoyed the hard work of making art. Artists, including child artists, were "respectful of their work," because they "put so much" into it.

Rita also made ample use of her CD player, weaving a variety of music into the school day. The local symphony, Bobby McFerrin, Cat Stevens, Ella Fitzgerald, Wee Sing, Sweet Honey in the Rock, Jimmy Cliff, and Joshua Redman were some classroom companions lying side by side in Rita's CD collection. She used contemporary folk to calm the children, jazz to get the work rhythm going, and varied genres, including gospel, to accompany study units. Rita also participated in the Arts in the Schools program, which included visits to the local symphony orchestra and classroom visits (and even performances) by individual members.

It was in this classroom, then, that I slipped into the cultural world of "the brothers and sisters": Marcel, Wenona, Denise, Vanessa, Noah, and Lakeisha, the latter who was less centrally involved in the project because she attended varied pullout programs for academic and emotional support.[1] The children's self-designation as "fake" siblings was linked to the use of the label "brothers and sisters" to refer to solidarity in the African American tradition, but it was much more literal. As already noted, the children engaged in elaborate narrative play, which they called "games"; in these games, and the imaginary world they constituted, the children were actual siblings.

Most relevant for the project, much of the children's play was informed by the media. The children presented a unique opportunity to explore the cultural landscape of a contemporary childhood and its links to varied sources of texts. I had come upon a semiotic gold mine and, fortunately, the children, their teacher, and their parents all allowed me entry to this mine. And so, in the fall of 1996, I began to document (through written observations and audio taping) the children's official and unofficial participation in school.

Data Collection Procedures

During the course of an academic year, I observed the children for 4 to 6 hours per week. I focused primarily on collecting classroom data during the morning language arts period, from 8:30 to 10:00, but I also followed the children out to the playground for morning recess. On occasion, I stayed all day, especially during the 2-week class study of space, in January, and of freedom, in March, when the children spent whole days involved in varied thematically linked composing activities. During the project year, they had no classroom computers on which to compose—but, I hasten to add, they most definitely composed in multimodal ways.

The brothers and sisters often sat together for at least part of the day. But for me, doing close observations of children's communicative and expressive activity (writing, drawing, talking, singing, often all interwoven with each other) requires anchoring those observations in the perspective of a particular child. So I distributed my attention among the children, devoting the entire day's observation to a focus on the perspective of one child or the other. In this way, my notes were organized around stable units of analysis—children's participation in official production events (e.g., doing a "writing workshop book" entry) and in unofficial ones (e.g., singing a radio song); those official and unofficial events overlapped, interrupted, and sometimes peacefully accompanied each other.

I composed my field notes as soon as possible after each day's visit, using my observational scratch notes, my audio recordings of child talk, and sketches and photocopies of children's work. (See Dyson, 1989, for a discussion of means of documenting children's writing and drawing processes.) I collected approximately 460 written products from the focal children, as well as all writing workshop entries ($N = 1,006$) from nonfocal children. Entries from the focal children's products were entered into a typed record.

My own relationship with the children evolved over time. I am a middle-aged White woman and I study in local schools, in which the social category of race, and its links to socioeconomic class, is consistently enacted. For example, no White child climbed down from those big yellow buses that arrived at the school each day with the brothers and the sisters; and no African American child walked to the school door hand-in-hand with a neighborhood parent. As is my way, in this project, I was initially quiet, unobtrusive, and reactive, akin to Corsaro (1985), but, unlike him, I made no effort to become one of the gang. I was "busy" with writing in my notebook, I was "interested" in "children," and I wouldn't "tell on them." So, as Rita taught a lesson, circulated among the children, or modeled working on her product, I sat, pen in hand, legal pad on lap, watching and writing without looking at the pad (a feat that never fails to impress first graders).

Among the brothers and the sisters, Denise was the first child to make some familial sense of me. She deemed me a "fake mama" and wrote me a letter declaring this fact. As far as I could tell, a fake mama could sit and listen and, when asked, her children could explain their ways to her. "Speak to me when you—ever you need to again," Wenona said, after I'd asked about her coach and her teams. I mainly spoke to the children at the end of the 90-minute morning work period, before they went outside for recess. However, if I felt I had no clue—no thread to hang on to—in following the goings on (which was sometimes the case when I observed Noah), I did intervene, trying never to interrupt any talk among the children themselves.

In the last 2 months of the project, the children developed a more active role in the playground data collection. The change was partly due simply to the passage of time and their familiarity with me and my more ostentatious note taking during recess (when no one but me was writing). For example, if I had not been at school the previous day, Denise would report any playground incidents she deemed worthy of my recording. "I got something for you to write down," she would say, before telling me of a boy-girl chase game, for example.

Some of the relational change, however, was due to a technological change. I typically recorded children, inside the classroom and out, using a lapel microphone attached to the shoulder strap of a tote bag. However, I decided to use a more powerful, and much bigger, unidirectional microphone on the noisy playground, in order to record their singing and radio station play. I explained to the curious children why I was using that big microphone, and they spontaneously reperformed all their songs for me. (I felt like a postmodern Iona Opie!) Denise, Wenona, Lakeisha, and Vanessa asked me to make them each a tape of their radio singing. Wenona was absent on the children's big day, and that is why, on the last day of data collection, in mid-June, she and I were out alone on the side of the school building, me just listening, her singing so wholeheartedly.

Media leads from the children were all verified, and original media sources documented, primarily through the efforts of project research assistants Soyoung Lee and, in the closing months of the project, Sheila Shea—and also, much help from the Internet. We were helped, too, by many kind souls at local video and music stores, not to mention friendly folks in varied public locations who happened to be singing to themselves in the style of a song we were trying to track down. (One such nonchalant singer works at my local grocery store—such luck!)

Fittingly, perhaps, this was not a project that could be accomplished by one lone researcher in a lone elementary school. In the classroom and on the playground, I could document the unofficial practices through which the media material became playful toys. But to trace that material back to its original sources, I had to venture beyond the school neighborhood. So, in the 2nd year of the project, I organized a parent meeting, which the parents of Denise, Noah, and Marcel were able to attend. I discussed with them my understandings of each child's writing and, thus, was able to confirm or clarify my inferences about the interests of each of them; in addition, I discussed with them their experiences with, and opinions about, the media and their children.

With Soyoung, I visited the children's favorite radio station and talked about the project with the deejay and the producer of the children's oft-referenced FM morning show. I asked them if, and what, they thought of small children as part of their radio audience. Given that the deejay had grown up in the children's neighborhood, I asked about his own knowledge of the children's playground rhymes and songs. Joined by Sheila, we also talked with an assistant coach of the Oakland Raiders football team. He, and his fiancée, helped us understand the local football culture (not to mention many of the symbols in the children's products) and the way that that culture was mediated by television. Finally, Soyoung and I talked with a professional writer who had experience composing scripts for children's animation. He responded to the children's cartoon-inspired productions and explained ways in which his professional composing challenges compared to those of the children.

In a sense, the same nonacademic material that mediated the children's entry into school literacy mediated my own entry into new social scenes. Before the project, I had never listened with careful attention to the children's hip-hop radio station. I had known close to nothing about the singers whose names were on the tips of the children's tongues. I had not been, and am not now, a football fan, nor a connoisseur of cartoons (although, through my last project [Dyson, 1997], I know quite a bit about superheroes). I would not claim to have been or to have become a media expert or a fan. But I would and do claim to have been open, curious, and persistent in following the children's textual threads. And I also claim to have carefully studied the children's textual productions through diverse data sources and perspectives, such diversity being a hallmark of a trustworthy interpretive study (Bogdan & Biklen, 1998; Emerson, Fretz, & Shaw, 1995; Erickson, 1986).

Data Analysis

To make sense of all I had seen, heard, and collected, I focused most intensely on those classroom observations featuring varied brothers and sisters. During each observation, the children had moved in and out of official and unofficial worlds—and in and out of each other's interactional space; they had used a repertoire of diverse symbolic tools (spoken, sung, or written words, drawn pictures, dramatic gestures) and an expanse of cultural stuff from all manner of mediated sources. Moreover, the data sets themselves stretched across the literacy activities of the classroom day and, also, across the time span of an academic year. Analyzing such a morass of data did not happen in a month—or even a year—but stretched over time. I aim, in these introductory comments, only to give a sense of the basic procedures, leaving the details to be spread more comfortably over the chapters to come.

To find my way into the textual tangles of the children's productions, I used as my basic organizational unit a child's production event, that is, all of the child action and interaction that occurred during the production (and/or the interpretation) of a text. The text—the configuration of signs—could be oral, written, drawn, enacted, or, most likely, a multimodal production. And the production event itself could be organized within varied participant structures arrangements ([Philips, 1972] e.g., a collaborative production or a singular performance). The event could be an official one, an unofficial one, or (as was most often the case) a hybrid event—some juxtaposition, interplay, or even convergence of the official and unofficial (as when, in the midst of an official writing workshop event, jokes, songs, or stories evolved, none of which were in any way officially sanctioned).

By studying these production events, I could untangle at least some of the intertextual threads that indexed the children's ongoing actions in their experiences, for instance, as (pretend) radio singing stars and, beyond that, as radio consumers (or video watchers, superhero enacters, churchgoers, and so on). I categorized all of the children's references to media by type (i.e., book, movie, music, television [cartoon, sitcom. sports show], video/computer game), and I also developed a taxonomy to describe the nature of the cultural material appropriated by the children (e.g., conceptual content, communicative forms, technological conventions [like graphic arrangements or icons], actual spoken utterances, and ideologies [including beliefs about race, gender, fame, power]). (The Media Bibliography section provides reference lists of appropriated movies, television shows, and video games, along with a bibliography of referenced songs, organized by singer.)

I paid attention not only to the content—the media references—of the children's production events but also to their interactional structure (Hymes, 1972). I noted who referenced what media material with whom under what kinds of social conditions, characterized by what kind of mood, to enact what kind of textual practice or genre. In this way, I gained insight into the social usefulness of the media in the children's school lives.

My aim, however, was not only to portray the cultural landscape of a contemporary childhood, but also to understand how this landscape influenced the children's entry into school literacy. I needed to understand how the children's appropriations of cultural material, and their movement among social worlds, changed over time. So, I organized chronologically all of my observations of each child. Within each data set (each case study of a child), I identified key production events. Within key events, the children's actions and interactions indexed the nonacademic practices or genres that informed their academic efforts and, also, made salient the tensions (symbolic, social, and ideological) that could arise when children drew on unofficial practices in official ones.

For each child, I linked key events by tracing the child's textual toys as those toys were appropriated from, translated across, and reframed within and across practices. Initially, the children participated in most official composing events by drawing and talking and by writing familiar words and officially modeled written forms (e.g., "I like . . . ," "I went . . ."). During these official events, the children's *talking* and *drawing* were organized primarily by communicative practices not explicitly taught in school, like collaboratively enacting a fantastic world or playing out a visual adventure; thus, the children's symbolic and social actions were centered in, or indexed, the children's unofficial world. Any *writing*, though, was a sociolinguistic nod to the official world, "the social matrix within which the [print] discourse" mattered (Hanks, 2000, p. 166).

Over time, the children's written texts began to mediate in more complex ways their efforts to declare and maintain themselves as playful, knowledgeable, powerful, and socially valued people in official and unofficial worlds. That movement "over time," just like the movement over space, happened through recontextualization processes—processes of differentiation, appropriation, translation, and reframing of cultural material across symbolic forms and social practices.

Although the children all shared a cultural landscape, they drew differentially on that landscape as they entered into school literacy. The particularities of their resources mattered, since different sorts of cultural material posed different translation challenges and lent themselves differentially well to reframing in varied school-preferred practices. Thus, though they used similar processes, the children differed in their developmental pathways (i.e., in the nature of their converging practices and the "options, limits, and blends" of practices thus made salient [Miller & Goodnow, 1995, p. 12]).

In this book, certain chapters feature certain kinds of cultural material (sports, animation, music) and, thus, certain children. As a whole, though, the book provides both the particular details that illuminate the complexly textured agency of individuals and, at the same time, the "concrete universals" to be found in those particulars (Erickson, 1986, p. 130)— that is, the common developmental dynamics of recontextualization. In sum, then, my broad research aims were

- to document the cultural landscape of a childhood culture, considering the range and nature of the cultural materials that were recontextualized in children's communicative practices;
- to analyze how (the recontextualization processes through which) children made use of nonacademic practices and materials as they participated in school literacy practices (and vice versa);
- to trace changes in how children used the resources of their cultural landscape over time and across the social spaces of official and unofficial cultural worlds; and, as a part of that tracing,
- to examine the consequences of—including the kinds of tensions that could result from—children's recontextualization of nonacademic material in school practices for individual and classroom learning.

A WRITING DEVELOPMENT REMIX: THE PLAN OF THE BOOK

In Chapter 2, I use the textual threads of the children's unofficial talk and play to map the cultural landscape of this contemporary childhood. I consider the range of cultural texts that the children appropriated, and the ways in which those texts marked the time-space dimensions of their childhood spaces. For example, the children's media references constructed childhood pasts (with their preschool shows and tunes, for instance); current links to family and peers (with their oral traditions of games and chants); and anticipated futures as teenagers (especially as mediated by radio songs). I consider as well the social purposes energizing the children's appropriations of cultural texts. From pleasantly passing the time to displaying admired expertise, the media served a range of functions in children's shared lives.

In Chapter 3, I move from the children's unofficial world into the official world of Ms. Rita and the language and literacy curriculum. Using the framework of the classroom study of space, I illustrate how the brothers and the sisters moved out onto the official landscape, describing what unofficial resources they brought with them and how those unofficial appropriations mediated official productions. Finally, I consider how the children's use of unofficial materials in official spaces made salient larger societal boundaries (e.g., those of gender, race, and socioeconomic class). A vivid example of this micro/macro connection is found in the differing classroom fates of two films—*Star Wars* (Kurtz & Lucas, 1977), sometimes considered "ersatz high culture" (Jenkins, 1992, p. 22), and *Space Jam* (Falk, Ross, & Pytka, 1996), considered a "best movie" by all the brothers and sisters).

In Chapters 4, 5, and 6, I move across time, using textual threads to reconstruct the nature of children's expanding pathways into school literacy practices. It is in these chapters that I foreground the developmental dramas energized by recontextualization processes (processes of transporting and transforming cultural material across practice boundaries). Each chapter features a particular cultural material and a particular child: "Sports Matters" (Chapter 4) features Marcel; "Animated Adventures" (Chapter 5) features Noah; and "Singing Stars" (Chapter 6) features Denise. The three featured children had the strongest predilections toward a particular kind of cultural material and, thus, were the most theoretically informative.

In Chapter 7, I weave together the data from all the case study children and re-present the developmental theory. The metaphor "a writing development remix" captures my aim in this chapter—to add a new dialogic rhythm to an old song about children building on what they know. And it captures as well the recontextualization processes that provide the generative beat of this rhythm.

Denise once explained remix to me as a way of composing in which one does not "make up" a song (more broadly, a text) but, rather, mixes up "words from another song" to make something new. New, but not invented out of nowhere through an imaginative inner eye. Invented out of somewhere, through alert eyes and ears. Sampling from the old and remixing for something new are basic to hip-hop culture's rap music (Rose, 1994), but they also link to Jones and Hawes's principle of antiphony, and to Bakhtin's dialogism—that is, to a willingness to respond to the current beat by transforming old moves. This willingness cannot be furthered by compensating children for their supposed lacks (the perceived absence of certain school-valued experiences) but only by recognizing the potential of their present resources.

Moreover, that potential is organized, furthered, or constrained by social conditions as interpreted by the children themselves. The particular developmental dramas I construct herein are, in the main, positive in tone, depicting children's expanding participatory powers in school. But these unfolding dramas were enacted within a fractured social landscape, one negotiated herein by a highly experienced teacher with an expansive curriculum and a critical, reflective disposition. Her efforts were also enfolded within a structured institution, the school, which is oriented toward the societal mainstream and which continues to be under enormous pressure to narrow the curriculum and the possible negotiating room for children and teachers. Against the cacophony of the present policy context for school literacy, state curricular documents and the general public discourse maintain a loud silence about multiple literacy practices, diverse learning pathways; indeed, about children as opinionated, active agents with a human right to a decent, satisfying present—a childhood (see Stephens, 1995). Thus, it is not hard to see the fragility of the observed children's situation and how, as described for older youth, schooling may become a "subtractive process," divesting children of their social and cultural resources and aggravating societal divisions (Valenzuela, 1999, p. 1).

Thus, in the closing chapter, Chapter 8, adult voices are brought to the foreground, including Ms. Rita, parents, and members of the children's mediated landscape. The adults' views encompass both a range of concerns about children, school learning, and contemporary media and, at the same time, a recognition of the role of diverse cultural sources in childhood (and family) pleasures and learning possibilities. "You've got to grow with your children," a young deejay told me, keeping tabs, talking about issues, and, I add, stretching minds and ways with words. That strong advice is the theme of that chapter and, moreover, the practical message of this book. The children are ready to jig in a world that they jointly make. The grown-ups might best flex their knees, bend their elbows, and show the children some new (literacy) steps as well.

2

Mapping the Cultural Landscape of a Contemporary Childhood

Noah and Marcel are working on their 100th-day-of-school project, pasting 100 tiny objects (Cheerios, mainly) in a shoebox top to make a design. As they work (but not while they are counting), they sing the catchy refrain from "Gangsters Make the World Go Round" (Westside Connection, 1996). Then Marcel initiates a round of the theme song from *Barney* (Leach, 1988), a children's television show.

MARCEL: (singing) I love you/ You love me.
  NOAH: Ew! (with disgust)
MARCEL: (laughs) I hate Barney [a sweet dinosaur].
  NOAH: I got the movie of Barney. I <u>love</u> it.
MARCEL: WHAT?!
  NOAH: Remember in kindergarten you watch Barney?
MARCEL: I did not!
  NOAH: Yes you did.
MARCEL: I did <u>not</u> watch Barney!
  NOAH: How about in preschool? How'd you like Barney?

The children's conflict is soon dissolved as both boys are swept up by a jingle from a Cheerios commercial that engulfs their table.

Both the textual remnant from a hard-edged gangsta rap and that from a saccharine preschool show were cultural stuff with which Marcel, Noah, and the rest of the brothers and sisters constructed their identities, expressive practices, and histories as children. This process of constructing a childhood cannot be detected by studying only the textual sources themselves—the radio songs or the television shows.

Popular images appeal, in part, for precisely the same reason they disconcert: they feature dominant desires and pleasures about, for example, power, wealth, and beauty, which themselves reflect interrelated societal constructions like age, gender, race, and class (Buckingham, 1993; Dyson,

1997; Fisherkeller, 2002; Hall, 1981, 1992; Willis, 1990). People do not simply take in media input—they interpret it, based on their pasts and the social contingencies of the present. In this way, popular culture becomes "a theater of popular fantasies . . . where we discover and play with the identification of ourselves" (Hall, 1992, p. 32).

Further, we do not experience this theater alone in the dark, despite the common stereotype of the television beaming directly into the head of an isolated child (see discussion in Spigel, 1998, and the cover of Levin, 1998 [in other respects, a practical book]). Voices emanating from human or electronic containers are organized themselves in varied kinds of genres (e.g., stories, raps, informational or persuasive pieces) and, moreover, they are experienced by children in the context of varied kinds of family and peer routines and practices. Children do not just listen to music, for example; they are encouraged, discouraged, or unnoticed as they participate in church service singing, morning routines involving radio airwaves, or an older sibling's sing-along sessions with a favorite radio star. Along with their family members, they may anticipate, watch, and rehash a televised sports show or a movie theater event. They may spend afternoons playing video games with a sibling or a friend, perhaps with after-school television shows as a backdrop.

Some of these text-involving experiences are directed to them. Vanessa's "granny *made* [her] watch Barney," or so she complained to her friends. Others are forbidden but sought out anyway as a kind of "stolen lipstick," to use a phrase from the poet Kenneth Koch (1998, p. 74). Using such texts is a way in which children can imagine themselves older and hipper; that is, those texts are toys for a kind of dress-up play. For the brothers and sisters, this was especially true of many radio songs for teenagers, although sports shows also offered material for imagining glamourous futures, particularly (but not exclusively) for boys.

The diversity—and seemingly contradictory nature—of children's textual appropriations has been observed in young children from diverse socioeconomic and cultural backgrounds. The master early childhood teacher Vivian Paley (1986) commented on her own students (primarily middle-class children at a private, university-sponsored preschool), "Themes from fairy tales and television cartoons mixed easily with social commentary and private fantasies . . . [to form] a familiar and comfortable world" for them (p. 124; see also Dyson, 1993; Garvey, 1990; Jenkins, 1988; Opie & Opie, 1959). Similarly, Marcel's mother noted that he was "bouncing back and forth between some nursery rhyme and [the rap music] his brother listens to," not to mention the songs he learned through his participation in the church choir and in the official world of school.

The pervasiveness of popular media in particular, including television, in children's experiences has been characteristic of American childhoods

since post World War II (Douglas, 1994; Seiter, 1993; Spigel, 1998). As
Spigel and Jenkins (1991) illustrated, adults' recollections of popular childhood media programs are intertextually linked not only with each other,
but also with their narratives of their experiences and feelings as children
growing up with family and friends (see also Fisherkeller, 1997, 2002).
For Spigel and Jenkins's interviewees, a cartoonish superhero (Batman)

> brought back a situational context, a scene that painted a rough sketch of
> places in the house, times of the day, and childhood relationships with fam-
> ily and friends. . . . The degree to which these people relied on shared cul-
> tural and social frameworks—family settings, childhood games, school yard
> contexts—suggests the relational aspects of popular memory, the attempt
> to use memory in a way that binds the individual to a larger community of
> ideas. (p. 134)

In this project, too, the children's appropriated texts mattered because
they were constitutive of their relationships with others and with their
positioning on the dialogic landscape as boys and girls, as kids from the
East Bay (not San Francisco), as African Americans, as brothers and sisters, singers and artists, players and serious students. Their interactions with
each other provided my means for constructing a vision of the "architecton-
ics of [their] answerability" to the voices that surrounded them (Bakhtin,
1919–1986/1990, p. 1); that is, of the ways in which they forged connections with each other, their family members, and with the wider world.

In this chapter, I first use child appropriations from nonofficial cultural practices to portray children's own constructions of their pasts as
preschoolers, their complex present childhoods, and their anticipated futures as "teen-age-ers." Although all three of the media forms highlighted
in this book will be included—sports media, animation, and music, the
latter features most prominently in this chapter. Music was woven through
most other media events and, moreover, it was an integral part of children's
participation in varied institutions; music was part of the ties that bind and
the threads that weave through generations in churches, families, schools,
and among children themselves. Thus, it was music texts, and the interactions in which they featured, which allowed the most insight into
children's perceptions of the voices surrounding them and of the locations
of those voices in time and space.

This mapping of the time-space dimensions of a childhood culture is
my deliberate goal, but it was not the children's. So, in the second major
section of this chapter, I consider the social ends that orchestrated and
guided their own appropriations of cultural texts.

In sum, in this chapter, I begin my investigation of literacy development by portraying the nature of childhood agency as exercised through

textual appropriation and manipulation. I present not child actions on the expanse of a piece of paper (the arena of most studies of child writing), but actions on the social expanse of "childtimes" (Greenfield & Little, 1979).

"CHILDTIMES"

> People are part of their time. They are affected, during the time that they live, by the things that happen in their world. Big things and small things. A war, an invention such as radio or television, a birthday party, a kiss. All of these experiences help to shape people, and they, in turn, help to shape the present and the future. . . . (n.p.)

This is the opening to Eloise Greenfield's and Lessie J. Little's *Childtimes: A three-generation memoir* (1979), their introduction to a book about their own family, about "kinsfolk touching across the centuries, walking with one hand clasping the hands of those who have gone before, the other hand reaching back for those who will come after. . . ." (n.p.). The child kin featured herein were also so located. By listening to their own naming of textual events and media genres, and their sense of the intended audience of those events and genres, I gained some sense of how the children were constructing their present, past, and future childtimes. I begin below with the children's "present" time and spaces, but, as will be evident, those present times were shaped by children who had long gone into their own futures.

Present Childhoods

"It's two more books that we can read with, you know, the voices," commented Vanessa, after she and Denise had sung a text from their basal reader, gospel-style, "like you're in church."

In related ways, the children's appropriations from available cultural materials—and available voices—situated them in their present lives as child participants in churches, families, neighborhoods and, most immediately, schools. The most evident child-initiated appropriation of *school* material involved songs. Generally, the children appropriated such songs during official events thematically related to the original ones introducing the songs. One child would begin a song, and the singing itself recruited other children, folding them into the ongoing rhythm. Such recruiting was audible and visible, for example, when Marcel began a rendition of "Mother Earth" (Rose, 1990) to accompany his assigned creation of an Earth Day crown.

Although less common, children's musical appropriations could situate them beyond the school walls and evoke their roles as *church* members. Not only had Denise and Vanessa "read" certain texts with singing "church" voices; occasionally they joined together for a "hymn," as in the following:

Vanessa and Denise are sitting side by side writing their observations of a silkworm. Vanessa starts singing:

1, 2, 3/ The devil's after me
4, 5, 6/

Denise joins in, and they sing the next verse together:

He's always throwing sticks
7, 8, 9/ He misses every time
Hallelujah, Hallelujah, Hallelujah
Amen

Denise, in particular, wanted to get church teachings right, and music may have informed her knowledge, or so Vanessa thought in the following data excerpt:

DENISE: Adam was the first person that got made, and he ate the apple.
VANESSA: And what apple was that? Shoot.
DENISE: I don't know, but I don't think he was supposed to, and he was the first man on earth, that got made.
VANESSA: He ate a apple, so what? Why wasn't he suppose to eat the apple?
DENISE: I, don't, know.
VANESSA: And who told you that somebody—oh that little old hymn.

Vanessa saw no sense in remarking on somebody eating just any old apple until she traced Denise's remark to its textual source ("that little old hymn") and, thus, to their shared textual knowledge as churchgoers (although to different actual churches).

In addition to church and school, the children's appropriations also located them as members of *families*. Some appropriated songs were from movies the family had seen. For example, one day, Lakeisha commented to Wenona, "Last night my mama had me singing 'I Believe I Can Fly' [Kelly, 1996, from the movie *Space Jam* (Falk, Ross, & Pytka, 1996)]. She *love* that movie. She *love* that song."

That loved movie featured African American basketball star Michael Jordan and Looney Tunes cartoon characters, and it was part of all the brothers and sisters' experiences during the school year. In the fall, those experiences could involve a much anticipated trip to the movie theater. For Vanessa, a planned trip was delayed when her mother had felt too sick to go, or so Vanessa sadly reported as she drew herself with tears streaming down her face. In the spring, those experiences could involve repeated viewing of the movie video with cousins and siblings. Noah hoped to bring the movie for the "whole class" to see as a treat, since his sister had already watched it "eight times and me and [fraternal twin] Ned watch it nine times. We watch it with my cousins." Noah's ability to do by memory the dialogue for whole scenes of the movie suggested the accuracy of his count. All of the brothers and sisters could sing songs from the movie soundtrack and did so with great frequency.

Children indexed family life when discussing television watching as well as movies. "You're not made out of glass" is what Denise said her family told her when they watched television together, and she sometimes discussed with Vanessa what she "had" to watch after school, when she and her brother negotiated their television viewing. As already noted, Vanessa had some disagreements with her granny about the suitability of *Barney* for a 6-year-old. Noah watched many afternoon cartoon shows with his brother Ned—and he could name lots of them. Once after he and Jamal were discussing the cartoon *Godzilla* (Wildey, Patterson, Urbano, Dufau, & Gordon, 1978), which I did not know, I asked him what station it was on. He told me and then said,

> You must watch it 'cause it got funny stuff on it. It's Bugs Bunny on it, Tweety Bird, Daffy Duck, Porky Pig, 'semite Sam. And it got Superman, Batman, Super—I mean Superfriends—um. I know all the names: Auto man—Auqa man, Fire man, Superman, Bat man, Robin, Wonderwoman. What's another one—Thunder man, and um and um—Wonderman. His neck is—his necks is all wet—all wings.

Noah was the only brother and sister, however, who talked at all about playing video games; that activity, too, was part of his after-school activities with Ned.

Unlike going to the movies, which was an anticipated family event and the source of retold stories, watching television shows was a recurrent event and, usually, the source of well-known characters. (Commercials, I should note, were the source of retold jokes, especially for Denise: "Have you seen that commercial that says 'We've been up since the crack a noon?'") Among well-known television characters were members of the comedy show *Martin* ([Bowman, Carew, Lawrence, & Williams, 1992] especially loud bimbo-ish Sheneneh, whose name, said in a playfully accented way, inspired giggles) and of the sitcom *Moesha* ([Finney & Spears, 1996] especially the teenage lead, played by the singer Brandy). Marcel's middle name was given after a character in a long-running sitcom about a loving, African American family.

Songs also could situate the children within family rhythms. The children reported learning songs from parents and grandparents, songs that were, in effect, folk songs. Interestingly, these were older, rhythmically riveting R&B songs. (For discussions of the permeability of folk and popular culture, see Mukerji & Schudson, 1991, and Narvaez & Laba, 1986.) The children knew mainly the hook or repetitive refrain and, typically, a child comment triggered a semantic connection to that hook. For example, when the first graders were looking through their kindergarten portfolios, Noah repeatedly commented that "I done that real good." Denise then broke into lines from a James Brown (1965/1971) classic "I Got You/I Feel Good." Denise, Vanessa, and Noah disagreed about the placement of the "so good"s and "so nice"s, but all compromised and sang "I feel good. I feel nice. I knew that I would." On another day, Denise was extremely excited about her upcoming family move and the possibility that, in this new place, she could have a cat; she gave a little shudder and then sang the hook—the memorable lines that grab listeners—from "I'm So Excited [. . . and I just can't hide it]" (Pointer Sisters, 1982).

In addition to movies, television, and songs, sports indexed family life as well. Indeed, Marcel was named after a football player, from the time when sports figures were "role models for our children," explained his mother. She no longer felt this was true, in large part because the media now delved into all aspects of sports figures' lives—their feats on the field no longer satisfied the popular media. Still, football was a part of Marcel's family life, and so it was for other children. Wenona, in fact, quite explicitly said that her family "like the [Oakland] Raiders, but we're still Dallas [fans, too]."

In addition to indexing family life, the children's references to televised sports situated them geographically and historically. Marcel was the biggest sports fan and typically knew the scores of the Monday night football game. These Bay Area children were not 49ers fans although they did sometimes mention the popular 49ers player Jerry Rice. They were Raiders fans and, moreover, Dallas fans. This surprised me, but it did not surprise my professional informant, an assistant coach for the Oakland Raiders, who was African American. In his view, the children's preferences indexed, in part, their identities as *East Bay kids* and, more broadly, as *fans—*

as participants in contemporary football culture, which is heavily mediated by the television.

There is a huge rivalry between East Bay Raider fans, who have a public stereotype as rowdy beer drinkers, and the San Francisco 49ers who, in the coach's words, are stereotyped as the "wine-and-cheese-crowd" and "golf clappers." His fiancée noted that during the Raiders games, fans roar with delight if the scoreboard flashes a 49er update showing them losing. Still, both Raiders fans and 49er fans may watch a great deal of Dallas football. Indeed, when he was a child, the coach, still a young man in his late 20s, was also a Dallas fan, although he was born in southern California. He learned about Dallas from watching television, just as the brothers and sisters did. He pointed out that Dallas games are often broadcasted, because of the team's popularity as a frequent Super Bowl winner and because of the popularity of its marquee players. (Indeed, the Raiders' home games sometimes are *not* broadcast, because their games do not always sell out, a National Football League requirement for broadcasted games.) For all these reasons, a small group of East Bay children with busy imagined lives as Dallas players and cheerleaders was not, in the end, as startling as I had initially thought. (Indeed, when I brought the topic up, my own mother, who lives in rural Wisconsin, told me the same facts about Dallas that this young coach in the Bay Area did—which also suggests to you, my readers, how on the edge of popular life I myself seem to be.)

In the preceding discussion about the textual threads between children's cultural resources and their lives as child participants in school, church, family, and a given geographical region, any material discussed belonged, at least initially, to adults—their teachers, parents, grandparents, and other older relatives. But one kind of material that children appropriated came, in fact, from other children and indexed their membership in *a child culture*. This material consisted of songs (also referred to as "games" or "play") learned from other kids, particularly neighborhood kids. Although all the children knew many such songs, the most prolific song producers were Denise and Vanessa. Denise sadly reported, after her midwinter move, that "things were different" in her new home in Oakland. Her new neighbors—two girls and a boy—didn't want to do anything, she said, except play tag, football, and catch:

DENISE: (describing catch in a voice expressing great ennui) Throw it up and down, up and down, up and down, and catch it, catch it, catch it.

DYSON: What would you like [the kids] to do?

DENISE: Play::.

DYSON: Play what?

DENISE: Play the games I used to play . . . like "Down by the Bank"
(a clapping game).

Unlike the previously discussed songs, and the ones to come, the songs
learned from other children, like "Down by the Bank," were almost exclusively playground fare. Scholars of such songs have tended to homog-
enize children's racial and ethnic cultures, emphasizing the raucous and
irreverent nature of children's oral cultures, passed on through generations of childtimes (for discussion, see Sutton-Smith, Mechling, Johnson,
& McMahon, 1995). Child cultures' songs and rhymes are notably more
vulgar, more raucous, more focused on sexual and power themes than
any material adults deliberately teach children.

Still, the children's repertoire included verses, especially jump rope
songs, which have been particularly (but not exclusively) associated with
the play of African American girls (Beresin, 1995; Gillmore, 1985). Indeed,
verses heard on the children's Bay Area playground were included in Bessie
Jones's collection, based on her own childhood in a Black farming community at the turn of the 20th century and dating back, she reported, at
least to her grandparents' childhood (Jones & Hawes, 1972).

For example, in the midst of the children's "Down by the Bank" came
lines (italicized below) from Jones's "Green Sally Up" (p. 25):

This is a clapping song, where partners alternately clap their own
and their partner's hands and, at the very end of the song, try to
tag the other's hand "out." Denise and Vanessa begin clapping and
singing together:

Down by the bank
said a hanky pank
said a bull frog jumped from bank to bank
said E-I-O-U
Feeling with the ding dong
See that house on top of the hill
That's where me and my boyfriend live
Smell that chicken
Smell that rice
Come on baby let's shoot, some, dice

DENISE: You're out!
VANESSA: Ma::n! Why you have to get me out?

Another song, "Rockin' Robin," echoed not only with contemporary
popular culture but also Motown music of the 1970s (Jackson, 1971b),

the rock 'n' roll of the 1950s (Day, 1958), as well as with old play songs, especially Jones's "Sandy Ree" (Jones & Hawes, 1972, p. 134), which is about tough farm life. Following are a few verses, transcribed from an audiotaped performance by Denise and Vanessa:

> Rockin' robin/ tweet tweet, tweet-a-leet
> Rockin' robin/ tweet tweet, tweet-a-leet [compare to Jackson,
>   1971a; and Day, 1958]
>
> Mama in the kitchen/ Burning rice
> Daddy on the corner/ Shooting that dice
> Brother in jail/ Raising H
> Sister at the corner/ Selling fruit cocktail [compare to Jones &
>   Hawes, 1972]
>
> Rockin' robin/ tweet tweet, tweet-a-leet
> Rockin' robin/ tweet tweet, tweet-a-leet
>
> Batman and Robin/ Flying in the air
> Batman lost/ His underwear
> Robin said/ I'll buy you a pair
> But you don't know/ What size I wear [parody of contemporary
>   superhero]
>
> Rockin' robin . . .

Such songs were fast driving, syncopated, and quite performative. Thus, it is not surprising that the children slipped easily from generations-old rhymes to the drama of very now songs, as in the interaction between Marcel and Noah that opened this chapter.[1] As I discuss below, that movement involved a turn to an imagined future as teenagers and, moreover, to a more explicitly racialized and gendered one.

Children's (Audio)Visions of Past and Future

In the preceding section, I emphasized the linkages between children's cultural appropriations and their participation in varied social realms— church, school, family, peer group and, more broadly, geographical region. Implicit throughout was the racialized and gendered nature of their appropriations. The children, for example, referenced primarily television shows and movies that include African American characters (very similar to children observed in another local school; see Dyson, 1997). Although boys were the more ardent sports fans, both girls and boys were participants in popular sports culture. Conversely, although girls were the main participants in playground songs, both boys and girls frequently sang (including Lakeisha, with her loud monotonic voice).

When the children's textual appropriations explicitly indexed their own early years, race and gender seemed to fade from view, and school and home seemed quite compatible. For example, songs of remembered pasts were associated with preschool, kindergarten, and home. When their cultural appropriations explicitly situated them in their anticipated teenage years, however, a very different social experience was constructed. Those anticipated years were more gender-divided in consumption, more explicitly linked to race-identified artists, and quite unconnected to school. Consider, for example, the following scene:

> The children are making Earth Day Crowns, decorated with nature scenes and sayings. There is a great deal of cutting and coloring, the sort of activities that lend themselves to spontaneous singing. Elizabeth, Denny, Cedric, Marcel, Wenona, and Noah are all sitting at the same table. Marcel begins singing the Mother Earth song, and others join in. Then Marcel moves on to a different song, which he sings soul-style:

> MARCEL: "Baby, baby, baby, baby/I need you so much." (I do not know what the song is. Wenona does, though, and she joins in.)
>   NOAH: (to Marcel) You like girl songs!
> MARCEL: No I don't.
>   NOAH: Well, how come you singing 'em?

> Noah, Marcel, and Cedric move on to a hip-hop crowd pumper, belting it out together:

> "Put you hands in the air/Like you just don't care . . ."

> Rita puts the Mother Earth tape on, and the children all sing along. She compliments the children on the time and thought they are putting into their crowns (which look very good to me, too). She suggests they walk around the school later, wearing their crowns and singing Earth Day songs. "Cool!" says Marcel, quite pleased. He works a while, and then has another song selection:

> MARCEL: Let's sing the Barney [1993] song. (singing) "I love you/You love me/We're a happy family. . . ."

> Noah joins in, to my surprise, since he has criticized Marcel for his enjoyment of the Barney song. This time Wenona offers the critique:

WENONA: Why are you singing a <u>preschool</u> song?
MARCEL: Whoops. (looking sheepish)

As is evident in the above example, the children used preschool songs to construct age, not gender, distinctions by declaring who could like, or sing, such songs. Barney, a sweet dinosaur with no ironic edges, seemed a particular magnet for disdain. The children appropriated with unchallenged pleasure songs like "Rubber Ducky" (Ernie [Moss, 1970]) and "C is for Cookie" (Cookie Monster [Raposo, 1973]) from *Sesame Street* (Singer & Stone, 1969), a more sophisticated preschool show designed for child and adult appeal. As *Sesame Street* composer Joe Raposo commented, "We're just dealing with a very short audience"(quoted in Borgenicht, 1998, p. 145).

The children were quite aware that teenage music was not age-appropriate for them. They reported learning that material primarily from radios, radios that provided the backdrop to morning routines and school commutes, radios in community center offices and public parks, and radios in the company of adolescents, cool people whom children admired. These appropriated songs reverberated with adult voices beyond those doing the singing; their parents were concerned about the content of certain "teen-ager" songs. When Denise drew herself as a singer in high heels and a slinky gown, Vanessa said,

I'm not putting high heels on me cause that's too fast, Denise. That's too fa::st. We're only 6 and 7. And that is too fast (with definiteness). Cause, Denise, I'm sorry if I'm breaking your heart. . . .

The children's parents were indeed concerned about "<u>too-fast</u>" music, with its "<u>negative images</u>" and <u>vulgar language</u>, to quote Noah's father. Similar sentiments were expressed by Noah and Wenona in the context of brother and sister play about what "Mama" said about the CD player:

Wenona has just said she listened to Noah's CD player at home:

NOAH: You can't listen to it, cause I'm bigger than you.
WENONA: I'm gonna look at your CD player.

   . . .

NOAH: CD player! It got—it got bad words on it.
WENONA: So?
NOAH: You can't listen to it cause I'm bigger than you.
WENONA: No you're not.
NOAH: Yes I am. (Starts singing the commercial jingle for a chicken product, perhaps to change or at least stop the topic.)

For the children, then, referring to teenagers' music seemed akin to dress up—to using "stolen lipstick" (Koch, 1998, p. 74). And dress up tends to mark gender, particularly in reference to girl clothes ("girl songs," as Noah said). Moreover, appropriated music seemed to index an African American cultural sphere, as well as a youthful one. The children referred to the names of 43 popular performers or performing groups, all African American (with the exception of Cookie Monster and Barney). Listen to Vanessa's response when I ask her about the group Immature, one of whom has the nickname "Batman":

> VANESSA: Not the Batman that flies through the air.
> Not the Batman that lost his underwear [as in the
> children's playground rhyme]
> But Batman. He Black and he fine.

Perhaps because of the transitory nature of most popular music and its relatively sophisticated content, as well as their monitored exposure, the children knew primarily the hooks and the choruses from those songs. Beyond the strongly patterned, rhythmic, and highly repetitive parts, children sang words that made sense in their own childtimes. In a segment of "I'm Going Down" (Blige, 1994), Denise sang that the rain was "slowly driving me inside," rather than "insane." In a verse from "Best Friend" (Brandy, 1994), Vanessa sang that it didn't matter "whether I lose or if I win" in the "good games and the bad," not in the "good times and the bad ones," as in the original.

Despite the word changes, and the concentration on hooks and choruses, the children did understand the aesthetics of these songs, their usual beats and melodic contours, their moods, and their usual consumers. In the course of their play with these teenage voices, the children sometimes slipped off the high heels and wiped off the lipstick and resituated themselves in their present childhoods:

> Out on the playground, Denise has been reciting her version of the refrain from "My Baby Daddy" (B Rock and the Biz, 1997). From my point of view, the song is about jealousy; from Denise's, the song seems to be about family.

> DENISE: K-M-E-L [hip-hop radio station] (whistles)
> <u>Who that is?</u>/ My baby daddy (softer)
> <u>Who that is?</u>/ My baby daddy
> <u>Who that is?</u>/ My baby daddy
> That ain't your baby daddy [not in original]

Denise then improvises verses to the same beat.

Oh Anne is my mama/Oh Anne is my mama
Oh Anne is my mama/Just my play mama

Oh Johnny and Robert/Oh Johnny and Robert
Oh Johnny and Robert/They always play together

Oh Joseph and Vanessa/Oh Joseph and Vanessa
Oh Joseph and Vanessa/They both cousins.

The children's musical appropriations, like "My Baby Daddy," most clearly constructed a youthful future of gender-marked relations, often on a racialized landscape, but these relations could become visible whenever any appropriated material indexed a perceived adolescence. For example, once Jamal with great sincerity told Wenona, her hair newly arranged in cascading braids, that she looked like the teenage sitcom character Moesha. On another occasion, in the midst of a discussion of the Power Rangers teams (featured on a television show involving coed, multiethnic teenage superheroes), Marcel and Zephenia declared their love for the African American teenage girls featured on the show; it was their attractiveness, not their physical powers, that received attention (for discussion of super-heroes, gender, and child play, see Dyson, 1997).

Although the children's appropriated material clearly situated them in an adolescence of reductive gender relations, I, the arranger of their voices in this chapter, urge caution upon what I imagine may be some concerned readers. The children, true to childhood cultures, were playing with cultural identities; as complex individuals, they could not and should not be reduced to the representational limits of their texts (Zumwalt, 1995). It is, after all, a societal truism that adolescence is a time of exploring gen-der relations. Moreover, as Walkerdine argues for working-class girls, media stars (including, I add, sports stars) and their cultural productions are ways that children imagine themselves beyond their daily constraints into glamourous, wealthy futures, surrounded by admirers both male and female. To quote Denise, "the girls will say 'Go girl; it's your birthday' (Luke, 1994) and the boys will say 'I love you baby.'" (The girls, by the way, wanted to be "a lot of things" when they moved beyond the teenage years; among them, artists, nurses, and helicopter pilots.)

Further, the children's appropriated images contested, as well as sim-ply adopted, stereotypical gender values and relations. For example, the children's attentiveness to female beauty as something other than the typical fair-haired Barbie look is, in and of itself, a contestation of hege-monic standards (standards adopted much more readily by the older children observed in Dyson, 1997). In addition, the complex panorama of media images include contradictory media archetypes (Douglas, 1994). In the children's interactions, the textual seams of differing ideologies could thus emerge. Wenona, for instance, appropriated cinematic coed sports teams (like that of Coach Bombay) when Marcel challenged her right to imagine a future of playing on organized sports teams, like the boys:

WENONA: When I grow up, I'm playing hockey.
MARCEL: Girls are not supposed to play hockey.
WENONA: Yes, they can. Like on the *Mighty Ducks* [Avnet, Claybourne, Kerner, & Weisman, 1994]? . . .
MARCEL: Oh yeah.
WENONA: I'm on the Migh ty Ducks. I'm gonna be a football player and a hockey player.
MARCEL: Girls can't play football.
WENONA: Yes they can.
MARCEL: No they can't.
WENONA: OK. On the *Little Giants* [Molen, Parkes, Schmidt, & Dunham 1994]? . . . They do have a girl on *Little Giants*. Ice Box [girl character's nickname].
MARCEL: I know.

In the world of the brothers and sisters, Wenona *was* on the Mighty Ducks team and, on that basis, she assumed the right to project herself into a future of sports. And Marcel could not disagree. (As will be clear in the chapters ahead, these exposed seams were sometimes pointed out by the children's teacher, Ms. Rita, in furthering a critical imagination, an ability to imagine that the world might be otherwise [see Freire, 1970; Greene, 1995].)

In sum, the children's socioideological landscape provided them with whole utterances, utterance types or genres, and particular words and phrases, and this textual and cultural material became the stuff with which the children could construct their present lives, remember their pasts, and anticipate their youthful futures. In so doing, they were, at the very same time, constructing complex selves who participated in varied social institutions and, more broadly, in particular social and cultural spheres.

In writing these complex selves, and urging readers not to reduce any particular child to a singular voice, I am remembering my own complex participation in Hall's "theater of popular fantasies" (1992, p. 32). I was a child in a farm town during the 1950s, and have no preschool media experiences in my memories. But I do remember that my "father" was Sky King (a do-gooder air pilot on a television show), my own having died too soon (Jack Chertok Productions, 1951); part of the appeal of that father was his being very busy, and so his ward and niece, Penny, actually had quite a bit of freedom (much the same appeal of the textual Nancy Drew's [Stratemeyer, 1930] usually absent father). I also remember my glamorous future as a teenage radio star, which competed with my sanctified future as a nun who would, nonetheless, have 12 children (following a bit enthusiastically in the path of Mary). One of my most vivid childhood memories is of standing outside, in full view of the neighbors, swinging a hula hoop on my hips and singing a spirited rendition of "She wore an itsy bitsy yellow polka-dot bikini," which I learned from the radio (Hyland, 1960/1994).

It is not some sort of singular child essence that I am searching for, in tracing the threads of the children's appropriations; rather, it is a vision, however fuzzy and tentative, of the landscape of voices to which the observed children responded in constructing their own childhoods. Like my own remembered childhood, constructed in response to a landscape of voices, the children's landscape, reconstructed through their appropriations, was a panorama of voices and, thus, a shared textual toy box.

THE SOCIAL USEFULNESS OF TEXTUAL TOYS

As is the case with analysis, my descriptions of willful children appropriating textual material are based on my own willful study of pages of field notes and accompanying transcripts. I studied the episodes in my data containing references to particular media materials and, by examining their content and interactional patterns, I developed a coding system or vocabulary for describing the intertwined social functions served by those textual toys.

First and foremost, the children's textual toys provided a source of *pleasure* or just stimulation, including during official work times. For example, as they worked on a class assignment, Wenona suggested to Marcel that they sing the movie *Space Jam*'s title song because "it's boring just sitting here." A dominant quality of their pleasurable singing was its fluidity, its movement from one topic to the next, one kind of song to the next. Moreover, appropriated songs were intermixed with their own playful creations.

Noah, who tended to be intense when he drew and wrote, with little off-topic talk, marked his completion of his Mother's Day journal entry with "Oh my. I'm done/I'm shun/I shake that little bunny./I'm done/I'm shun/A little little bunny." He then joined Vanessa on the repetitive hook of a rap—"Somebody's sleeping in *my* bed, messing with *my* head" (Hill,

1996). Vanessa announced that she knew how to spell *apple*, and the children were off again:

> DENISE } A-P-P-L-E.
> VANESSA }
>   DENISE: (rapping) I want to A-P-P/About my fam-i-ly.
>   As I walk these streets/Something scar-ing me.
>   NOAH: Yeah. Right here. (Points to the scary dog's face he has
>   drawn in his journal)

The spelling A-P-P reminded Denise of the opening line of a TuPac rap (under the name of Makaveli, 1996), which actually begins with an "A-P-B on my thug family." In addition to that change, Denise mixed his line "Since the outlaws run these streets" with a related one from a Coolio rap (which Vanessa explicitly noted). In both raps, something was scaring somebody, and Noah playfully suggested that it was the big dog in his journal entry.

As is common in children's early symbol-making (Golomb, 1992), children's playfulness with, and pleasure in, their own voices was in productive tension with their desire to create more ordered products. Thus, a second function of textual appropriation was to provide material for *personal expression and performance*. Of course, any use of language is a kind of performance (Hymes, 1972), but that term typically suggests an "aesthetically marked and heightened mode of communication" that lifts it apart from other voices and puts it on display for an audience (Bauman, 1992, p. 41). The most elaborate efforts at coherent performances occurred on the playground and, most often, they were based on the raps and love songs of teenage music. The children's efforts included both group performances, with backup and lead singers, and individual efforts for friends and me.

For example, one day Denise and Vanessa were concerned about Elizabeth, a classmate, "spying" on them. During recess, Denise "made up" a "rap" about this situation (although the rap may have been influenced by MC Lyte's [1998] *In My Business*). The driving beat and aggressive tone of her performance contrasted her typical interactional style, which was playful and, during conflict, intent on compromise. Denise's effort to maintain a pattern of syllable stresses and rhymes led to some lexical nonsense, which she soulfully admitted during her performance:

> DENISE: It's called, "Why You in My Bus'ness?" (sternly)
>
>   (rapping) Why you in my bus'ness?
>   Cause I got you/In my far is-nius
>   And I had you/In my char-is-mus/ my bus'ness
>   Why you gotta be/In the bus'ness?

> Can you get one of your home-y?
> And you know you spy on me
> I'm gonna get your home-y
> Cause I know/How much/You spy on me
>
> (In an R & B style) That is true: oo
> That is true: oo/Yeah
> It is, true: oo oo

And after rapping again about her business, she sings:

> I don't know these words I'm saying
> So please forgive me for my words

The rap performance contrasted with the following more soulful "make-up song," to use Vanessa's name for an improvised song. During this recess performance, Vanessa took the role as lead singer, Denise and Wenona assumed backup for the "love song" (one of the children's genre terms):

VANESSA:	I'm gonna sing um a make-up song. Y'all gonna sing with me, right?
DENISE } WENONA }	Yeah.
DENISE:	What do you want us to say? [And when Vanessa has no particular directive to offer . . .] We gonna say "I love you."
WENONA:	Yeah.
VANESSA:	Heck no!
WENONA:	Yeah.
VANESSA:	No no no. (firmly)
DENISE:	We gonna say, "Baby." (definitively)
VANESSA:	No. (equally definitively)
WENONA:	"Baby boy"? (tentatively)
VANESSA:	Ok, ok.

Having agreed, Vanessa, as lead singer, now reissues that agreement as a directive:

VANESSA:	OK. Y'all gonna say "baby boy," OK?

Then she does the count down and begins singing:

VANESSA:	1, 2, 3. (spoken) No body can tell me

> to tell me who I see
> to tell me when I move
> OO oooh
> . . .

And the backup soon comes in, soft and smooth:

DENISE
WENONA } Baby boy (backup)

Even though the children's efforts were "make-up," they composed coherent stanzas through semantic consistency and repetitive structures that were genre appropriate. (On another day, Vanessa's "make-up" love song included the lines: "I knew that I could be/echo with reality"—not the usual 6-year-old fare.)

Performances did not have to be elaborate, and brief spoken ones could "breakthrough" (Hymes, 1975) almost any time, especially when the children were working in small groups. They might begin by pleasurably recalling a commonly viewed audiovisual story but, then, appealing character utterances would be lifted out of the story for recontextualization in the children's own performances. Indeed, such recontextualization of liftable utterances (e.g., those expressively and rhythmically marked [Tannen, 1989]) within new performances is the basic process undergirding folklore and everyday aesthetic activity (Bauman & Briggs, 1990; McDowell, 1995; Willis, 1990).

For example, Noah and Tommy were discussing the film *Space Jam* when they slipped into the voices of the film's monstrous space alien (Swackhammer) and his space lackeys (the Nerdlucks):

TOMMY: We need something—looney! Looney! (enacting the gruff voice of Swackhammer as he decides, upon seeing the Looney Tunes on his television sets, to kidnap the 'toon characters to enliven his amusement park)

NOAH: What if they can't come? (enacting the small voice of a Nerdluck)

TOMMY: Can't come!? Make 'em!

On another occasion, all of the brothers and sisters were recalling amusing scenes (from their point of view) in the film *Matilda* (Bregman, Peyser, & DeVito, 1996) as they worked in their writing journals. At one point, Noah had trouble drawing an image of the gorilla Donkey Kong and, after expressing his frustration, he voiced a popular line from the film *Matilda*, which led to joint performances (and a slight correction from Vanessa):

> NOAH: And the gorilla is really hard. (commenting on his
> drawing) "And there's nothing you can do about it"
> [from *Matilda*].

Denise, Vanessa, and Noah expressively recite the "Matilda" line,
which was spoken by the film's "mean teacher." Then Vanessa
recites the teacher's preceding line:

> VANESSA: "I'm big, you're small. I'm smart, you're dumb."
> NOAH: "And there's not nothing you can <u>do</u> about it."
> VANESSA: No! "And there's nothing you can do."
>
> NOAH }
> VANESSA } And there's nothing you can do.

Sometimes the children's textual toys allowed them *a context for dramatic play*. For example, in enacting radio play, this social goal organized
primarily the talk around the singing, rather than the singing itself (which
sometimes did not even occur). In the transcript below, recorded on the
playground, Denise is being a radio deejay <u>and</u> a star. The play contains
varied genres heard on her regular radio station, including teasing (sometimes insulting) exchanges with on-air personalities and spontaneous raps,
along with song introductions:

> DENISE: OK, K-M-E-L, 1–0–6. Everybody turn on their radio, right
> now. 1–0–6. Listen to this. Stay tuned. Somebody's gonna
> sing, "Who Can Love You Like Me? [Nobody]" This is
> Denise Ray.
> You remind me of eating. Yeah, right. The song is beginning.
> (Denise then sings a brief rendition of "Nobody" [Sweat,
> 1996].)

On another day, Denise interviewed herself:

> DENISE: (assuming a polite, interested tone) Denise. Tell us why do
> you like to sing—and your friends?
> DENISE: (rapping) We want to be a star/In the store
> We want to be on stage/For our cage.

As already noted, sports media also provided rich contextual material for unofficial play, because in addition to playing hockey for Coach
Bombay, Marcel played "for Dallas," and Wenona "cheerleads for Texas."
Wenona, Marcel, and Noah engaged in extended planning of their complex lives as students, peers, and team members. Below, Wenona and

Marcel sing a round of "We are the Champions" (Queen, 1986) and then reminisce and commiserate over their grueling schedule:

> MARCEL: 'Member they [San Jose] lost to us last year? We went to the world champions.
> WENONA: We <u>was</u> the world champions. . . . We gotta play at night time, you know.
> MARCEL: And my football game is at night. . . . We gotta play at Arizona, Texas, San Fran//cisco//—
> WENONA: //cisco// um Stockton. That's a long way. . . . Now, how we kids gonna do our homework?

In addition to pleasure, performance, and play, the children's textual toys were also a source of *displayed knowledge and expertise*. As already illustrated, Noah knew the names of a wide range of cartoon heroes. Marcel, Samuel, and Zephenia often repeated football scores to each other, after an opening "Did you see the game?" Moreover, the children knew, and noticed who knew, particular songs. They sometimes referred to the artists who sang certain songs, always accurately. Indeed, some musical knowledge seemed important if one was to be seen as a reasonably aware person. For example, when Marcel, Noah, and Lakeisha discussed the death of the rap star TuPac, Noah playfully disagreed with Marcel, to Marcel's irritation. But Noah quickly became serious when Lakeisha agreed with him, asking her, in effect, to be reasonable:

> MARCEL: [TuPac] died in 1996 [which is correct].
> NOAH: No he didn't.
> MARCEL: He died in 1996.
> NOAH: He died before we was a baby.
> MARCEL: No he didn't.
> NOAH: Yes he did. (laughs)
> MARCEL: No he didn't.
> LAKEISHA: Yes he did. (definitively)
> NOAH: No he didn't. (with aggressiveness) No he didn't. He— How come he made some more songs? He made some new songs.

Interrelated with all the social uses listed above for the children's textual toys was this one: to serve as a means for constructing relationships and, more particularly, for both *social affiliation and differentiation* in varied, sometimes overlapping social spheres. Within their friendship group, textual toys were primarily resources used to affirm and sustain group affiliations through collaborative practices of dramatic enactments, story-telling, and singing. On occasion, though, those toys could be effectively used to differentiate or distance one child from another. Once, for example, Lakeisha had threatened to tell Rita about a rule violation of Wenona's. Wenona just shrugged, "Yeah. So you can be a 49er. Forty-niners tell, not Dallas." Lakeisha, at least for that moment, was no longer on the team.

As previously discussed, the children's unofficial media use could construct and make locally visible societal boundaries. If Marcel, for in-stance, began singing a song taught in school, like "Mother Earth" or "I Got Shoes" (Sweet Honey in the Rock, 1994), then he would soon be joined by many children in the classroom, across race and gender lines. But, if he began a song learned from the hip-hop radio station, he was joined only by selected children (and since the volume did not become so loud at his immediate table, the singing did not spread beyond that table). His sing-ing mates were only African American children, with the exception of European American Tommy (whose older brother had a hip-hop CD col-lection). Even a widely popular song like the Grammy-winning "I Believe I Can Fly" (Kelly, 1996) from *Space Jam* had the same interrelated class- and race-differentiated pattern in this classroom.

The issue at hand, however, is the children's *intentional* use of media preferences (i.e., taste) to differentiate themselves socially. Beyond the already specified (and not always enacted) regulation of age and gender boundaries, such use was not a common occurrence. But it did happen. Vanessa was especially sensitive to relational nuances and to local racial boundaries constructed around music.

The most dramatic illustration occurred during an attempt at enact-ing a multiethnic girls' club. During the fall of the year, Denise, Vanessa, Wenona, and Lakeisha frequently made "girls' club" artifacts (e.g., sheets of paper decorated with their initials and drawn hearts). But, in the late spring, Denise decided to spend a classroom activity time (i.e., a time for self-chosen projects) to plan a girls' club with Vanessa, April, and April's good friends Nanette and Elizabeth, both European American. (Wenona and Lakeisha were occupied with other activities.) April, who was of Chinese and European heritage, was considered by herself and others as "part African American" because her father was Chinese (i.e., "African American" was equated with "not White," a confusion Rita eventually un-tangled). April had previously chosen on occasion to sit with Denise and her close friends. But Nanette and Elizabeth had not.

Denise took the lead in the group's planning, posing the decisions that needed to be made about the club. When she asked about the club's password, Vanessa suggested the radio call letters KMEL, a "word" only Denise knew. Moreover, as Denise continued to focus on the "club," Vanessa continued to use music to highlight her special relationship with Denise:

> Denise is giving directions for making the pages of the club book. Ariel, Nanette, and Elizabeth are attending and responding to Denise with their own suggestions. Vanessa starts singing a "bouncy song," seemingly inspired by Mase (1997), a popular rap artist:

> VANESSA: Look at those girls . . .
> OO:: they look so fine
> Look at those girls
> OO:: looking so fine

> Denise is concentrating on the pages.

> VANESSA: Come on, Denise. (to group) She's my best friend. She's hecka fun.
> DENISE: After you're done [with your page for the book, I'll sing with you].

And she did.

Finally, the children's textual toys could provide resources for *participation in school literacy events*, particularly for composing events. It is this latter function that is highlighted in the chapters to come. However, the children's diverse forms of agency, including their playful, performative, and socially regulative aims, will all be evident as well. As Vygotsky (1987) suggested near the beginning of the last century, children come to understand the symbolic nature of written language only if they have some sense of the functional work—the social ends—driving, requiring, and organizing the manipulation of those drab print symbols into speech, or, as I would say, into voices positioned in a dialogic world (Dyson, 1993).

VENTURING OUT FROM A CHILDHOOD LANDSCAPE: TOWARD SCHOOL LITERACY PRACTICES

Beginning with Noah and Marcel, who, in the opening vignette, discussed Barney over their papers full of Cheerios, in this chapter I have aimed to illustrate how children constructed their childtimes and the diverse cultural resources that that construction entailed. The children's expressive practices, social intentions, and articulated ideologies were all produced as they drew upon their shared histories and discursive resources to engage with each other within institutional spaces: an unofficial dimension of those spaces, most certainly, one outside the direct control of Ms. Rita, not to mention their parents and grandparents, preachers, and older siblings. But, nonetheless, the studied childhood culture—the world of the brothers and sisters—was produced in school.

In the next chapter, I reposition myself and the children and gaze out from the children's landscape onto that of the official school world. For the children, and for me, this world was not miles or years away—it was a social turn away, a change in footing or frame of reference (Goffman, 1981). Moreover, that social turn involved participating in the official "cultural production of an educated person" (Levinson & Holland, 1996, p. 1), but it did not stop the children's unofficial production as educated—as knowledgeable and skillful—participants in a particular childhood culture, itself dynamically linked with family, community, and communal (or popular) cultures. As Chapter 3 will illustrate, in their efforts to participate in the official world, they drew strongly on the unofficial one, with its diverse forms of agency and meaningful symbols. Thus, forms of childhood pleasure, performance, and power—all in evidence in Noah and Marcel's opening anecdote—as well as those familiar textual toys will be surfacing on the official landscape in the chapters to come.

But there was more involved in the children's development as writers—as participants in official school literacy events—than moving textual material from one sociocultural landscape onto another. That material, and the social practices it mediated, posed complex questions, for me as researcher but also for the children. Among the questions were: What exactly did the children appropriate from their cargo of resources for movement in the official school world? That is, what did they view as relevant for what? Through what compositional means did they transform that multimedia material into written prose? Moreover, what social ends organized the children's official written efforts? And what were the symbolic, social, and ideological consequences of those efforts, for both official and unofficial relationships?

The social turn to the official world, and to school literacy practices, is not just about learning a new code for representing meanings. It is about entering new social dialogues in what, educators hope, are expanding life worlds. As such, written language learning is inevitably a part of learning about social and ideological worlds and about the place of children's own relationships and experiences in those worlds. With that in mind, then, it is time to meet the children as they turn toward the official school landscape that they shared with Ms. Rita and their classmates in Room 10.

3

The Brothers and Sisters in the Classroom Family: Entering School Literacy Practices

I noticed that everyone who talked about [the book *Mama, Do You Love Me?*] was serious and, you know what? You didn't tell me that you knew your mom loves you because she buys you things. And I'm proud of you for that. . . . But now it's a different kind of love that I have for you. It's not like your mom's love, is it? But I have affection for you because you're my class and you're my classroom family. And I kind of hope that you have the same for me. And that you know when you get into trouble and you do things it doesn't mean that I don't like you. I don't love you any less than I did before. (Ms. Rita's comments to her class)

"Just look at her!" Denise said to me one day, when I asked why she and Vanessa liked Ms. Rita so much (as they had just declared). I wasn't sure what Denise and Vanessa saw, but I saw an energetic woman in her early 50s, short in stature, strong in voice, moving around the room, leaning over to talk with this child and that one, keeping up with her "classroom family."

Denise and Vanessa, members of "real" families and a "fake one," were also members of what Rita considered her classroom family. As such, they and other members of their unofficial family sometimes voiced a sense of sharing in Rita's encompassing view during, or in anticipation of, official events. After a work period one day, Rita gathered children on the rug for a "How did it go?" discussion, in which the class shared their sense of accomplishments and problems, as well as any actual finished products. Rita had just voiced words of praise and gratitude for the class's hard work when Vanessa spoke up:

> VANESSA: I'm going to bring a movie to thank you guys for being so good. . . . I could even bring some pop corn.

Vanessa spoke up with no hesitation, slipping into Rita's appreciative gaze at "you guys" (the rest of the class). But Vanessa was not 50-something, like Ms. Rita, nor did she have Ms. Rita's explicit intention of disconnecting affection and accomplishment from material rewards. From Vanessa's vantage point, as a fellow child, this class deserved a treat—the pleasure of one of her textual toys, complete with popcorn. (Rita thought this treat would be fine, some Friday afternoon when the class had an activity choice time.)

Vanessa's response to her class is a metaphor for the theme of this chapter: the complex interrelationships between unofficial and official communicative practices and materials. What was at stake in this "antiphony of . . . the child and the grown-up" was not only children's active entry into school literacy but, moreover, their entry into the communicative practices that bound together a classroom family complexly situated in an urban community (Jones & Hawes, 1972, p. 191).

The unofficial family, of course, was itself not always a smoothly functioning one, as illustrated in Chapter 2. It had its own relational complexities. Just a sampling: Marcel and Wenona were, in Marcel's terms, "soul mates" as well as fake siblings. Noah was their consistent fake brother. Denise and Wenona were real cousins as well as fake stepsisters—a step removed because Vanessa wanted to be Denise's only sister. Denise called Vanessa her "best play sister" or "best fake sister." Denise and Vanessa considered Marcel and Noah fake brothers, although Noah sometimes became overly affectionate toward Denise (by proposing marriage, for instance), in which case he was temporarily removed from the family due to Denise's irritation.

A functioning, lively social unit does not mean a consistently harmonious one devoid of potential divisions and power plays. It does suggest *a membership*, a sense of belonging through mutual understanding and reciprocity. Denise, Vanessa, Noah, Marcel, and Wenona knew where the other was coming from, so to speak. They shared a cultural landscape and common communicative practices. And they consistently watched out for each other. "I got your back," one might say to another, before telling a teasing other to "stop it," or even "leave my sister alone." Belonging to the brothers and sisters entailed active participation and contribution and a sharing of textual toys (not to mention any literal treats one might happen to have).

Developing a sense of belonging to the larger classroom family also entailed becoming an active, contributing member to the common pleasure if not the common good, and being seen as such a member. In a first-grade classroom, that participation and contribution inevitably entailed negotiating an entry into classroom literacy practices. In so doing, the children brought themselves, their relationships, and their cultural resources. Those very practices and materials of child agency could give form to potentially productive tensions for individual and collective learning in Ms. Rita's evolving classroom family.

In this chapter, I provide an initial panoramic vision of the children's negotiated entry into school literacy, saving the developmental narratives for the chapters ahead. The vision is displayed against the backdrop of Rita's language and literacy curriculum and, more specifically, the classroom space study unit, which welcomed the children back to school after the winter holidays. In the sections that follow, I first describe Rita's curriculum, emphasizing both the necessity for and the existence of its "permeable" quality (Dyson, 1993, p. 30), that is, of features that allowed a dynamic interplay, an antiphony, between the worlds of children and adults to evolve.

The unfolding of this interplay, so exciting to me, the observer and "fake mama," could sometimes be disconcerting to Rita, understandably enough. On occasion, when she reflected with the children on how a work period had gone, she told them she "struggled" with their talkativeness. It was hard to know whether or not the children were in control and concentrating on their work and discussing it with a peer, or out of control and abandoning their work for other interests. From my vantage point, as an observer, not a teacher, the children did not spin out of control, but they did sometimes spin beyond Rita's direct control, centering their actions in the unofficial world.

To illustrate the children's shifting orbits, in the second section to follow, I provide a taxonomy of the kinds of cultural materials appropriated from the unofficial landscape as the children turned to the official one, and then, with that taxonomy in hand, I offer a sampling of the children's participation in an official composing activity of the space unit. In so doing, I introduce the complex interplay between the official and unofficial worlds, as their respective communicative practices—and their resources—were juxtaposed, blended and, indeed, temporarily abandoned.

In Bakhtin's terms (1981, pp. 272–273), this interplay was energized by the simultaneous and contradictory pull of centralizing or "centripetal" forces, emanating from official practices, experiences, and values, and the decentralizing or "centrifugal" forces emanating from the unofficial world. The former normalized the composing efforts of Ms. Rita's classroom family; the latter interrupted this unity and, moreover, made visible its socioeconomic, gender, racial and, ultimately, cultural complexities. Any individual child's textual utterance was shaped by the "contradiction-ridden, tension-filled unity of [these] two embattled tendencies in the life of language" (Bakhtin, 1981, p. 272).

In the closing section of the chapter, I consider the intertextual tracings of these micro-macro relationships in the products of all classroom members. To do this, I describe how children appropriated two space-related popular texts—*Star Wars* (Kurtz & Lucas, 1977) and *Space Jam* (Falk, Ross, & Pytka, 1996) during open-ended classroom writing workshop times. In this way, I suggest that ways of weaving oneself into the classroom family may involve, at the very same time, emboldening the textual threads of distinctions. Rita's classroom family was not fermented in a melting pot, but woven together in a homemade quilt.

ORGANIZING THE CLASSROOM FAMILY: INTRODUCTION TO OFFICIAL SPACE

"I like a little bit of tension around learning," Rita told me one day when I asked her about how to make a classroom family. "I notice a lot of kids, they don't have a way of being a learner, and I don't want them to be scared, but I want them to have a little commitment. . . . 'We've got to get it together here, and I'm gonna be asked to tell my opinion or read my story any minute now.' It's not just the passive, teacher's-telling-you-to-do-everything."

A classroom family, in Rita's view, was a group of people who not only cared about each other but had a commitment and a sense of responsibility to what they did together. Indeed, part of Rita's own interest in integrating the arts throughout the day was her sense that in making art— a picture, a sculpture, a composition, a play—children could become committed to a production in which they had some personal stake: they had imagined its possibilities, made decisions about how to bring it to fruition, anticipated the pleasures of sharing. Rita's emphasis on student commitment and decision making had been influenced by a British educator she had worked with as a young teacher, Henry Pluckrose. From him, she said, she had learned that teaching was about how one talks with kids and, more generally, helps "them feel that [the school] isn't an institution but an extension of their life."

Below I locate Rita's children against a traditional evaluative horizon— that of teacher judgment of reading proficiency. This initial official viewing of the children dramatizes the importance of curricular qualities that are not traditional and which supported the brothers and sisters' involvement and commitment to the classroom family: (1) the teacher's responsive interactive style, (2) a diversity of structures for participation (cf., Philips, 1972), (3) a breadth of official literacy practices, and (4) an explicitness about how to participate in those practices and, indeed, in the classroom family.

An Official Regrouping of an Unofficial Group:
The Brothers and Sisters in Reading Groups

At 8:30 in the morning in early January, the brothers and sisters in Rita's room are wide awake (unlike the fake mama slipping in the door). They are spread throughout the small reading groups that meet in the opening 20 to 30 minutes of the day. (Figure 3.1 depicts the brothers' and sisters' unofficial classroom landscape.) Over with Rita, at the table underneath the city map, are Marcel and Wenona. Marcel is the tallest, and Wenona is a bit shorter, with more baby fat. (If Lakeisha was present, she would be sitting here, too, her lanky body almost as long as Marcel's more muscular one.) Robert, Cedric, John, Eddie, and Jamal are also there. These are the children about whose literacy skill Rita has been most worried. She works with them first thing in the morning.

Rita and the children read through trade book sets designed for beginning readers and through linguistic readers that emphasize shifts of "starting" and "ending" sounds in patterned words. Besides reading for sense and for enjoyment, Rita has worked on basic concepts of print, emphasizing the names of letters, sounds, and voice/print match (how to point with one's finger and voice at the spaced letter groups called "words," something Wenona in particular needed to figure out). Rita will soon have Marcel try morning reading with another group of children, as he is beginning to read with ease. But he prefers to read with Rita and his sister Wenona; indeed, the two children often choose to read together at other times of the day.

Marcel is the tallest child in the class, but his fake brother Noah is the smallest. A tiny, wiry child with big brown eyes, Noah sits at a round table in the middle of the room with three other children—Nanette, Denny, and Tommy. Led by a parent volunteer (Denny's mother), the children chorally read a *Little Bear* (Minarik, 1957) book. Noah enjoys the book, reading with great expression—although he becomes frustrated with Denny's mother: "You're going too fast!" (I am often irritated myself at how fast parent volunteers read, given many young children's need to deliberately coordinate voice and print.)

Denise and Vanessa are near the front of the room sitting at pushed-together desks with Ron, whose father is leading them through another *I Can Read* trade book. Denise is the taller of the two girls, Vanessa only

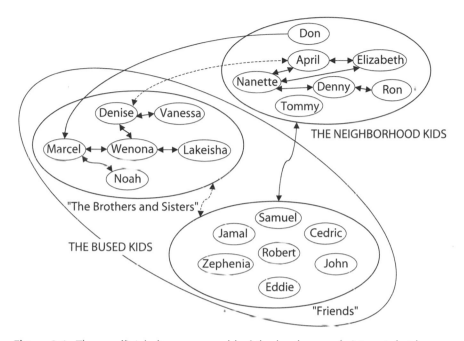

Figure 3.1. The unofficial classroom world of the brothers and sisters. Lakeisha, as already noted, was not consistently in the room. Don had birth defects that led to developmental difficulties, particularly with speech and motor control; he greatly admired Marcel and sought his company because Marcel, like Don, was a football fan. The "friends" were seven boys who typically sat together and interacted easily; they were friends with the brothers and sisters, but they were not members of the family. Denise and Vanessa considered one of the "friends," Zephenia, their (secret) boyfriend. Tommy was best friends with Samuel. Sometimes Tommy sat with the "friends," but Samuel never chose to sit with the neighborhood kids. Double-headed solid arrows indicate particularly intense, ongoing, reciprocal relationships. The single-headed arrow indicates an intense, but one-way, attraction. Double-headed broken arrows indicate children who were not in the same peer group (i.e., they did not regularly choose to sit together) but did sometimes seek each other's company.

slightly shorter and a bit wispier, although both are slim. Denise and Vanessa collaborate so closely in most all tasks that Rita has found it hard to know them as individual literacy users. But Denise finds encoding and decoding easier. Soon she will have the option of meeting with Samuel, Zephenia, April, and Elizabeth, who read their chosen books without an adult monitor. Like Marcel, however, Denise will often choose to read with her best fake sibling, Vanessa.

Even as I have laid out the preceding vision of the children spread throughout official classroom space, the children have disrupted my attempt at order. The brothers and sisters did not choose each other as fake siblings based on perceived proficiency in school literacy tasks. In not choosing friends based on reading levels, they acted similarly to other children from their neighborhood whom I have observed in classroom ethnographies in different schools in the district (e.g., Dyson, 1993, 1997). And they differed from portrayals of children in studies of friendship patterns in culturally homogeneous classrooms (e.g., Beaumont, 1999) and among middle-class European American children, who do gravitate toward other children of similar perceived proficiency (e.g., Rizzo, 1989; for a helpful discussion of friendship patterns in early childhood, see Ramsey, 1991).

In Rita's class, I came to know children from the local middle-class neighborhood mainly in whole classroom events, and also, in those interactions when their paths intersected with those of the brothers and sisters. These common events and intersecting paths, however, did make salient the local instantiation of generally observed differences. As a friendship group, the local neighborhood children, all living in the surrounding economically comfortable area, sometimes distinguished themselves from others based on perceived literacy skill (e.g., by quietly mocking Rita's words of praise to another child for a good effort, as in "Nice holding your pencil, Cedric").

The brothers and sisters were quite capable of teasing and joking and general unkindness—but teasing about academic proficiency was explicitly and consistently ruled out-of-bounds. Once Denise made a disparaging comment to John (in retaliation for his own such comment), and Vanessa was quick in response:

Denise has just asked if anyone knows how to spell *want.*

JOHN: You don't know how to spell *want.* (sigh)
DENISE: You don't know how to read (sigh) that good.
VANESSA: Is that funny, Denise? I can pick out a book that you can't even read.
LAKEISHA: You go, girl.
DENISE: I can pick out a book that you can't even read.
VANESSA: And don't act like you all that good because you can read. You ain't.
DENISE: You ain't either.
VANESSA: I didn't say I was, did I?
DENISE: I didn't say I was, did I?

The connections between the brothers and sisters were grounded and sustained by their common cultural landscape and by familiar and shared forms of pleasure. They could not have maintained themselves as an unofficial family if they had accepted teasing based on location in an official school hierarchy. By early spring, four of the five focal children in this project (Marcel, Noah, Denise, and Vanessa) were reading and writing with evident ease (and Wenona would do so by mid–second grade), as the chapters to come will amply illustrate. But two of them, and many of their friends (including their sister Lakeisha) had been or were in that group Rita met with early in the morning, that group about which she worried, although none of the local neighborhood children were, nor did they have any regular companions who were in that group.

I hasten to add that, in the official classroom family, Rita herself explicitly discussed and strictly censured any teasing based on ridicule of any kind. Indeed, she responded much as Vanessa had: If she wanted she could make any one of them look like she or he didn't know anything—and somebody else could do that to her. Moreover, she explicitly noted that "there's nothing wrong with mistakes"; they are evidence of thinking. Not everybody in the class was equally good at talking, at writing, or at drawing, Rita explained, but "everybody's good in this class at thinking," and they all had ideas to share. Moreover, they were all good people trying to get better in varied ways:

Rita is talking with the class about their New Year's resolutions. It is Lakeisha's turn to give her resolution:

Lakeisha: To always do my homework.
    Rita: Did you do it? . . .
Lakeisha: I left it at home.
Vanessa: At least she did it. (in an upbeat tone)
    Rita: Well at least you did it. Yeah.
  Jamal: (offering his resolution) I won't be bad every day.
    Rita: . . . "Bad" is a word I wouldn't use for any of you. . . .
           Everybody is good. It's just occasionally (pause)
Zephenia: You're playful. (a verbal spin that Rita does not disagree with)

. . .

Wenona: My resolution is that (pause) keep on doing hard work and being good and do my homework always.
    Rita: I like that doing hard work. . . . I want things to be hard but I don't want them to be hard so you get frustrated. . . .

Like, was putting this [bulletin board] up easy for me?
["NO," the children say.] And I was proud of it when I
was done! I had to read the instructions! I was tired.

As the discussion continues, Denny offers that his resolution is
"getting stronger," and Rita responds:

RITA: You mean in your body? working out? (Denny nods.)
That's definitely mine too. . . . Remember when we have
looked at our Being Smart Wheel [a construction paper
wheel that indicates varied ways of being smart, among
them "Picture Smart," "Word Smart," "Body Smart,"
"People Smart," "Number Smart," "Self Smart"]? The
Body Smart is something that I'm always trying to be
better at. . . . I'm not good at those things some of you are
good at. I can't ride a bike. I don't know how to swim.
ZEPHENIA: I know your resolution should be to keep working at it.
RITA: Yeah, I think that's right.

In the above exchange among all the children in the class, Rita's use
of an inclusive and responsive interactive style is in evidence. Even in the
large group format, Rita allowed and expected every child to participate;
participation meant not only listening and responding to Rita, but listening
and responding to each other. This and other features made her curriculum permeable and, thus, able to become "an extension" of children's
knowledge, know-how, and relationships. The children's writing development was itself dependent on this permeability, since it involved recontextualization of their practices and resources in school. Thus, I now
move the traditional aspects of Rita's curriculum to the background (without in any way devaluing the importance of providing focused and needed
help) and consider how else the children were organized and reorganized
in this permeable curriculum.

Diversifying and Linking Participation Structures:
Organizing for Commitment

For the children's early-morning school activities, they were organized in
small groups and closely monitored and guided either by Rita or by another adult. Right after those opening groups, the children gathered on
the rug for teacher-led whole group activities, in which their official roles
were more complex than performing correctly, as illustrated by the above
New Year's resolution discussion. In whole class events, Rita and the children could, for example, read and discuss the sense and orthographic fea-

tures of Rita's written message for the day, which detailed class plans. They could consider directions for a project or compose varied kinds of texts—for example, class thank-you notes, to-do-lists, story starters.

Most importantly, large group events were bookends to those organizational structures in which children themselves assumed the dominant organizational role as Rita worked with selected students and circulated among others. Included in these organizational structures were student-led small groups collaborating on a single product—a poster, for instance, or a mural; pairs of collaborating partners, reading a selected book, for example, or composing a common text; or collegial arrangements, in which individual children worked on separate projects in a common space (e.g., a table, an area of the rug), sometimes seeking or offering each other varied forms of feedback and help. Among these latter structures were those most central to this project: writing workshop time, which was generally a collegial arrangement; and assigned writing projects for social studies or science, which were generally collegial but sometimes small cooperative group affairs.

These student-organized times were always preceded by large group meetings in which concepts were taught, plans were made, and directions were given. And they were always followed by a large group meeting, in which finished work was shared or progress evaluated by both Rita and the children. For example, after the daily self-selected reading time, when children read independently or in pairs, there was a whole-class meeting for book sharing; in this latter meeting, children could share in varied ways, including by reading the book word by word, by retelling a story in dramatic fashion using voice and pictures, or by some combination of both approaches.

The linking of interactional structures—and thereby of spaces and times to connect individual efforts to a common community—was critical to building that commitment so important to Rita. No activity was left hanging, no child was unaccountable for their plans and products. As will be evident throughout the child dramas, this commitment was especially evident in children's anticipation of, and plans for, a public performance—a form of agency central to the brothers' and sisters' family (see Chapter 2)—as well as to the classroom family.

As a collegial small group event, the writing workshop was especially valuable to Rita and to me. During this event, the children controlled topic and genre and, in fact, they could rework a participant structure from a collegial to a collaborative one. In Rita's view, this event allowed her an important opportunity for assessment; she could see how exactly the children went about planning and encoding a text. She kept notes on particular goals for particular children; for example, she aimed for Wenona to move beyond repetitive sentences and, moreover, to apply her budding sound/symbol knowledge to take a guess at a spelling. She wanted Marcel to finish his sentences, rather than stopping an idea in grammatical mid-air. And she thought (as did I) that his writing would be ever so much easier to read if he would leave space between words. Rita thought that Vanessa's and Denise's texts were often so very brief, and Rita hoped that writing questions on their entries would lead to longer, more coherent pieces.

For my purposes, the children's organizational control of writing work-shop was also critical. But Rita, as teacher, had her eyes firmly on the children in the frame of her instructional goals. As researcher, I had one eye on the children within the official school frame, the other on their actions within the unofficial one. I used my wandering eyes to trace the kinds of communicative practices and textual materials the children were weaving into their composing time efforts. To further appreciation of those efforts, I now briefly consider the breadth of official composing practices in Rita's room. And, to exemplify this breadth, it is time to bring into focus the class involvement in official outer space.

Incorporating a Breadth of Genres: Broadening Possibilities

> RITA: I was sitting on the floor, surrounded by books, and then I'd stop . . . "Wait a minute. Why is [the galaxy] called the Milky Way?" And then I started to read [this book]. "'You can't see the separate stars without a telescope. . . . People living long ago, before the telescope . . . made up a story that this white band [of stars] was a river of milk. The Milky Way is part of a great collection of stars called a galaxy' [Rosen, 1992, pp. 7–8]. WOW! I didn't know that!"
>
> ZEPHENIA: Hey! That's what's up there!

Zephenia was pointing to that space unit bulletin board that Rita had worked so hard on. One side was labeled *Fantasy*. On a piece of tag board were the words "A long time ago in a galaxy faraway . . ." These words are the well-known opening of the *Star Wars* movie (Kurtz & Lucas, 1977); accompanying them was a picture of characters from that film, among them Luke Skywalker, Princess Leia, and the robots R2-D2 and C3PO. The other side was *Fact*. And on its tag board was the word *galaxy* and the defi-nition Rita had just read.

As the bulletin board suggested, Rita's space unit had as its central theme what I would call a stance toward reality, and what Rita called a concern with what is considered "fact," "fiction," or "opinion." It is, she explained, "really hard to tell" what's real or not on the topic of space. Thus, as already suggested, the unit was expansive enough to include both details of the night sky and the planets ("facts" that seem like "fantasy") and the film *Star Wars* (a "fantasy" that includes some "facts").

The children were officially guided into galactic space through a myriad of activities, involving varied symbolic tools and diverse genres. Of these, there were two key writing activities: composing fictional worlds (or stories) and reporting information (or "What I Learned"). These, along with varied genres about personal matters (e.g., reporting personal experiences ["I went . . ."] or evaluations ["I like . . ."]), were the central, but not the exclusive, official composing genres of Rita's class during the academic year.

The children's first space unit composing task was to produce illustrated facts, either alone or with self-selected partners; these productions were to yield displayed classroom posters, like Rita's illustrated fact on her bulletin board. The second assignment involved space fictions, an assignment preceded by varied activities. The children visited a local junkyard to find assorted materials with which to construct space robots or aliens. In small groups (organized by Rita, although honoring originally formed partnerships), the children invented home planets for their aliens, drawing them on large sheets of paper. And then, as collegial individuals, they named their creatures and wrote their creatures' food and activity preferences.

The children also engaged in a series of events that were variants of the "I Learned That" practice, in which they were to perform as knowledgeable students for interested others. They played dialogue games in which partners asked other partners, "Did you know that . . . ?" They also reported "I learned that . . ." to Rita and the class (and, in a homework assignment, to their parents). At the end of the unit, the children wrote in their writing books about what "I learned."

I have named and briefly described Rita's plans for the children. What is more critical, however, is that these were not "passive, teacher's-telling-you-to-do-everything" activities, to use Rita's words. They were activities in which "you have to think"—imagine alternatives and make decisions. Nonetheless, as I explain below, they involved much explicit guidance.

Making Decision-Making Explicit: Supporting Involvement

Rita guided the children's participation in the classroom's communicative practices and social relations and, thereby, in its familial values of commitment and responsibility to each other and to their own efforts. The children were to be decision-making colleagues, partners, group members, and "loving" family members. Sometimes Rita explained the decisions students had to make before an activity ever began. Just as often, however, decision making was part of the follow-up discussion of how things "had gone." Consider, for example, the following unfolding of the dialogue partner activity.

The activity began with Rita and the children gathered on the large rug. They first reviewed a chart of studied facts. Rita led the class as they read through those facts, pointing to each word as she did so; in the process, Rita and the children both offered comments and clarifications.

"'The first astronaut walked on the moon in 1969,'" read Rita.

"That's when I was born," said Zephenia (which prompted clarifying comments from Rita).

"'Astronomers are people who study stars and planets.' And that ['astronomer'] is a very long word," said Rita.

"Bigger than me," Noah said.

Rita continued: "'Jupiter is the biggest planet'"—

"In the whole galaxy!" added Marcel (not quite correctly, of course, but a game effort at that key word "galaxy").

"'Astronauts explore space,'" read Rita.

"DUH::! We know that," said Vanessa.

After this review of facts, the children played the "fact game." In pairs, the children picked a fact out of a bag, read it, and then, cocktail-party style, they circulated around the room, asking other pairs, "Did you know . . . ?" The appropriate response was either "Oh, I didn't know that" (which no one said) or "Yes, I did know that" (of which a variant, "I know that," seemed most popular).

The pairs worked differentially well, and people streamed up to Rita to vent varied complaints about one unfair act or another. So Rita called everyone together for a discussion. She asked them to think about how pairs went about asking their question.

Zephenia and Samuel volunteered to come and act out their procedure for the class. In front of the children on the rug, Zephenia turned the written fact into a question as Samuel watched. When Rita asked someone to explain how exactly the boys had proceeded, Ron commented, "quietly," and April described, "One person was talking, and the other person was just watching."

Rita asked for more volunteers. Vanessa and Denise went to the front of the room and chorally transformed their statement into a question.

"They do it together," observed Jamal.

Then came Nicole and Elizabeth who, they noted, "divide it up," each saying part of the fact.

"Those are three important ways" to do this activity, said Rita. Partners needed to make a plan for the activity so that everyone would feel "part of it" and no one would be "coming up saying 'Jamal didn't let me have a turn.' Nobody's in charge. Talk to your partner about how you are going to do it."

Rita, however, *was* in charge. In fact, one day when Rita returned after leaving a substitute in charge, Vanessa exclaimed "Hallelujah" because, as Denise said, "Rita knows how to control." She did not control like the classroom's just-learning student teacher and its seemingly out-of-practice substitute—by disciplining one individual child after another as the others raised their voices under the adult's stern demands. Rita centered the group through explicit guidance toward both social and academic involvement.

Rita offered similar explicit guidance about composing, the most immediate concern of this book. For example, when the children were to write "what I learned," she explicitly discussed, and asked them to plan for, varied aspects of the task at hand. She asked them to consider where they were going to sit and near whom, considering both the enjoyment of talking about their topic and of mutual helping, as well as the need to concentrate. She asked them also to consider the topic, the facts that they found interesting; they should write for people who would be learning about space by reading their work. And she noted avenues of help for spelling (e.g., words on the tag board in hanging charts, books, and their own sense of sound/symbol relationships). If all a child could manage was the first letter heard in the pronunciation of a word, that was ok. The class even practiced writing a few words together, listening to sounds. After the children fanned out into the classroom's workspaces, Rita circulated, urging individuals to reread their efforts and thereby monitor their messages and never to copy a word that they could not read.

With all this effort, one might imagine that perhaps, set on the right path, little reports about space would neatly unfold on children's papers.

But no. Not at all, as the chapters ahead will illustrate. Nor should such a display of neatly ordered children in compositional tutus be expected. After all, Rita had developed a permeable curriculum, one in which children were to think, take action, make decisions. If the children were to assume such agency, they would need to rely on the guidance of past experiences and familiar practices and tools, even as they responded to the new, not-yet-familiar ones. Moreover, the children were not just Rita's students; they were each others' peers, friends, and fake siblings. As they oriented themselves on the official school landscape, and negotiated the unofficial one, I followed the trails of their textual toys as official and unofficial practices were juxtaposed, blended, and differentiated.

CHILD JOURNEYS INTO OFFICIAL SPACE

Denise and Vanessa are illustrating their chosen space fact: that "the earth orbits the sun." As they work, they consult a picture in a reference book, and then they try to reconcile the heavens above, populated with "Great Grandma, my grandpa . . .", with the pictured expanse of the Milky Way, which, perhaps, people in heaven use for "milk in their cereal." When the girls are nearly done with their planet-filled, multimodal text, they add a space robot—who soon gets long hair and a T-shirt, becomes a singer, and has a little girl robot named Precious. And when those robots get antennas they look, for heaven's sake, like radios! "It's K-M-E-L [the local hip-hop radio station]," they say. Then they slip from the official school space into the unofficial one and, under the expansive buzz of classroom voices, they sing the opening to Coolio's (1995) "Gangsta's Paradise" rap: "As I walk through the valley of the shadow of death. . . ."

In my detailing of Rita's official introduction to the space unit, I made no reference to heaven above, to valleys below, nor to human stars on a hip-hop radio station. In this multimodal production event, Denise and Vanessa evidenced their attentiveness to Rita's official practices and her guidance, but they drew as well on the cultural materials that figured into their lives as children, and they did so in ways that reflected familiar forms of agency and communicative practices.

Before delving further into their response to official space, I offer below a look at the children's cargo of unofficial resources.

The Children's Cargo of Unofficial Resources

The particularities of children's appropriations from each of the media sources featured in this book (sports media, animation, and music) will be given in the following chapters. At this point, however, I provide a taxonomy of the children's varied appropriations and describe their compositional use. The categories are not mutually exclusive, but they do capture the rich variety of appropriated materials. They are based on an analysis of all the children's written products, from January of the school year onward (when they were, in the main, much more readable). For the brothers and sisters, those products were studied within the context of observed production events. Most of the products and events evolved during writing workshop times, rather than during study unit assignments.

The children's resources yielded five major kinds of appropriations. First, the children appropriated varied forms of *content*, among them, for example, names of sports teams and singing stars; entire media events; plots or plot segments of narrative material; and categories of conceptual knowledge, such as a sports team's recent wins and losses or a singer's songs.

Names are a comfortable and familiar element for child writers, and the observed children readily inserted them into a personal text offering an evaluation (e.g., "I like . . ."). Similarly, events could serve as topics of personal experience and/or evaluative texts, in which a child reported watching and/or liking a media event. They could even be embedded in written exchanges with peers or adults, in which a child sought another's opinion or team preference. Plots or plot segments could be retold or appropriated into a new story.

Varied types of content knowledge could be recontextualized within school-modeled writing practices, including composing lists (e.g., of teams' home cities and/or states), information reports (e.g., "I know that Michael Jordan is a superstar . . ."), and fictional accounts (e.g., "Michael [Jordan] plays on my team"). Such knowledge could also be recontextualized as reference points, scaffolding children's learning of school-valued tools and knowledge (e.g., using teams' home cities or states as reference points for exploring maps).

Second, children appropriated *communicative practices*, or genres, for instance reporting game results, improvising love songs, or enacting superhero adventures. These practices could serve as guiding frames for their efforts. To varying degrees, the children could appropriate particular textual features of these genres; for example, the violent action verbs of sports reports, in which one team might have "whipped" another, the repetitive lines of love songs and other musical texts, or the frequent exclamations in superhero cartoons (such as "Help!").

Third, the children appropriated *technological conventions*, particularly graphic displays (e.g., of football game scores on television, in which team names or cities and their respective scores are arranged in vertical columns) and symbols (e.g., icons of teams and commercial products [a sports shoe's graphic swish] or of letter symbols indicating radio stations or rap groups).

Fourth, the children appropriated *actual lines*, the particular words spoken or sung by characters or singers. These could be either embedded in a child's own retelling or unembedded—that is, not reframed by a child, but lifted (e.g., a child writes only "Don't ever call me doll!", an utterance taken from the movie *Space Jam*).

Finally, the children appropriated *ideologies*, among them, those of gender, wealth, and power. Ideologies were also recontextualized in child talk, drawing, and writing, as in, for example, pictures of singers with slinky dresses or of muscular football players. More strikingly, they could become the focus of official and critical discussions among children and their teacher, as when Rita discussed gender preferences for sports media with the class.

To gain access to, and make use of, these diverse kinds of cultural materials, the children engaged in a variety of recontextualization processes, among them the differentiation of, appropriation from, translation across, and reframing within communicative practices involving diverse symbolic forms. Most basically, to become compositional material, audiovisual material had to be "entextualized" (Bauman & Briggs, 1990, p. 73), that is, differentiated from its original source and rendered liftable, as it were. The most liftable forms are bits of texts that call attention to themselves through formal properties of speech or graphics (rhythm, rhyme, layout) and thus stand out from their interactive surrounding (Bauman & Briggs, 1990). In Rita's classroom, children sometimes appropriated bits of songs, commercials, and superhero themes and wrote them on their papers, without reframing or combining them with any additional written material (e.g., "Go Go Power Rangers"). Like the name of a family or a friend, a bit of a known popular text could be meaningful in and of itself.

Audiovisual material also had to be translated in some way—processed—if it was to be written. In contrast, the most common means of appropriation from book media was simply to copy sections of books; this compositional means was used primarily (but not exclusively) by children still untangling basic concepts of print, like voice/text match and the alphabetic system. Such unembedded appropriations (i.e., appropriations not combined with any other text) accounted for two-thirds of all writing workshop products intertextually linked to specific books (i.e., 20 of 35 products).

Given these recontextualization processes, children's production events and written products tended to be kinds of Bakhtinian hybrids; that is, their symbolic stuff, including their written words, established relationships to a complex of overlapping social worlds. To clarify the interplay of official and unofficial sources in the children's school composing, I return below to Denise and Vanessa's illustrated fact and to a sampling of the brothers' and sisters' midyear participation in official space.

Sample Journeys into Outer Child Space

Although not a task requiring the generation (as opposed to the copying) of written text, the children's responses to Rita's assignment to illustrate a space fact exemplifies the diversity of children's resources. Denise and

Vanessa, for instance, appropriated unofficial content, technological conventions, and actual lines (not to mention embedded ideologies of heavenly rewards and earthly pleasures) in the course of producing their space fact, as earlier illustrated. Those appropriations linked their efforts to their out-of-school experiences as church members, radio fans, pretend singers, and usual play companions.

At the same time, however, Denise and Vanessa's efforts were also linked to their experiences with official resources and their related practices. For example, the girls consulted a reference book to examine the placement of the sun, just as Rita had earlier when she showed the children how she studied books to produce her space illustrations for them. They added *U.S.A.* (and a flag) to the earth, an illustrative convention used in another class reference book. They even stopped to act out a concept Rita had taught them, making one fisted hand the sun, the other the orbiting earth, while they repeated the relevant "orbit" fact. After drawing their figures, they made pop-up book flaps to cover those figures; this convention was inspired by their secret "boyfriend" Zephenia (even Zephenia did not know!). Zephenia had himself taken the idea from a *Star Wars* pop-up book Rita had shared (its flaps, however, were not decorated with hearts and rainbows). In the end, the girls' pop-up space illustration became a guessing game in the unofficial world, in which they asked others to "guess" what was behind the flap.

Neither illustrating nor reporting written facts was, in and of itself, a familiar genre or communicative practice for these girls at this point in the school year. They had a task to do, and they situated that task within intersecting spheres of meaningful action. Official relationships with their teacher, experienced through practices of book consulting and class concept discussions; their unofficial relationship as friends, realized through practices involving collaborative play (e.g., drawing, singing, naming secret boyfriends); their community relationships as churchgoers who participated in practices enacting beliefs about a heavenly afterlife—all these relationships were indexed by the cultural material evident in the children's hybrid event.

Not all of the brothers and sisters participated in such a freewheeling way in this event (shifting so fluidly from official to unofficial social spheres). If a child situated a task within a guiding (and familiar) communicative frame, that child's efforts were more coherent or unified—but not necessarily more attuned to official purposes. Consider, for example, Noah's "illustrated fact" event. Noah's efforts yielded a more coherent product than the girls' did; but those efforts seemed to unfold in an unofficial world primarily juxtaposed to, rather than intersecting with, the official world.

Noah's physical artifact, a drawn scene featuring a laser duel, could have been an illustration of the listed fact that "The movie *Star Wars* came out nearly 20 years ago." Noah's fact, however, was "There are nine planets," which he neither copied nor orally referenced. At the beginning of the work period, Noah sat down and immediately began drawing, enacting a dramatic intergalactic space battle (with the open admiration of his peer Cedric). Indeed, Noah drew intergalactic space battles for all of the space unit-composing activities, including a thank-you letter to the woman at the junkyard, and a homework assignment to share space facts with family members.

The apparent coherence of Noah's event came from its situatedness within a familiar communicative practice—enacting a superhero adventure, which Noah saw as relevant to the official task. After all, as he explained, many "real" cartoons have characters from space, "even Fox Kids [children's programming on the Fox television channel]." Noah's production event included the usual content and the symbolic conventions of his many media-inspired and drawn dramatizations: good guy, bad guy, and victim characters; and a battle symbolized by graphic swirls of "fire power" (in this instance, a clearly labeled TNT blast—not the result of space-age technology).

As Denise and Vanessa blended and Noah juxtaposed unofficial and official practices, Wenona seemed to abandon any evident connection with official space. With Rita's guidance, she and Lakeisha read their fact (about the meaning of "galaxy") and learned to make stars. Once Rita left, they filled their paper with stars, but their talk veered off into the unofficial world, in which they anticipated an evening dance performance on a stage in their neighborhood park. The R&B star Monica was going to be there, they said; in fact, every girl on the stage would be named Monica—including them! (They each signed the name "Monica" to their space fact paper.) Outside any apparent perceived need for planning or decision making about the conceptual stuff of space, the girls' talk abandoned the official world for the playful, performative one of unofficial space, in which *they* were stars.

Marcel, like Vanessa and Denise, seemed to delve deeply into the conceptual stuff of outer space, although, like Noah, his composing actions were relatively coherent and situated in a guiding frame. Marcel was a knowledgeable sports fan, and he frequently displayed football game scores in his writing workshop book. He seemed to find the "illustrated fact" event an appealing opportunity to report information through visual display. Marcel copied most of his fact (about the origins of the word *galaxy* in the Greek word for *milk*). But, after consulting one of Rita's space books, he proceeded to display all the planets and their names. Indeed, this practice of organizing and displaying information, especially through the communicative form of a list (used but not foregrounded by Rita), seemed to grip Marcel's attention. He listed planet names for composing tasks about space as regularly as Noah enacted dramatic adventures (whether or not such behavior was, in Rita's view, task appropriate). As Chapter 4 will illustrate, for Marcel, this listing practice became a major means for organizing unofficial conceptual content.

In this brief tour of children's responses to the official space unit, the brothers and sisters were always engaged, but not necessarily, and not exclusively, within the official classroom world. Within that world, Rita's goal was for writing to become a substantive tool in children's symbolic and social repertoire, so that they could use it to deliberately reflect, organize, imagine, and communicate. She explicitly connected this academic goal with the need for a classroom community: child engagement, through any symbolic means, is dependent on agency—on a role to be played, decisions to be made, products to be prepared for a community to which one belongs.

As illustrated by the children's responses to Rita's offerings, a sense of agency cannot be conferred simply through explicit guidance, as helpful as that guidance may be; it cannot be engineered through inclusive social and academic arrangements and responsiveness, as critical as those qualities are. Nor can it be guaranteed through offering a diversity of recurrent practices and possible symbolic tools, as important as that diversity is.

Children's sense of official requirements must be negotiated over time, as children make sense of what is expected. In Chapters 4, 5, and 6, the dimension of time will be added, as I trace the trajectories of converging unofficial and official practices undergirding children's negotiated participation as writers.

In Rita's classroom, this negotiation involved both the centralizing forces of a classroom's common cultural ground—its own history of experiences, routines, and established practices—*and* the decentralizing forces of the children's common ground within their circles of friends. It was these latter forces, linked to socioeconomic, gender, and cultural divisions, that made clear the sociopolitical and ideological dimensions of learning to participate in such seemingly straightforward literacy practices as reporting facts, composing fictional worlds, and even sharing personal experiences and opinions. In the last section of this chapter, then, I resituate the brothers and sisters in the classroom family. To do so, I am going to examine not Rita's offerings about outer space, but the children's offerings in the context of the more open-ended writing time: Writing Workshop.

TEXTUAL BORDERS IN PERMEABLE SPACE:
THE CONSEQUENCES OF *STAR WARS* AND *SPACE JAM*

He's [Bugs Bunny's] on fire like M. J. [Michael Jordan]. Bugs is in [the game.] M. J. [is] on the ball. Bugs slaps the ball away. Bugs is tide [tied] with Michael Jordan['s] sore [score].

Denise and Vanessa's boyfriend, Zephenia, wrote the above text, which was inspired by the movie *Space Jam*. It was his own story, however, written as a broadcaster's commentary on a basketball game between Bugs Bunny and Michael Jordan; the writing accompanied a cartoon-style rendering of the dramatic moment.

Zephenia's text is one of many that suggest the permeability of the Writing Workshop event. This was an event in which the children were expected to and did use their interests and experiences as the stuff of their official school writing. In their appropriation of material for this event, the children made salient both their interconnections and their potential boundaries in the classroom family (see also Buckingham, 1993; Dyson, 1997).

For example, gender boundaries were constructed as children appropriated specific cultural material from textual practices involving sports media (especially basketball or football), a social action taken by 54% of boys from January of the school year onward, but not by girls. Conversely, racial boundaries were visible in differentiated patterns of song appropriations: about a third of the children of African American heritage appropriated songs (all from the local hip-hop radio station, KMEL), but no European American heritage child did. Moreover, the small group of girls from the middle-class neighborhood (April, Elizabeth, and Nanette) rarely appropriated *any* popular media material for free composing.

Even experiences with the movies, a source of composing time appropriation for 85% of all children, yielded clearly differentiated patterns. Using findings based on a frequency count of written products (and not on the accompanying oral "cotexts" [Hanks, 2000, p. 166]), the intersection of gender and race axes becomes quite visible. Beginning in January of the school year, boys of African American heritage produced the bulk of the texts containing identifiable film material (53 of 73, or 73%), although they comprised less than half (45%) of Rita's children. Boys of European American heritage produced a proportional amount (14, or approximately 20%), followed by African American girls (7 texts), and European American girls (only 1 text).

These statistics, however, based only on the general category of "film appropriations in written texts," provide only a partial picture. Highlighting the *nature* of the film material appropriated, as well as the *compositional means* for so doing, emphasizes not only race (and, in Rita's room, its interrelated category of class), but also variation in children's experience appropriating and playing with media material.

Although Rita officially introduced the topic of outer space, unofficially children's media also features space, particularly in adventure stories (Kline, 1993). During the project year, Rita's children appropriated from a range of media sources involving outer space as they participated in official and unofficial events; among the film sources were *Independence Day* (Emmerich, Emmerich, & Fay, 1996), *Mars Attacks* (Burton & Franco, 1996), and, most especially, *Space Jam*.

The single most dominant source of textual toys for the brothers and sisters was the movie *Space Jam*, particularly in the spring of the year when the video was released and available for repeated viewing. The stars of the movie include basketball player Michael Jordan (a well-known African American sports figure), the Looney Tunes characters, especially Bugs Bunny and the newly introduced Lola Bunny (source of the frequently revoiced "Don't ever call me doll" line), and a group of goofy space aliens sent to kidnap the Looney Tunes for an alien entertainment park.

For the brothers and the sisters, seeing this film was an anticipated family event and a reported experience. It was also the source of jointly reenacted plot segments, mimicked voices, and many group singing events. (Its featured song, "I Believe I Can Fly" [Kelly, 1996], won an American music award—the Grammy.) However, only one European American child, Tommy, had seen the movie (until Wenona offered it as an end-of-school treat).

With the exception of Tommy, only—and almost all—African American children appropriated material from this source for free composing. With this material, they composed personal texts about their experience with and feelings about the film, informative texts listing characters or the score's musicians (all by Marcel, as readers might anticipate), texts composed of plot retellings or perceived funny character lines (e.g., "Don't ever call me doll!"), their own related stories (like Zephenia's), and combinations of the above.

As discussed, Rita herself included *Star Wars* in her official space unit, although most children were already familiar with it. Indeed, this is one reason she chose it as an example of space fiction. This film, sometimes considered "ersatz high culture" (Jenkins, 1992, p. 22), features the savior of the galaxy (and of Princess Leia), Luke Skywalker (who, interestingly, is also her brother). Unanticipated by Rita in January when she planned the space unit, the film was rereleased for movie theaters later that spring, 20 years after the first release in 1977. *No child* appropriated from this movie for open-ended composing until it became part of the nonschool world; that is, until it was rereleased in the theaters.

Although three African American boys and Tommy appropriated material from both space films (gender clearly figuring into the attraction of male superhero material [Dyson, 1997]), the two children who appropriated only from *Star Wars* were European American (see Figure 3.2). Both children rarely appropriated media material—and both wrote only personal pieces about liking the film (e.g., Ron's "I like the dazins [dozens] of star wor's spases sips."). Ron had in fact never been to a movie theater before he had gone to see *Star Wars*. As he explained to Noah, "That's the only movie I've ever watched on the big screen. I'm really fussy about movies cause I like to be smart."

"I've seen a whole bunch," responded Noah, who, at that very moment, was drawing a cartoon-inspired story about a giant dog who became a superhero.

Ron, like us all, was a complex character. He spent weeks drawing spaceships in his journal after the "big screen" *Star Wars* event. *His* fussi-

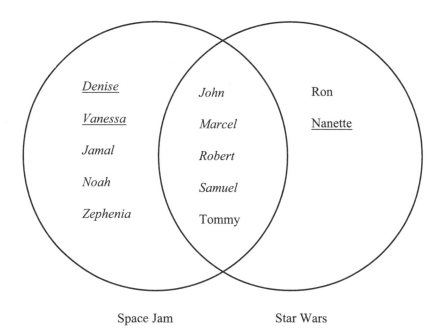

Space Jam   Star Wars

Figure 3.2. *Space Jam* and *Star Wars* media appropriations by the children. African American boys' names are in italics; European American boys' names are in plain text. African American girls' names are in italics and underlined; European American girls' names are in plain text and underlined.

ness was thus at some tension with both his relative powerlessness in the choice to avoid movies and his relative power in the choice to play and replay his singular cinematic experience with projected speed, might, and space heroes.

Ron's comments linking moviegoing frequency with smartness did not necessarily reflect the views of anyone in Rita's classroom family other than himself. But his comments both reflect and contradict the patterns and processes evident in how Rita's children and, more particularly, the brothers and sisters appropriated from popular media texts. Children from the local, economically privileged neighborhood made less official use of such sources. In this way their behavior, like Ron's comment, was compatible with the stated views of many upper-middle-class parents (Seiter, 1993) and with the traditional goals of the language arts curriculum.

The traditions of that curriculum still have remnants of the 19th-century educator Matthew Arnold, who saw education as a means through which the minority elite could civilize the masses who, nonetheless, would always be satisfied by less than "the best" (cited in Storey, 1998, p. 26). In such a vision, there are clear categories for art and for groups of people; there is no sense of cultural fluidity or of the "dance and dialogue" between what is considered "high" and "low" (Varnedoe & Gopnik, 1991, p. 12). Moreover, children of more privileged social classes may tend to align themselves accordingly in official school settings, offering opinions like those of Ron's—although, in *unofficial* places, they may offer very different points of view (Buckingham, 1993; Dyson, 1997).

In contrast to those curricular traditions, the child culture of the children studied most closely, the brothers and the sisters, entailed no such clear categories for media forms. Their childhood culture was open, not closed, and linked to complex networks of relations that stretched far beyond the classroom walls (cf., Massey, 1998). More specifically, their involvement with popular literacies did not negate an openness to media and textual forms stressed in school.

Indeed, the only class members to appropriate material from an officially introduced book for free composing (beyond simply copying a text) were Denise, Vanessa, and Noah. These children were attracted to the discursive features in book media, which attracted them in other media forms. Denise and Vanessa appropriated material from the poetry books of Eloise Greenfield, regularly performed by the children in Rita's class. As will be illustrated in Chapter 6, the emotion and musicality of the poems, and their featuring of African American characters, were textual features similar to those of their appropriated radio songs. Noah appropriated from the *Little Bear* (Minarik, 1957) book series, whose lead character, a bear drawn in the iconic style of a cartoon character, reminded him (as he explicitly said) of Donkey Kong (Stamper, 1986), a gorilla from a favorite video game set.

In sum, for many children, particularly the brothers and sisters, media material provided textual toys that permeated the unofficial world, and that could be drawn upon for participation in the official one. Their use of this material, so central to childhood cultures, evidenced discourse flexibility and sociocultural adaptiveness. Those qualities undergirded the pathways of the children featured in the chapters to come: namely, Marcel, Noah, and Denise.

TOWARD SITUATING CHILDHOODS IN COMPOSING SPACES

"You are my classroom family," Rita told her children. She knew that working toward such a family was not sentimental, but rather deeply practical. In order to learn, children must be engaged in making sense of new information, new symbolic tools, and new ways of organizing, communicating, and taking action in the world around them. And this kind of human agency is generated by, and becomes meaningful within, a community with expectations for participation and production. This was Rita's view, based on her professional history and personal experience. It is a view compatible with that of cultural and developmental psychologists (Bruner, 1996; Miller & Goodnow, 1995) and, moreover, with that of curriculum theorists and psychologists who stress that feelings of alienation from school have profoundly negative consequences, particularly for minority student achievement (Nieto, 1999; Steele, 1992; Valenzuela, 1999).

Denise and her close friends were members not only of the classroom family but also of a "fake" family. That family was also formed in the classroom, but it was founded on a cultural landscape with deep roots in churches, families, neighborhood parks, and in the forms of pleasure, power, and companionship they found in those places. The school family was, potentially, on much more fragile ground. Its practices and symbols were organized in relationship to curricular and instructional expectations removed from the particularities of children's lives; those institutional concerns usually do not involve children's pleasure, power, and companionship.

The brothers and sisters, however, did not approach Rita's curricular offerings as though they had nothing to do with their experiences and relationships with each other. On the one hand, they actively worked against any attempt to glorify oneself, or insult another, by seeing a person only in relation to the official school landscape. On the other hand, they used their familiar cargo of resources, including their textual toys, to take intellectual and social action on that official landscape. The resultant antiphony between the classroom family and the "fake" (but no less real) family provided the central rhythm of the children's development. Recontextualizing material from one family to the next, across social relations, symbolic tools, and ideological values could do just what Rita hoped— help the children understand their choices and become more skillful, more deliberate decision makers and communicators.

But it was a rhythm that clearly had to be maintained by an alert conductor and a skillful teacher. The very resources that energized and organized the children's participation in school marked the complexities of their identities and, more particularly, the socioeconomic and cultural complexities of Rita's children. In the following chapters, I highlight the brothers' and sisters' textual journeys, but Rita will be there, providing opportunities, guidance, and critical discussions as she builds and maintains her classroom family.

4

Sports Matters: Marcel and the Textual Mediation of Coach Bombay's and Ms. Rita's Worlds

It is nearing the end of writing workshop time. For his workshop entry, Marcel has written about the San Francisco 49ers' loss to another football team, the Green Bay Packers: "Green Bay [not San Francisco] is the World Chpn [Champion]." At the bottom of his entry, he draws neither a Packer nor a 49er but a Dallas Cowboy (Figure 4.1). Marcel himself is a Dallas Cowboy and, also, a Mighty Duck—a hockey player for the cinematic Coach Bombay, whose team is based in Minnesota (although they played in Los Angeles in one of their movies). Throughout the writing workshop period, he and his teammate, Wenona, have been reviewing their team plans.

Wenona has written "I gotogo." During a conversational lull, I ask what she is writing. "I'm going to the Water World [amusement park]," she says, explaining that she hopes to go in the summer. Marcel immediately pipes up:

MARCEL: But if we win, we gotta go to the playoffs! <u>Then</u>: we gotta go—
WENONA: We going to Water World. Don't you remember?

Wenona then remembers her own "forgotten" plans:

WENONA: You know I'm thinking about going over to [a relative's] house today but we gotta play games. I forgot. We playing hockey. Today we playing hockey.
MARCEL: Cause we gotta play hockey. (agreeing)
WENONA: In Los Angeles—no—
MARCEL: It's in Los Angeles. (affirming)
WENONA: It's in Pittsburgh <u>and</u> Los Angeles.
MARCEL: I forgot. We gotta play Pittsburgh.

Figure 4.1. Marcel's Dallas Cowboy player, No. 88, Michael Irwin.

WENONA: In Pittsburgh. (That is, they are going to play the Pittsburgh team in the city of Pittsburgh.)

MARCEL: Pittsburgh is real weak.

WENONA: They don't play good.

MARCEL: They don't even practice.

The discussion continues, the children "remembering" and "forgetting" as a means, not of monitoring individual memory, but of
collaboratively constructing a busy world of responsibilities, challenges, and triumphs. Soon, though, Rita comes by and calls the

children to account in another busy world of responsibility: the official classroom one.

WENONA: Remember when you was watching the game. I was playing. And you was sitting on the bench. And it was only me and one girl playing—

MARCEL: Cause I made a touchdown.

WENONA: It was only me and one girl playing. (Wenona is correcting Marcel; her "memory" seems based on a scene from a Coach Bombay movie, in which two hockey players from opposite teams squared off in an overtime play for a championship game.) And um I won—we won. We won.

MARCEL: Oh yeah, I forgot. We won.

RITA: (just coming to the table) Wenona, I want you to put the date [on your page]. . . . And I don't want you to spend the whole time talking with Marcel while you're thinking about what you want to write. . . .

As Sylvia Ashton-Warner (1963, pp. 103–104) said, "the worst enemies to what we call teaching . . . [include] the children's interest in each other. . . . If only they'd stop talking to each other, playing with each other, fighting with each other and loving each other. This unseemly and unlawful communication! In self-defense I've got to use the damn thing" by harnessing it.

As detailed in the previous chapter, Rita, like Ashton-Warner, harnessed the children's interest by centering them within recurrent, explicitly guided, and permeable literacy practices. And, as also explained, if Rita's efforts had been counterproductive—if they had worked against child agency, decision making, and performing—the brothers' and sisters' world would have collapsed. Instead, the children's development was evidenced by their use of written language to move more deliberately among social scenes and societal boundaries. The beginnings of such social maneuvering with written text is evidenced as the "writing Water World" event continues below. To reorient readers within Rita's classroom, I begin by repeating her words of concern to Wenona:

RITA: (to Wenona) I don't want you to spend the whole time talking with Marcel while you're thinking about what you want to write. . . . What pretty nails! (Wenona's nails are painted a glittery pink.)

WENONA: Thank you. Actually, I was starting on this page. I was starting to write—I don't know how to write "water."

RITA: Well, what is it you're trying to say?

WENONA: I'm saying, "I am going to go to Wa ter world."
RITA: Can you say the word and see if you can hear the beginning sound? (Wenona does so.)
WENONA: W.
RITA: You got it!

Rita helps Wenona figure out the spelling of "water," advising her, "That's the secret, to say the words to yourself." After Rita leaves, Wenona rereads her words again, and then Marcel deliberately resituates Wenona's text back within the unofficial world:

MARCEL: We can't walk to Water World. (a comment linked to an earlier discussion of how the children might travel to their varied destinations)
WENONA: Yes.
MARCEL: What do ya' mean? We gotta walk to Water World?
WENONA: We're driving. "I'm going to Water World." (Wenona rereads, pointing to the words. She realizes that she does not have the word "world.") How do you spell "world"?
MARCEL: W. W-O-R-L-D (*World* is a word Marcel spells quite a bit.)

Wenona listens to her own slow pronunciation of the word. She does not detect that "w" at the beginning of the one-syllabled "world" as easily as she did the one at the beginning of the two-syllabled "water." She disagrees with Marcel:

WENONA: Werl::::: L! Right?
MARCEL: L-D. (Wenona looks doubtful.) Whatever.
WENONA: "Wa ter World. Wa ter World."
RITA: (to the class) Here's the deal. We're gonna have 5 minutes silent writing now, and then we'll have time for sharing.

Wenona and Marcel stop talking. Wenona stops writing. Wenona draws a water slide, and Marcel finishes his football player.

As Rita feared, the children's talk was, in a sense, distracting them from the official world. But when talk stopped, writing could as well. The children's talk was constitutive of a universe of meaning that allowed them agency, social connection and help, and potential textual stuff. As young children, relative newcomers to official school communities and their literacy practices, the brothers and sisters paid attention to Rita, but they were guided as well by the sense and agency afforded by child-controlled worlds.

In each case history of a brother or a sister, children moved in and out of official and unofficial spheres of activity. And, to varying degrees, writing served as a mediator of their participation in both spheres. But in moving among worlds, children were "exchanging one set of interpretive procedures for another" (Stewart, 1979, p. 30). Wenona's expression, in the official world, of her personal hope for a trip to Water World could, in the unofficial world, be a report of her team plans for life after the playoffs.

In this chapter, the first of three chapters offering developmental tales, I feature Marcel, the most ardent sports fan of the brothers and sisters and, perhaps, of Rita's children as a whole (with the possible exception of Zephenia, who was an intense basketball fan). Marcel's case is both an exemplar of the breadth of literacy resources children may appropriate from a localized cultural resource (i.e., sports media), as well as a particular case of general trends in the children's recontextualization processes.

In their early forays, the children tended to reframe unofficial material within stiff written utterances appropriated from the official school world (e.g., "I like . . . ," "I went . . ."). In contrast, their talk and drawing was situated within unofficial communicative practices, and it accomplished complex mediational feats: with great ease and interactional skill, the children exercised their will through the verbal stuff of grand cultural spectacles like playoff games and hit movies. They did take some control over written utterances, but not without varied symbolic, social, and ideological struggles.

In Marcel's developmental narrative, conceptual and textual resources are embedded within the collaborative construction of life on Coach Bombay's team. This practice, and those resources, provide guidance and substance for Marcel's entry into school-mediated practices, especially those involving reporting information, composing fictional worlds, and sharing personal experiences. His blending of unofficial and official practices and resources provides productive—if not fully resolvable—tensions. These tensions are as much about Marcel's identity as a member of Rita's classroom family as they are about his control of print symbols and written practices.

Below I provide a brief introduction to the potential resources of sports media. Then I begin the featured developmental story in the fall of the year, when Marcel—brother, sportsman, and team traveler—was just beginning to compose through writing.

THE TEXTUAL RESOURCES OF SPORTS MEDIA

From something as simple as the small red scorebook in which I inscribed the narrative of a ball game, I saw the inception of what has become my life's work as a historian. (Goodwin, 1997, p. 10)

Doris Kearns Goodwin traces the roots of her passion for history to the afternoons she spent as a 6-year-old, huddled by the radio with pad and pencil, recording the names of baseball players and the numbers of inning scores. She would use these jottings to jog her memory when she retold the game for her father. In a related way, Marcel's interest as a 6-year-old in watching televised football games supported more academic interests, including meteorology. As I will illustrate, embedded within Marcel's engagement with football media was conceptual knowledge (especially of mathematics and geography), as well as textual knowledge. Those football teams, like the funnel clouds and hurricanes with which he became fascinated, traveled the states according to forecasted routes.

Just as Goodwin's involvement with sports media grew from and supported her relationship with her father, Marcel's was clearly rooted in his home, too, as his mother affirmed. But it also was functionally linked to his relationships with friends, peers, and adults in school.

In Rita's classroom, sports media materials were not the most widely appropriated media for official writing workshop composition—films were, by 17 of the 20 children. In contrast, 9 children, 8 of whom were boys, produced texts based on televised sports events. All of the focal children, however, participated in some talk about sports media and, in addition, all wrote about at least one sports-related film.

Further, a diverse range of material was appropriated from televised sports media, all of which will be illustrated in Marcel's case. The children could appropriate varied forms of content, including names of teams and players, entire events, and sports knowledge itself. They could appropriate communicative practices, like announcing upcoming games and reporting game results. Among the textual features of the resulting products were the presence of location adjectives before team names, as in "Dallas Cowboys" or "Minnesota Vikings"; the proliferation of time adverbs and adverbial phrases, as in "Tonight, [Dallas] will play at Miami"; the dramatic, sometimes violent action verbs, as in "The 49ers got whooped on Sunday"; and omitted verbs, as in "The Bulls 304 Warriors 463" (cf. Hoyle, 1989).

The children could also appropriate technological conventions, especially graphic arrangements (e.g., of game results on television) and symbols of teams and commercial products. In addition, they borrowed actual lines spoken by broadcasters or fans. And finally, they appropriated ideologies of gender and power. These were embedded not only in the sometimes tough, even violent sports discourse, but also in images, like pictures of musclebound football players.

Knowing what the children appropriated from the media does not allow insight into how their resulting texts mediated their school participation, nor into how such texts could generate potentially productive tensions. To these ends, I turn now to the case of Marcel.

MARCEL AND THE WRITTEN WORD

In September of his first-grade year, Marcel was 6 years and 8 months old. Under the school district's latest desegregation plan, Marcel could have attended a school closer to home, but he rode the bus to Rita's school. This was the school to which his two older brothers had been assigned, and it was also the school his younger sister would attend in the years to come. The school was a part of his family's history and, indeed, this was also the case for Wenona, Noah, and Denise.

The bus ride to and from school was sometimes transformed in the children's talk into a van ride with Coach Bombay or his assistant. ("Fake") life was busy for Marcel and the brothers and sisters, full of all kinds of necessary travel and obligations to relations of one kind or another. Marcel and Wenona had a special connection, since they were "soul mates," in Marcel's words. Wenona was the child whose name was first written in his writing book, the child he most often sat by, and, with Noah, his most frequent companion in the world of the brothers and sisters. Yet out on the playground, Marcel usually played organized games, like basketball and kickball, with other boys.

Like almost all of his classmates, Marcel initially explored the graphic look of print through mock writing (Clay, 1975), copied appealing words from bulletin board or white board (e.g., *black widow spider* from an insect unit), and also wrote known initials or whole names of family members and friends. Unlike most of his peers, however, Marcel also wrote the names of football teams and the numbers of favorite players (like 22, the Cowboy Emmitt Smith, and 88, another Cowboy, Michael Irvin). A drawing of a football field (Figure 4.2) suggests some of the complex knowledge embedded in his sports entries, much of it school valued (e.g., counting by tens, writing and reading 2-digit numbers, graphic design and paper arrangement, labeling, and symbol use).

First Contact: Texts as Place Holders, Means, and Filters

After the first few weeks of school, Marcel, like his classmates, began to write more extended prose in his book. He did this by appropriating brief forms from the class-generated "things to write about" list as framing devices for his messages (e.g., "I like _____", "I went _____"), inserting names or other chosen content into the blanks. For some children, these

Figure 4.2. Marcel's detailed football field.

brief texts served more as place holders than communicative means; that is, the texts did not necessarily have a direct link to the writer's intention. Wenona, for example, used "I like cats" as her fail-safe for the entire year (i.e., her place holder—what she tended to *write* automatically or when her plans outstripped her success at securing help). She *drew* and *talked* about varied topics, but very seldom was the topic "cats."

Marcel, however, used his texts of experience and evaluation to comment on varied events and people, including those involving football. Moreover, by December, Marcel began to engage in media-influenced communicative practices: reporting sports results and announcing upcoming games. The resulting products were short and manageable, given his encoding skills (visual and emerging alphabetic encoding skills). Although his initial efforts were syntactically awkward, they did contain key information and structural features, as illustrated in the following example:

> The Dallas Cowboys and the 49ers and Texas g [against] The 49ers got Wt [whooped] on Sunday

Marcel's texts, however, were deceptively simple; they did not entail the straightforward reporting readers might imagine. Below, I elaborate on Marcel's production of the "Dallas Cowboys" texts and illustrate the social and symbolic complexities it involved, complexities evident to varying degrees in the composing time experiences of all the brothers and sisters.

Filtering social spheres. Marcel's "Dallas Cowboys" text took shape most immediately within an unofficial communicative practice—the collaborative enactment of a fantastic world. In that world, Marcel's talk was focused on an actual and playfully reenacted Monday night football game (one in which the 49ers most definitely did not get whooped). Marcel recontextualized the genre of sports reporting within the unofficial world of the brothers and the sisters. His product, seemingly an information text, was mediating primarily his participation in unofficial play, not knowledge display, as exemplified in the following excerpt composed from field notes and transcript data:

> As Marcel discusses with Noah the 49ers' recent win over the Falcons, he draws a Dallas Cowboy. (As readers may recall, Marcel "plays for Texas"; like Wenona, he "hates" the 49ers.) Noah, in an apparent act of affiliation, decides to draw a football player, too:
>
> NOAH: Oh! Are you making a football [player]? I'm gonna make a football [player].

Noah's player soon becomes "me. These are my muscles." He also adds an invented "baby brother" football player. As he draws, he narrates a version of the Monday night football event, "Forty-niners tackle the Atlanta Falcons."

Marcel responds to Noah's play with "Jer ry Rice. Jer ry Rice," and then draws that 49er. He soon returns, however, to the Cowboy figure and to Dallas ("Noah, look! This is Dallas."). Marcel pronounces the final score "20 to 23, Dallas." As he begins to write his report, Wenona comes over and shows Marcel her journal piece— a drawing of a cheerleader (Figure 4.3). Marcel explains:

MARCEL: She cheerleads for Texas. (I look puzzled.) For me.
ANNE: Oh, she cheerleads for you. Where?
WENONA: In Texas.
MARCEL: Mm m.
WENONA: And sometimes we go to um Grove St. Park to practice. Sometimes.

. . .

WENONA: This is where I'm cheerleading. I'm on the side but I came to the field to talk to Marcel.

Marcel appropriated a genre from sports media practices for use within his unofficial world. And that peer world intersected with the official one of writing workshop time. However, Marcel's final product contained no dialogic traces of the unofficial world that could be recognized beyond its borders. When Marcel read his text within the context of official sharing, it became a communicative *filter* as well as a communicative means—the voices of unofficial play no longer "sounded" (Bakhtin, 1986). The familiarity of Marcel's textual form allowed others to understand *his* text in *their* terms. During sharing time, no one questioned the details of Marcel's "informational" text; and "Dallas" was simply a football team. In a similar way, Vanessa and Denise wrote unquestioned "personal experience" texts about going to each other's homes to play, although neither sister had actually been (nor ever went) to the other's home.

To a certain extent, textual forms always function as social filters, preventing certain meanings from slipping through the chosen words (Bakhtin, 1986; Vygotsky, 1962). This is especially so when those words have to mediate between people whose "thoughts wander in different directions" (Vygotsky, 1962, p. 141). In Marcel's case, as in that of all the brothers and the sisters, this dynamic relationship between textual forms and filters played out on the border of child and adult worlds, of unofficial and official frames. This relationship, revealed when children recon-

Figure 4.3. Wenona cheering for Dallas.

textualized material across social and ideological borders, contained the seeds of productive tensions and potential literacy growth. As the school year progressed, these tensions would be about the ways in which varied social spheres judged the value of particular cultural material and the competence of its user and, moreover, about how varied "truths" become visible on official literacy stages.

Unsettling knowledge. Marcel's use of cultural material from sports media brought symbolic as well as social boundaries into high relief. He needed to translate the names of football teams from their audiovisual source to the printed page and, needing help, he sought out a states map, an available and officially valued cultural tool. This simple act stopped him in his tracks, so to speak. On the map's symbolic canvas, his extensive knowledge of football team names—including the Kansas City Chiefs, the Dallas Cowboys, the Oakland Raiders, the Minnesota Vikings, and the Arizona Cardinals—was unsettled: not all of those names were readily visible, as I illustrate below.

> Wenona and Marcel are sitting together during writing workshop. It is early December. Wenona quickly writes "I like"; when no one at her table can provide her with *Christmas*, she finishes the sentence with *cats*. Marcel, who aims to write about football, needs spelling help, too. But he avails himself of a classroom graphic resource—a states map (approx. 18" × 24"). At first Marcel looks for Kansas City on the map, but then he spots a familiar place.

> MARCEL: And there's Texas right here! (He *is* pointing to Texas.) And Oakland, where's Oakland? Is this Oakland? (turning to me)
> ANNE: That's Oregon. Oakland's gonna be in California. Here's the Bay. You see the Bay? Well, Oakland's right near the Bay, right?
> . . .
> MARCEL: Where's Minnesota?
> ANNE: It's right here.
> MARCEL: Good. Here's Texas.
> WENONA: Texas! Where? (She leans over the map, head-to-head with Marcel.)
> MARCEL: Go like this, going down, straight down (running his finger down the map from Minnesota to Texas). You got to cross the whole town. You gotta cross the whole town to get to Texas.

Marcel has abandoned his writing now and is completely absorbed in the map. He shows Wenona another route, a longer one, through California.

MARCEL: Go like this. Go down. Go down California, cut across here. And there's Texas. That'd be a long way from California.

WENONA: I want Oakland.

MARCEL: Oakland is easy to find. (pointing to map)

. . .

ANNE: That's Oregon.

MARCEL: OH MY GOD! . . . Here's Arizona. . . . Is this Minnesota?

. . .

WENONA: Yeah! Like on Mighty Ducks. They say "Minnesota something." (Notice how Wenona is locating Minnesota in a dimly recalled utterance from a movie, just as Marcel's notion of unfamiliar states is rooted in sports media utterances and, more specifically, team names.)

MARCEL: From Minnesota—from Minnesota to Arizona takes a long time. . . .

With Wenona, Marcel returned to a common theme of his unofficial world: team travel. But the geographic information embedded in that talk was unsettled and reorganized, as it was recontextualized within, and in fact became a reference point for participating in, the literacy practice of map reading. As his finger traversed the borders of states, the distinction between city names and state names was becoming an issue ("OH MY GOD!"). (Later that same day, Marcel returned to the map and, Rita reported, she explained to Marcel that it was a *states* map.)

For Marcel, the map seemed a kind of nodal point between his fake and real worlds and, moreover, between his location in the Bay Area and the wider world. His interest in maps continued. Within a few weeks of the above event, he wrote the sports report shown in Figure 4.4. That text has a clear symbolic link to its media resource: the teams ("Minnesota" and "Dallas") and their respective scores are laid out as they would be on a TV screen, rather than prose style, as in print media. Moreover, Marcel's talk during this event revealed his grappling with the place of those teams on the geographic map, as well as their place in unofficial and official social spheres and their respective reporting practices. In the following vignette, all references to geographic concepts are italicized.

Figure 4.4. Marcel's sports report.

Marcel is sitting by Lakeisha and a parent volunteer, Cindy.
Lakeisha is his sister and understands that he plays for a winning
team—Dallas. Cindy is not a relative; she understands that Marcel
is a little boy who seems to have the facts about Dallas's playoff
fate wrong. I, as fake mama and researcher, am not sure whether
or not Marcel knows that, in the official world, Dallas lost, but,
listening to his talk, I am quite sure he understands that he is
negotiating different social spheres.

MARCEL: (to Lakeisha) I know what I want to write about. "The
Dallas Cowboys (beat) Carolina."
. . .
CINDY: They [Dallas] <u>lost</u>. Did you watch the game?
. . .
MARCEL: They're out! Out of the playoffs?
CINDY: They're like the 49ers now.

Marcel changes his writing plans. He begins, *The Dallas*, then stops,
gets the states map, and begins to copy *Minnesota*, the team Dallas
had beat the previous week. (See Figure 4.4.)

MARCEL: (to the table generally, as he looks at the map) *It's got all
            the states right here.*
            (to himself as he writes *Minnesota*) *Minnesota, Minnesota,
            Minnesota, Minnesota . . . to the city of dreams. Minnesota,
            Minnesota, Minnesota, to the city of dreams.* (Pause) *Dallas,
            Texas. Dallas, Texas. Dallas, Texas.*
            (to the table) *This has all the states, right here. I have all the
            states, right over here. . . .*
            I'm writing "Dallas against Minnesota."

Marcel writes *Minne* for "Minnesota," positioning that truncated
word under *Dallas*, column fashion, just as it would be on the
television screen. He rereads "Dallas against Minnesota." Marcel
then recites "Dallas, Texas" several times before writing *in Texas*.

MARCEL: It [the score]—it was, 15—no 15 to 48.
LAKEISHA: Where's Berkeley [on that map]?
MARCEL: In California (pointing). (Notice Marcel now expects only
            the state name on the map, and he knows the state name
            is *California*.)

Marcel rewrites *Minne* and *Dallas* in another column, placing the
scores after them, again, following the technological conventions
for display on a television screen. Also consistent with those
conventions, he adds the team emblems—the horns for the Minnesota Vikings and the stars for the Dallas Cowboys. At one point,
after searching for varied team names on the states map, including
"Pittsburgh," he recalled the first letters of that team and placed the
Pittsburgh Steelers' emblem underneath that team name. (See
Figure 4.4.)

MARCEL: (to Cindy) This says, "Dallas against Minnesota. In Texas.
            15 to 48." *It has the cities of the teams. . . .*
            (to Lakeisha) I be home tomorrow, only me and Wenona
            will be home late. 'Cause me and Wenona got practice. . . .
            I still got to go to football practice. . . . Wenona got cheer-
            leading.

Marcel and Wenona will both be home with Mama and Lakeisha
tomorrow—but they'll be late. The Cowboys may be out of the
playoffs, but Marcel's "still got to go to football practice," and
Wenona's still got to go to cheerleading.

As the year progressed, the negotiation of symbolic and social boundaries evidenced by Marcel was displayed in varied ways by his classroom

siblings, as will be elaborated upon in the chapters to come. To briefly illustrate, Denise wrote that she owned the "*Space Jam* [video]. The song goes like this." She didn't actually write the song because, as she explained, she was going to sing that part during sharing time. On another occasion, Noah, who was fascinated by animation and video games, puzzled over titles: he could not figure out whether to call his second video game-inspired story "Chapter 2" or "Donkey Kong II," the first a prose style, the second a video game style. And once Wenona had the following exchange with Denise, seemingly seriously:

> WENONA: (rereading the names of family members that she has just written) Mom, Wenona, Christian, R-O-B—
> DENISE: Rob and James [the last written name].
> WENONA: We don't call him Rob. We call him R-O-B.

Apparently, the written language convention of orthographically interpreting grouped letters (i.e., *Rob*) was leading Denise to make an erroneous conclusion.

Through such reflective moments, the children demonstrated that, as communicative mediators, written forms shape, as well as are shaped by, writers' intentions, challenges, and enacted practices (Wertsch, 1989). That is, the written symbol system's communicative possibilities require the intentional use of particular technological and semiotic conventions. Thus, when children translated cultural material (e.g., names, informational displays, kinds of texts, text sequencing conventions) across the boundaries of different practices involving different semiotic technologies, they could be stopped short, as the textual and conceptual knowledge embedded in their everyday and playful practices was disrupted and brought into reflective awareness.

In sum, even during the very first months of school, Marcel and his close friends were sensitive to the importance of *written* material in school contexts. When writing, they reframed the names and textual content appropriated from nonacademic sources with textual frames quite literally lifted from school (e.g., "I like . . .", "I went . . ."). Marcel was atypical in that, in his early school writing, he made use of genres themselves appropriated from media sources; these were informational genres whose textual forms were, on the surface at least, valued in school.

All these early forms served as communicative means (and sometimes as simply place holders) and thus helped children make contact with the official world. At the same time, those neat forms filtered out from official view the complexity of the composing time interplay of official and unofficial spheres and the potentially productive social and symbolic tensions thus generated. Marcel in particular used reporting practices in the service of a larger, overriding one—collaboratively enacting a fictional world. But outside his unofficial sphere, his resultant product was potentially subject to interpretive procedures involving different truth criteria. Marcel's efforts to textually negotiate between social spheres (by exchanging *Carolina* for *Minnesota* after the parent's correction of his fact) foreshadowed more complex, and more public, negotiations to come.

Orderly Transformations: Texts as Containable Hybrids

By January, the focal children were becoming more comfortable writers generally, exploiting resources in the room (like word charts) and their own growing orthographic sense to produce longer texts (all averaging about 24 words per entry from January on—with the exception of Wenona, averaging 8).

The children continued to make use of the media. For example, from January onward, approximately two-thirds of Marcel's completed writing workshop texts contained references to the media (30 out of 45), and approximately half (24) had references to a media sports show (e.g., Monday night football). Among the focal children generally, unembedded utterances from hip-hop songs and popular movies began appearing occasionally, as well as new communicative forms (e.g., R & B songs and horror stories, inspired largely by the *Goosebumps* books and related *Goosebumps* TV series [Protocol Entertainment & Stine, 1996]). Nonetheless, their writing book entries continued to be framed primarily by textual forms highlighted in school: along with statements of apparent (not necessarily actual) personal experience, evaluation, or reported "facts" came written exchanges, more extended reports, and stories.

As I will illustrate, their new length and diversity contributed to the complexity and power of the children's texts as communicative means and, moreover, as dialogic hybrids (Bakhtin, 1981); these hybrids recontextualized material from diverse social worlds within official literacy practices. There was little evidence that *children* initially conceived of themselves as textually bringing diverse social spheres "in contact with one another" (Bakhtin, 1981, p. 326). For the most part, any symbolic and social tensions were smoothed over by the filtering textual frames and performance conventions of school. Nonetheless, through their composing, the children were transforming the official world—they were introducing material not anticipated by the curriculum.

A number of these more elaborate but containable hybrids were generated by the space unit Rita introduced in early January (see Chapter 3). As readers may recall, the unit's early lessons were accompanied by displayed lists of planets and charts of space facts; sometimes those facts were reviewed in a dialogue game in which pairs of children asked other pairs, "Did you know that . . . ?", and then reported during sharing time that "I learned that . . ." Marcel had seemed quite taken with the ways in which Rita, and the colorful reference books, had displayed information. He had used the "illustrated fact event" to organize and display planets' names. And, in response to Rita's first assignment to report "what I learned," he listed planet names—after Rita explicitly told him *not* to write about the Dallas Cowboys.

In his writing workshop events, Marcel also began to engage in list making, fact reporting, and written exchanges (which Rita had already initiated with Denise and Vanessa). Indeed, he began to fill his writing workshop book with lists—lists rooted in, yes, football and in his efforts to untangle cities and states. Map reading had already made salient this geographic information embedded in Marcel's play on Coach Bombay's team. Now, through list making, this knowledge began to be further distanced from that context and recontextualized within official practices subject to different truth criteria (i.e., the facts reported had to be viewed as accurate by those outside of Coach Bombay's world).

First in Marcel's list-making efforts was a list of teams ("Green Bay, Dallas, Bears, 49ers"), and then a team list that included locales (e.g., "The Green Bay Packers and the Carolina Panthers, the Dallas Cowboys, the New York Giants, the New York Jets"), and finally, a list of just states (see Figure 4.5):

The state of Texas
The state of Arizona
The state of New York
The state of Minnesota
The state of Kansas

Marcel's named states, and their accompanying illustration of a helmeted man, left little doubt as to the origin of his efforts. Thus, his football team expertise continued to be reorganized and recontextualized in taxonomic form, not only through the support of a symbolic tool (a map), but also through a new communicative practice (list making).

In addition to list making, Marcel began writing information texts that displayed his football expertise; these texts were more elaborate and more officially truthful than his reports of game results. His first such text (50 words, twice his, and the class's, average) began modestly with his announced intention to write that "Desmond Howard made 3,079 touchdowns."

Figure 4.5. Marcel's list of states, all of which are affiliated with football teams.

"Yeah, right," said Noah skeptically. Then Jamal declared that Desmond Howard played for the 49ers.

"He didn't play for the 49ers," Marcel said firmly. "He played for the Green Bay Packers [but not, as it happens] for his whole life."

Marcel recorded Howard's identity as a Packer, wrote about a player whom he knew switched teams, and finally, reported the Super Bowl results:

Desmond Howard made 300079 Touch Downs.
He playd for the Green Bay Packers.
Dion Sanders plaid for The 49ers and The Dallas Cowboys.
The Carelon [Carolina] Panthers playd in the Spbol [Super Bowl].
But they lost the Spbol ag [against] The Green Bay Packers.
    [Actually, the Packers played the Patriots.]
And The Green Bay Packers wr [were] the World Chpins agn
    [again].

"I did more. I did more writing," said Marcel to Noah when he was
done. "Rita's gonna be so proud of me. . . . That was the tightest story I
ever told."

"How many football players do you know about?" asked Vanessa
when he shared.

"I know about 29," replied Marcel, looking very pleased with himself.

In addition to lists and reports, Marcel also attempted to affiliate with
a student teacher intern, Tami, through a written exchange. Taking the
role of the expert, Marcel wrote about Emmitt Smith's and the Cowboy's
gained yards and then asked,

Now? Do you got the game
Sow hr [So here] is a question for you
[Tami] what team Do you like
Do you like The Cowboys
Do you like The 49ers
Do you like The Eags [Eagles]
Do you like The Jag [Jaguars]
Do you like The Brs [Bears]

Marcel's expertise in football, his interest in travel across states (especially Texas), and his experience with lists and reports, seemed to cul-
minate late in the year when he became fascinated with a book about
tornadoes read by Ms. Sheng, the school librarian. The book includes both
a states map and an illustration of a television weather person pointing to
a U.S. map (Bramley, 1988). Marcel's end-of-year thank-you letter to
Ms. Sheng incorporated the teacher-suggested evaluative statement about
his favorite book, but then, quite quickly, became a report on tornadoes'
travel across states, old familiar states:

Dear Miss Sheng:
I love the book of tornados.
Becous the tornado.

suks [sucks] up things thats gots [gets][1] in its.
way The tornads are very very.
dagtras [dangerous] becous it can suk you.
up and throw you in the clod [cloud].
Thats the tornados clod job.
When the tonrd [tornado] is don, it gos back.
to the clod and thir [they're] tornads.
in Florida Ther may be some tornads.
in Arizoney. But ther no tornads
in Berkeley Calfony Becous it is so
hot in spring the sun is so hot
on the news ther were [was] a twister
in Texas yesterday in the moreing [morning].
A tornado in the morning.

                                        from Marcel

When Marcel was in the second grade (a year after he wrote the above text and began his fascination with the weather), his mother told me that he still checked the sky each morning for funnel clouds in his assumed role as family weather forecaster, and he still considered "the tornado" book his favorite.

Although they rarely composed lists or informational reports about media-related figures or events, Vanessa and Denise engaged in many written exchanges and even dialogically (through alternating turns) composed R&B songs and a horror story; and Wenona and Lakeisha coached each other through an exchange about their liking of *The Hunchback of Notre Dame* (Conli, Hahn, Trousdale, & Wise, 1996). Most impressively, Noah produced a lengthy report on *Space Jam* (Falk, Ross, & Pytka, 1996) and Michael Jordan ("one of my favorite men," he wrote). It began, "I know that Michael Jordan is a superstar and he know that he goes on Space Jam. . . . He gots the moves. . . ." (The report was 94 words—over four times longer than his average entry.)

In sum, the children exploited school-valued practices to organize and display knowledge appropriated from an expanding range of un-official sources. In Marcel's case, appropriated school practices included list-making and reporting, and they involved the use of cultural tools, including geographic taxonomies and representations, which allow one to trace movement across space. The children's texts were hybrids, however carefully contained: they were constructed from the symbolic stuff of elite and common culture, and that material mediated children's participation in overlapping official and unofficial worlds. Not sur-

prisingly, then, the recontextualization of material across social and symbolic boundaries did not always go so smoothly, as I illustrate in the next
section.

Contested Transformations: Texts as Unruly Hybrids

Sometimes children's texts were unruly hybrids, less compatible with official textual structures, and uncontained by official school practices. Those
texts were not such efficient filters; meanings rooted in children's unofficial world seeped through to the official one. These unofficial meanings
could generate —and sometimes were deliberately exposed in response to—
symbolic, social, and indeed, ideological tensions. The public display of
tensions was not necessarily negative. In our socioculturally complex
world, becoming aware of social boundaries, and more deliberately negotiating them, is key to successful literacy learning (Dyson, 1993, 1997; The
New London Group, 1996).

Indeed, as the school year progressed, there was evidence that all of
the brothers and sisters were becoming more deliberate about using writing, as a cultural tool, to negotiate boundaries—and that their teacher Rita
was critical to this socioideological learning. For example, the children were
becoming more sensitive to the cultural material appropriate in particular contexts. During the space unit, as earlier noted, Rita cautioned Marcel
against football as a topic for his science text; and Noah and Wenona objected firmly when Marcel suggested they name their invented planet
(another assigned task) "Pizza Planet," based on the movie *Toy Story*
(Arnold, Catmull, Guggenheim, Jobs, & Lasseter, 1995).

Sensitivity to judgments about writing's context appropriateness goes
hand in hand with a sensitivity to writing's potential for managing social
boundaries (see also Dyson, 1993). And the children were most definitely
aware of these boundaries. They engaged, for example, in surreptitious
writing. They made lists of "club" members, which they stashed in their
backpacks or their cubbies. Marcel's was named the "BC" club, after the
radio station KMEL's BC (Breakfast Club). These clubs tended to be more
exclusionary than those Rita advocated (i.e., "Everybody Clubs"). The
children also made what might be called "double-coded symbols," symbols that were intended to function as filters in the official school sphere.
For example, one day Wenona wrote a *2* in her writing book, which was
"how old her nephews were" on the official school stage but how many
times she, Marcel, and Noah would "beat up" Jamal on the unofficial one.
(This was more a "snap" than an actual threat, since hitting was forbidden—but "remember, Mama said she don't care if we snap at somebody.")

The more children used writing as a functional tool in their social lives, the more deliberate they became about minding social boundaries of appropriateness and the more potential they had to exercise power by heightening border tensions. Tensions could be heightened if authors abandoned double-coding and openly read an alternative meaning; tensions could also be heightened if authors made salient unofficial (and potentially unacceptable) sources or if addressees resisted the recontextualization of material from particular sources.

In the two examples below, border tensions between social worlds become evident as Marcel recontextualizes first an image and then the narrative and discursive stuff of his Coach Bombay play to official contexts. These tensions, however, do not originate from Ms. Rita's—or any adult's—objections, but from other child members of the classroom family. The examples thus illustrate children's potential interconnections and borders and, moreover, they highlight the power issues embedded in differing judgments about what can be legitimately said (or written or drawn): issues of access and competence in the official world, of identity and belonging in unofficial ones and, moreover, of textual value and truth (cf., Bauman & Briggs, 1990). These are issues whose public display is dependent upon unruly textual hybrids.

Hey Arnold, Hey Lincoln. In March, the class studied Harriet Tubman and the Underground Railroad. The study was an historical one (and it featured that states map so intriguing to Marcel; Rita and the children traced some of the routes of the escaping slaves as they moved from the South through to freedom in Canada). The study, however, was also grounded in the broader context of what "freedom" meant to the children as children. On this day, the assigned task was to construct, in cooperative groups, a poster about freedom. In Rita's words, the poster could be about "history or it can be about you."

Marcel sat down with his assigned cooperative group partners—his fake sister Denise and classroom peer Denny (a child from the immediate neighborhood). On Denise's suggestion that they write about "freedom [being] when people get away," Denise herself drew cotton (which looked like her regular happy-face flowers), Denny began the grass, and Marcel, on his own initiative, began to draw a large figure preparing to traverse the states: He drew an escaping slave "going out to the Underground Railroad in Canada."

Marcel's escaping man looked like a cartoon figure he had used before for football players. Indeed, Marcel himself commented that the figure looked "*like* [not *was*] 'Hey Arnold,'" with his sun-ray hair and his broad face (Snee-Oosh Inc. & Bartlett, 1996). When Denise mistook his escaping slave for a white overseer, Marcel responded that "White people not supposed to be" running away and, to clarify his picture, he began to color the figure black. When Rita came by, Marcel seemed to have other concerns about possible misinterpretations. He quite spontaneously assured her, "It's not no football player," apparently assuming that would be her concern. He was stretching a cartoon image, usually used for football players (with heads shaped like footballs) into a daring historical figure.

Marcel did not, however, anticipate Denny's concern. After Rita left, Denny asked:

> DENNY: Are you still drawing Hey Arnold?
> MARCEL: No. I'm drawing a person walking. They have strong muscles. . . . All I'm drawing is one person trying to get away.

Marcel sings a Pete Seeger song about the Underground Railroad, which Rita had taught the class, and an apparently invented one about Abe Lincoln getting shot, all the while working on the big, bold figure; that figure gains a Nike sign—"the sign of a football player"—on his shirt, Nike gloves, and "check this out," he has "tight shoes," too. Denise comments that she likes the drawing and that she hopes to go to the opening of the Nike store in the city this weekend. (Denise's smiling cotton flowers have now sprouted dialogue signs saying "I love you", the flowers are happy not to have been picked.) Although Denise is appreciative, Denny is not; he says nothing about Denise's loving flowers, but he persistently points out that "we're not talking about TV shows." Eventually Marcel responds in a firm voice, with a defiant edge:

> MARCEL: It's Hey Arnold. It's my idea.

Marcel then writes "Hey [not Arnold but] Lincoln" and, next to that, "Hey George [Washington]."

The tension between Denny and Marcel continued the next day, when the children returned to their posters. Denny had resisted the (albeit not complete) recontextualization of material from a "TV show" for a freedom poster, and Marcel responded by escalating the tension . . . within limits. He consistently referred to his drawing as "Hey Arnold," *except* when a grown-up (other than me) was around—when it reverted to the figure on the Underground Railroad. Marcel seemed to be playing on the now reinforced boundary between official and unofficial worlds to irritate Denny. Finally, Denny complained to Rita about Marcel's identity-shifting figure (i.e., his double-coding).

When all the children came to the rug with their posters, Rita asked them to explain their posters and, also, their experiences "cooperating." In their turn, Denny, Marcel, and Denise quite cooperatively reported the tension they'd had; in Marcel's words, "Denny didn't want me to draw my favorite character." Therefore the drawn figure, begun as only the image of a cartoon character, now *became* that character.

Some children responded to the reported dispute by shaking their heads, frowns on their faces. Others, like Vanessa, openly admired the big colorful drawing. Marcel grinned at his peers and chuckled, apparently enjoying the moment. During the previous composing periods, when the nature of his chosen symbol seemed to filter its school-valued meaning from Denny's view, Marcel had initially aligned himself with the official world: "All I'm drawing is one person trying to get away." Now, during the public sharing time, Marcel seemingly accepted with pleasure his place at the margins of official acceptability; he abandoned the figure's identity as an escaping slave.

For her part, Rita did not engage in a power struggle with Marcel, which would have been inconsistent with her responsive, group-centered style. She in no way heightened the tension; rather, she embraced it. She was not aware of the figure's more complex identity, but she seemed aware of issues at the heart of the tension: issues of whether or not Marcel's composing decision was a competent one, whether or not his product should be valued and, most importantly, whether or not Marcel himself, given his current stance, belonged in the official world. Rita responded,

> RITA: Well, there are two ways of looking at it [this problem]. You could say, "Well, I'm free to draw whatever I like," right? An artist and writer can draw or write whatever they like and . . . try to publish it. . . . [But] I might say, "Marcel, you are working in a group, and the assignment is to do something about your knowledge about freedom. . . ." And he might come back and say, "Well I disagree with you. I think my idea of freedom is to be able to draw something I want to draw." . . . There's no answer that's right or wrong.

And, on that note, the children continued to explain to each other how groups had interpreted the assignment and the points of disagreement that had surfaced.

Denny's objection, which was not unreasonable, pushed both Marcel and himself to articulate a boundary, constructed through media material, between official and unofficial worlds. Moreover, that articulated boundary became an official and public manifestation of potential social and ideological differences among the children themselves. Marcel and Denny were unique individuals but, as discussed in Chapter 3, differences in their textual choices reflected differences in their cultural memberships and in the interrelated categories of race and class.

In response to the public drawing of a clear boundary between reasonable and unreasonable responses, Rita blurred the line. She deemed Marcel's response an occasion for reflection; it could, she argued, be viewed as reasonable, too. (In fact, one child group had included watching television in their poster of favorite activities they were "free" to do.) Rita thus redrew the boundary of the official classroom world, bringing in both boys, the disputed symbol, and the larger issues at the heart of their disagreement.

This redrawing was not unusual for Rita. When, for example, Noah and Wenona objected to Marcel's "Pizza Planet" suggestion, Rita cautioned them to "remember you can get good ideas from books . . . and movies, and you can get good ideas from other people. . . ." On another day, when Jamal commented that only boys liked football, Rita discussed sports preferences with the class and invited local female athletes to talk with them, too. Rita also "interviewed them," to use Vanessa's words, about their film preferences and about the meaning and use of codes like PG and R (with which the children were quite familiar).

Rita did not resolve tensions; she brought them out into the open where the range of opinions undergirding them could be made audible. And this process of naming and discussing diffused power struggles and promoted social and intellectual discussions of text types and preferences (cf. Dyson, 1997). I offer below one last, brief example of textual media tion, one that suggests the importance of not resolving tensions, of giving children leeway to define themselves in complex public spheres.

Marcel and the playoffs. One day in June, Marcel stood before his class and read two pieces that were, on the surface, personal experience texts. In one he reported watching "the playoffs" on cable all weekend "till 6:30 in the morning" on Monday. In the second, he himself was in a nighttime playoff game and "made 3,000 touchdowns":

On The Weekend I.
Was play[ing] FootBall My.
Koch [coach] was saying that.
Our tham [team] wood have to play.
In the Night The game was.
Over at Mait Nigth [midnight].

We was in the play offs.
I maDe 3,000 thcH [touch] Downs

In producing this text, Marcel recontextualized much more than an image or even a genre used in Coach Bombay play (e.g., reporting game results). Rather, Marcel appropriated the discursive substance of the play itself, including key characters (e.g., the coach, himself as football player) and typical plot elements (e.g., making the playoffs, scoring touchdowns, and winning the championship). Coach, for the first time, spoke to him in a space mediated by writing, and Marcel (not Emmitt or Dion) responded with ample touchdowns.

But, as illustrated below, this new development—this new option of recontextualizing narrative material from unofficial play for official written display—seemed to position Marcel himself awkwardly between worlds. Being in playoffs and making touchdowns were important in the unofficial brothers' and sisters' world but, during sharing time, Marcel's text was situated in the official world. His presentation of dubious facts about himself—not some distanced team—led to peer objections, objections that emphasized Marcel's status as an adult-dependent child:

> JOHN: (responding to Marcel's reading) When you said you stayed up, did your mom know that you was um staying up til late?
> MARCEL: I I I was in the playoffs.
> JOHN: Yeah, did your mom know?
> MARCEL: No. . . .
> . . .
> JOHN: Is that a made-up story?
> MARCEL: No.
> . . .
> ZEPHENIA: Marcel, why were you out by yourself?
> MARCEL: I wasn't. My dad was the coach of my team.
> VANESSA: O::h. So you went with your dad. Your dad coached your team. . . . (nodding at Marcel and, then, at her classmates in an affirming way)
> MARCEL: I was on the team.
> ZEPHENIA: You're not on those teams. (That is, you cannot be on the kind of city teams coached by parents, since, as Zephenia soon notes, Marcel is too young.)
> RITA: Well he was in that writing.

Zephenia has an accusing tone in his voice. Rita allows Marcel refuge in his text, but Marcel is not claiming to be a football player only in his text. Still, Marcel, under pressure, has lowered his sights. He does not claim to play for Dallas but, rather, for:

MARCEL: Peewees. (Marcel is referring to the city teams for children.)
ZEPHENIA: Peewees are 8 to 9.
MARCEL: I know, and they're 7 in second grade, and in first grade.

Rita thanks Marcel and moves on to the next child.

Marcel's genre or communicative practice in the above event is an unruly hybrid and thus not easy to name or contain. John and Zephenia, two friends interested in sports, responded to both of Marcel's pieces as though they were personal experience texts which, on the surface, they seem to be. Their response reflected the usual interpretation of a piece shared in public that began "I was," "I like," or "I went." It would be non-sensical to ask an author of a fictional story about a grandiose child action, "Did your mother know where you were?"

In fact, Marcel's text *did* constitute personal experience in the broth-ers' and sisters' world, a serious world, the routines and games of which were seldom acknowledged as just play; that world was about being power-ful, responsible, and competent. But now, blending official and unofficial worlds in this public way seemed to "undermine the suspension of doubt needed" to sustain Coach Bombay's world (cf. Stewart, 1979, p. 17). Given his sharing time audience, Marcel attempted to negotiate a "true" context for his piece, supported by his sister Vanessa. He did not, however, in any way allow his text a once-upon-a-time frame. He remained a football player, although he did constrict his place in the world. He traveled around the city, not around the states.

As an older relative of the brothers and the sisters, an affectionate fake mama, I noted that it was only the neighborhood middle-class children who reported traveling beyond state borders for family events (i.e., a weekend skiing trip to New Mexico, a plane ride to Grandma's in South Carolina). As Marcel negotiated his identity in this public place, I felt pro-tective of his links to a larger landscape, even as the teacher in me appre-ciated the probing questioning of Zephenia and John, and the way they and Rita worked to understand what kind of communicative genre—what kind of space—Marcel was offering.

Marcel was not the only child to engage in this public negotiating. When a classmate asked Noah during sharing time about his small drawn football player (earlier noted), Noah named the figure "my baby brother." Rita articulated the official composing time boundary between what was true "in your story" and "in your family." For whatever reason—saving face in this public place or simply maintaining his overlapping location inside the unofficial world (where invented siblings were common)—Noah did not let go of that invented brother. When Rita inquired as to the baby's name, he (like Marcel) negotiated with the adult world: "My mother didn't got his name yet."

ON COACH BOMBAY'S KIDS AND WRITING

It is after all so easy to shatter a story. To break a chain of thought. To ruin a fragment of a dream being carried around carefully like a piece of porcelain. To let it be, to travel with it . . . is much the harder thing to do. (Roy, 1997, p. 181)

Unlike Roy's children in *The God of Small Things*, Marcel and the brothers and sisters did not use dress and makeup to create new realities and identities for themselves; they used talk and, more particularly, shared references to popular media. A favorite movie provided a coach, televised football provided them a team and an itinerary, and less emphasized in this chapter, the radio provided them group songs. Still, their world, too, struck me as paradoxically fragile. Their voices were strong and sure whenever they were in that world, and yet they worked hard to maintain the coherence of their constructed reality. Moreover, outside that world, others could view the texts mediating that reality—and the shared symbols through which it was built—as quite dubious in value. Noah somberly hanging on to that football-playing baby brother, Marcel straightforwardly negotiating a public place where he could still be in the playoffs—these were not, at that moment, lighthearted children, but quite serious ones.

The tensions resulting from children's awkward placements amid worlds all reveal something fundamental about childhoods and writing. At the heart of child cultures is the desire for a space in which children, not adults, have control. If writing is to be a useful childhood tool, as Vygotsky (1978) recommended, it must be about mobilizing agency and available resources in familiar, intention-driven communicative situations. Thus, Marcel did not need to read football books to learn written language, nor did he need a football fan as a teacher. But he did need to use familiar textual practices, and the embedded knowledge they contained, to mobilize his agency and resources and to orchestrate his evolving literacy knowledge.

Analysis of Marcel's composing events revealed the potential hybrid nature of even the earliest of children's written texts; those texts could be situated within overlapping social worlds, which themselves drew upon a diversity of cultural texts, including those of the popular media. Inherent in this hybridization were developmental challenges related to the symbolic, social, and ideological nature of children's diverse resources and pleasures.

In their initial forays into writing, the children in Marcel's classroom coped with the demand that they "write" by drawing, talking, and writing familiar words and by appropriating written forms and patterns from school. This is a common child pattern: when in doubt, observe what others do, say (Fillmore, 1976), and write (Bussis, Chittenden, Amarel, & Klausner, 1985; Clay, 1975; Dyson, 1989; King & Rentel, 1981). Their appropriations from the media consisted primarily of content—names and events that could be "liked" or to which they could have "went." Marcel appropriated communicative practices whose resulting textual forms, sports reports and announcement, were salient to him and manageable—liftable—for a just beginning writer.

Early texts, even when communicative in intention rather than simply place holders, were also filters. For Marcel in particular, outside the constructed boundaries of the brothers' and sisters' world his dream fragment—his transformed identity as one of Coach Bombay's kids—did not sound; it lost the backdrop of unofficial voices that allowed his own to resonate (cf. Bakhtin, 1986). Nonetheless, Marcel's early composing did reveal the semiotic tensions possible in translating material between audiovisual (television) and prose graphics, and between the narratively organized sports events (where two teams do battle and one wins) and academic tools and practices (where two teams identified by their locales could end up on different lists, not to mention different maps).

Over time, children's texts began to mediate in more complex ways their efforts to declare and maintain themselves as playful, knowledgeable, powerful, and socially valued people in unofficial and official worlds. They appropriated a diverse range of cultural material from unofficial as well as official worlds. The children's agency—and the symbolic texts through which that agency was exercised—could generate social and ideological as well as symbolic tensions. These tensions could be hidden through double-coded symbols or surreptitious writing. They could be reduced through authors officially framing unofficial information ("I know that Michael Jordan is a superstar") and through others socially allowing, or even critically discussing such recontextualization. And tensions could be heightened through rejecting recontextualization or ruling it out of bounds ("We're not talking about TV shows"). Such rejection could lead to anger or righteousness, a forced choice between social worlds.

The social and ideological tensions that Marcel, and all the brothers and sisters, encountered were critically important, even though they may not be resolvable. To negotiate literate participation in complex classroom cultures, children must differentiate not only phonological niceties and textual features but also social worlds—the very social worlds that provide them with agency and important symbols. In Marcel's classroom, Rita could help transform such tensions into classroom discussions of social relations and authorial and artistic choices.

Within the frame of this book, Marcel has now introduced the basic processes of recontextualization—processes of differentiation, appropriation, translation, and reframing of cultural material across symbolic forms and social practices. In the next chapter, Noah will come out from the background and take center stage. With his strong sensitivities to visual media, as well as his desires to be a proper schoolchild, Noah's case foregrounds the resources and challenges found in visual media forms, which, unlike sports media, are specifically directed to children (especially to boys). Noah, even more so than Marcel, wanted to be seen as proper, as good, by Rita. With his ear increasingly attuned to official-sounding prose, and his mind's eye replaying the visual scenes of his favorite animated pleasures, Noah negotiated a distinctive course through the social waters of his first-grade class.

5

Animated Adventures: Noah's Textual Ark

Noah is adjusting the dangling eyeballs of his space creature, who is named, appropriately enough, "Eyeballs." He cannot resist making his space creature, and thereby the eyeballs, dance. But those Styrofoam balls are secured only by thin strings themselves attached with awkwardly placed swatches of tape. A few dance moves, and the eyeballs swing loose and roll on the floor. Despite all this dancing and retaping of eyeballs, Noah writes the officially required information: his space creature's name (IYBS [Eyeballs]), its favorite food (PZZ [pizza]), and its play preference (NITDOAT [Nintendo]).

Sitting across from Noah, on the long back table, is Wenona and her space creature, Julie, named after a girl member of the cinematic Mighty Ducks hockey team (Avnet, Claybourne, Kerner, & Weisman, 1994). That space creature, constructed from well-attached toilet rolls, is resting comfortably beside her. But Wenona is struggling to write Julie's food preference. As illustrated below, she and Noah maneuver between official and unofficial frames, Noah helpfully guiding her in the official world and playfully bickering with her in the unofficial one (where he most definitely does not have the upper hand).

Wenona is staring at her paper. A circulating adult (a new student teacher) asks Wenona what her alien likes to eat, but Noah immediately takes over. Wenona responds to him, not to the student teacher, as illustrated below.

> Noah: What you like to eat? What you like to eat? Pizza? Uh, candy canes? Um—
> Wenona: Candy canes! . . . I'll write "candy canes." How you write it?

NOAH: Um C. C-A. (saying word to himself) No no no. Yeah.
    A-N-D. That's all.
WENONA: That's [CAND] "candy cane"? (Wenona is rereading
    word.) That's not right.
NOAH: Yes it is.

Marcel has come by to show his robot to his fake siblings. Noah
pretends the robot is attacking him with his antennae
("AHHHHHHHH!") and, then, with his fire-spewing belt ("EEE EEE
EEE EEE"). Marcel slips back to his seat at another work table, and
Noah helps Wenona spell "hockey," the game preference of her
space alien. Then:

WENONA: I'm finished!
NOAH: Draw a picture. If you want to, you can draw a picture.
    (Wenona begins drawing.) Making a candy cane?
WENONA: No.
NOAH: What ya making?
WENONA: A hockey thing.
NOAH: Oh, a hockey stick?
WENONA: A hockey stick. Uh. I might play at football.
NOAH: (not missing a beat after Wenona's turn to unofficial
    concerns) You don't want to play it, 'cause you can't go
    outside.
. . .
WENONA: So. I don't care.
NOAH: [I can go outside] 'cause my room is already clean. I
    cleaned it up [and so their Mama will let him go out and
    play].
WENONA: So, I messed it back up. Now what you gonna say? And I
    don't care what Mama say either. Cause I ain't about to
    get my hands dirty [cleaning some more]. Mm mm
    [no]. . . . And you better not get in my diary.
NOAH: I did. I threw it in the garbage can.
. . .
WENONA: No you didn't.
NOAH: The old one. 'member the old one?
WENONA: But don't tell me you looked in my new one!

Like Marcel, the sibling featured in Chapter 4, Noah was a skillful member of the brothers and the sisters family. With evident ease, he played
with the cultural stereotype of the mischievous brother. At the same time,
though, Noah, more so than Marcel, appropriated Rita's teacher voice. In

the preceding vignette, Noah guided Wenona's decision making through the varied steps of the assigned task and modeled word analysis for her.

Noah's case thus revealed in particularly dramatic fashion the way in which children's developmental histories are shaped by the contradictory forces emanating from official practices and unofficial ones. Like his fake siblings, the talk and drawing that dominated during Noah's early production events were organized primarily by familiar childhood practices. As the creature Nintendo and his dangling eyeballs might suggest, Noah was highly attentive to visual media; he seemed to view the expansive space of a blank page in his writing workshop book as an irresistible invitation for constructing a visually dramatic world. His production events typically yielded a multimodal drama.

However, the connection between those dramas and Noah's accompanying brief written statements was often tenuous indeed. Those statements were Noah's nods to the official expectation to write. Even more so than Marcel, Noah seemed to prefer to render to Caesar the things that are Caesar's, so to speak—and Caesar controlled the serious tender of writing. As I will illustrate, Noah initially seemed to bring no motive to school writing other than gaining Rita's approval and, thereby, that of his parents. After all, the motives that language users bring to language situations are the result of cultural learning—of knowing what practices are for (Halliday, 1980; Miller, 1982; Schutz, 1970). In Noah's case, these purposes initially seemed homogeneous and divorced from any childhood pleasure or purpose (other than appeasing and pleasing adults).

Moreover, Noah's preferred textual toys—those of animated media— allowed him no manageable communicative practices to blend easily with official practices (unlike Marcel's sports reporting). In his video games, creatures did not talk; and even in the cartoons he watched, where creatures did talk, the dialogue could be stiff and sparse.[1] Thus, in addition to the social and ideological challenges posed by Caesar's world, there were the semiotic challenges of translating visual symbolic forms into print media (see also Dyson, 1989).

Below I introduce the potential resources of animated media, which Noah drew upon to enter school composing practices. Then I begin his developmental story in the fall of the year, when Noah, like his fake siblings, was just beginning to construct written texts. As will be demonstrated, Noah did develop as a writer—as a decision-making participant in the practices of Rita's official school family. But, like Marcel, Noah never abandoned his identity as a playful brother in the unofficial world. Rather, as his composing actions were channeled by the socializing forces of Rita's official practices, Noah found those practices more meaningful—that is, less vacuous, more identifiable as kinds of communicative situations. And, just as with Marcel, as Noah understood the communicative possibilities of literacy practices, he was more likely to use his textual toys deliberately to exploit those practices for familiar childhood ends, like play, pleasure, and performance. Noah thus negotiated particular, playful communicative spaces through what initially seemed the stiff, routine exigency of Caesar's words.

THE TEXTUAL RESOURCES OF ANIMATED MEDIA

> All children in those small-town, unhurried days had a vast inner life going on in the movies. Whole families attended together in the evenings, at least once a week, and children were allowed to go without chaperone in the long summer afternoons—schoolmates with their best friends, pairs of little girls trotting on foot the short distance through the park to town under their Japanese parasols. . . . My sense of fictional comedy undoubtedly caught its first spark from the antic pantomime of the silent screen, and from having a kindred soul to laugh with. (Welty, 1983, p. 37)

Eudora Welty spent lovingly remembered afternoons at the movies with her brother Edward, collapsing in laughter at the visually displayed shenanigans of silent comedies. In her memory of family and popular media, she locates a potential source of her adult predilections to craft words in comedic ways. Like Doris Kearns Goodwin, whose childhood memory of baseball helped introduce Marcel's case, Welty helps me, as author, create a space for consideration of a certain kind of childhood pleasure foregrounded in Noah's case.

As readers may recall from Chapter 2, Noah was an expert on the "funny stuff" one could find in varied visual forms, among them television cartoons, movies, and video games. These forms of pleasure were shared with his fraternal twin Ned and, sometimes, with his cousins, who, he said, came over to watch that funny stuff with him. During his writing workshop events, Noah referred to many animated animals—flying dinosaurs, urban adolescent turtles, mischievous chimps, loony animals of cartoon fame, and even an apparently invented superhero dog. It should be noted that Noah also enjoyed real animals of many kinds, including creatures in the bay and in the zoo, not to mention his family dog, Frisco, and his puppy, Chopper. And, in the case history to come, Noah will be seen grappling with the geographic habitat and the pet-potential of real versions of virtual creatures, analogous to (although less intensely than) Marcel's grappling with the geographic location of football teams.

In addition to the embedded conceptual material about the nature and habitats of varied creatures, Noah appropriated from animated media varied sorts of cultural material for his multimodal production events. Indeed, many children appropriated from visual media during composing time, especially from movies (from January through June, 17 of the 20 children). A smaller but substantial number appropriated from television cartoons (8 children, mainly boys), but only 2 appropriated characters from video games. For Noah, however, all these forms of media offered animated animals and potential pets.

From media involving animation, children could appropriate varied forms of content, like names (e.g., of characters or particular media shows) and themes (e.g., saving the world, rescuing the threatened, or using superhuman capacities associated with real or mythic animals, like breathing fire or flying). Among other appropriated content were the actual watching of a show as itself a reportable event and, also, particular plot segments. As Welty might have predicted, the children seemed drawn to comedic, slapstick scenes, including unabashed displays of physical affection, like kissing—a kind of vaudevillian humor, in many young schoolchildren's view.

The children could also appropriate communicative practices from animated media. In Noah's case, enacting a superhero story was a particularly common practice. He appropriated certain textual features of such stories, including heavy use of exclamations ("AAAAH!", "Help!") and grand summarizing claims ("Godzilla saved the world"), although the bulk of the action was carried visually.

The children could also borrow technological conventions, like stylized print, directional indicators, and symbols of potential and enacted power (e.g., jagged lines, swirls). Moreover, they could revoice actual lines spoken by characters. In both their oral and written texts, children could feature the easily differentiated and lifted lines of dramatic, often funny bits of dialogue. Particularly popular during the project year was Lola Bunny's "Don't ever call me doll," said with drop-dead seriousness by the svelte Lola to the smitten Bugs in *Space Jam* (Falk, Ross, & Pytka, 1996).

Finally, as that Lola Bunny line suggests, the children's appropriated media material contained embedded ideologies of gender and of physical power and love. These were embedded not only in lifted lines, but in images (like Lola Bunny herself) and, moreover, in recurrent plot sequences (like a physically powerful superhero rescuing weak others, who were not necessarily female).

The following case history of Noah displays the potential resources of visual media and, also, the developmental challenges inherent in their recontextualization. Noah did bring his animated creatures onto his blank page—his textual ark—as he ventured further into the official literacy practices of Rita's family. But, as I will illustrate, keeping that ark afloat took some alert maneuvering through the symbolic and social currents of his classroom worlds.

NOAH AND THE WRITTEN WORD

In September of his first-grade year, Noah was 6 years and 1 month old. He was 1 minute younger, he said, than Ned, his fraternal twin. Ned was in another classroom at the school, as was his older sister, Leslie.

As already noted, Noah was a visually attentive child. Sometimes he even included labels on his drawn characters' shoes and the initials of hip-hop groups on their shirts. Moreover, Noah often became deeply involved in his own visual adventures, as he drew melodramatic happenings involving power swirls and fire bursts.

And yet, as the vignette with Wenona suggested, Noah was also very responsive to others. He moved easily from amusing and playing with friends and fake family members to helping them (not that others always wanted his help). When his friend Jamal responded to Rita's request that he write more by muttering that he didn't want to (after she was out of hearing range), Noah urged him on:

> NOAH: Want a long story? (sweetly)
> JAMAL: I'll just start it, "Harriet the Spy" [the title of a movie he had just seen].
> NOAH: Then when you take it home, you can show your mother you did a lot of work! (enthusiastically)

Noah was also attentive to Rita's needs, as he understood them. Once when Rita could not get the tape dispenser to work, Noah offered, "I got some tape at home. I give you one. I give you a pack of tape." He even tried to get Rita mulberry leaves for the classroom silkworms from a neighbor lady's yard, a story his father confirmed:

> NOAH: (to Rita) I was fixing to get some [mulberry leaves for you], but that lady—I was gonna get a lot, but that lady—a lady said "Don't get none of those mulberry leaves." (brief pause) I can get some tomorrow.

Noah's expressiveness in the above vignette—his use of dramatic dialogue, his explicit references to his own intentions—was quite characteristic. Moreover, as his sibling rivalry with Wenona suggested, Noah was verbally as well as visually playful. He enjoyed singing popular radio songs with his fake siblings and friends, and he could recite great chunks of movie dialogue, especially of the Looney Tunes characters in *Space Jam*. That ability to get a voice just so was also evident in his reading, where expression mattered to him; he tried to appropriate the adult readers' intonation patterns.

Visual and verbal playfulness were in evidence when Noah first ventured into his writing workshop book. *Written* playfulness, however, was not apparent. In fact, as is no doubt already evident, Noah was quite serious about meeting official expectations. His playful drawing of "funny stuff" combined with his serious writing efforts to yield hybrid productions that only a child maneuvering between social worlds could construct. In the sections below, I illustrate this hybridity, the communicative resources constituting it, and the developmental challenges generating from it.

Multimedia Adventures and Textual Commentary:
Entering Alien Waters

Like most of his classmates, Noah talked and wrote his way into the classroom writing workshop. And, also like his peers, Noah's writing workshop entries evidenced his attention to the written names of important people in his life, as well as to the surface features of the written system itself. He wrote mock letters (Clay, 1975), copied words, and recalled family member names, especially his own and that of his fraternal twin, Ned. Names, squiggles, and seemingly random letters were usually placed under his drawings of dogs, people and, in the fall, dinosaurs. There were dinosaurs on hills, dinosaurs showing their teeth to small boys, and one magnificent dinosaur between two palm trees which looked exactly like a scene from the film *Jurassic Park* (Kennedy, Molen, & Spielberg, 1993), in which deadly dinosaurs escape their cages. Noah's first clear phonologically based spelling was the label, JRSK PRK [Jurassic Park].

By October, Noah began to write more extended prose. To do so he again, like most of his peers, appropriated brief forms from the class-generated "things to write about" list. As in Marcel's case, Noah's tendency to anchor his writing with such appropriated forms led to personal experience texts that were, in fact, about virtual, rather than actual, events; that is, they were inventions or stories. "I wt [went] to tll [the] zoo I sa[w] Dinosaurs," Noah wrote which, one would have to say, was not likely.

Noah's brief (pretend) personal experience texts usually accompanied elaborate, action-packed drawings. He drew in a common style of visual dramatists—one that could be called a moving picture or a cartoon style (Dyson, 1989): Successive events were layered on his single-framed pictures. As the actions piled up, Noah provided a running commentary and, if sitting by a fake sibling or a friend, he called attention to his efforts. His commentaries revealed stories that were "phantasmagorical," to use Sutton-Smith's (1997, p. 151) very apt word—fantastic, sometimes fragmentary, usually "disorderly and exaggerative" (p. 158). The intertextual threads between the theatrical, multimodal utterances and the brief written ones could be quite thin indeed.

For example, Noah drew and partially narrated an "emergency": Cars crashed into his friend's dinosaur—a small dinosaur that "don't bite." As he later told me in explaining his picture, "The cars . . . was going fast, and they crashed into the dinosaur, and then the dinosaur was dead. He's dead now. From the emergency." Note the squiggles over one dinosaur in the picture in Figure 5.1. The flying baby dinosaur headed toward the emergency in Figure 5.2 is Godzooky, from the cartoon *Godzilla* (Wildey, Patterson, Urbano, Dufau, & Gordon, 1978]).

Noah said that his mother told him about the emergency. She said, "'You need to get out of bed and run fast far from—far from home.' And then I did. I went over to my auntie's house."

Despite all this narrative adventure, Noah wrote a variant of earlier written utterances: *I what to the pruc.* [I went to the park.] (See Figure 5.2.)

"Is this still about the emergency?" I asked when he wrote it.

"Yes," he said. "It was at the park."

Noah's drawing and accompanying talk was organized by his sense of visual storytelling and constructed with borrowed characters, plot elements, and visual images from the popular media. Those resources supported Noah's play with compelling themes of good and evil, villains and heroes, physical power and physical vulnerability, including vulnerability to unexpected but still frightening accidents. Noah knew a hero dinosaur featured in earlier compositions (from the *Godzilla* cartoon), a sweet baby flying dinosaur (Godzooky, from the same cartoon), and monstrous ones that were indeed at the park (in *Jurassic Park*); he knew about car accidents (and had been in one) and other emergencies where one was to run to a relative for help.

On the openness of a page, Noah fashioned carefully detailed creatures and disorderly swirls, linking characters and events in loosely intertwined events. He pushed toward tighter narrative coherence primarily in response to my queries or, in other events, to those of a confused peer or a puzzled teacher. In the fall of the year, the push toward writing was also a response to official expectations. In the emergency example, all of the action happened "at the park." He seemed on secure footing when producing his visual adventures but adrift in alien waters when he turned

Figure 5.1. Noah's pictured emergency at the park.

Figure 5.2. "I went to the park."

to writing. Noah anchored his written efforts with familiar official frames, as he worked to organize written graphics (which seemed harder to control than dinosaurs run amuck).

Differentiating Social and Semiotic Waters

As the winter months began, Noah gradually took control of the literacy practice of reporting personal experiences in written texts. He seemed to gradually swallow his stiff official frames, infusing them with a genre-appropriate conversational stance.

This change was not due only to Noah's increasing comfort with the written system, his improved visual memory of words, his more fine-tuned ear for orthographic connections. It was also due to participation in the public sharing time practice. In that practice, as noted in Chapter 4, written texts consisting of "I was"s or "I went"s were treated as statements of personal experience and, thus, any fictional meanings were filtered from view. Moreover, the children generally treated such texts in this way even when Rita herself did not. Consider, for example, the following vignette:

> Noah spent the composing period enacting a dramatic visual adventure, in which Godzilla, with the assistance of Godzooky, rescues some "little kids" from a "bad guy" dinosaur. His accompanying text reads: "I saw a Godzilla. The man shot his Godzilla. Godzilla saved the world." During writing time, Noah's friend Jamal questioned why a man would shoot Godzilla. Noah's response implied that Jamal (not he) had made the mistake; Noah pointed to his picture, explaining that the man had shot the evil dinosaur. Now, after having officially read his text to the class, there are no such questions:
>
> RITA: Your pictures always tell stories. (admiringly) (It may not occur to Rita that it is odd for someone to shoot Godzilla, whose fictional persona was not originally so kindly.)
> NOAH: Um, April. (calling on April, as she has raised her hand to ask a question—an appropriate audience response during sharing time)
> APRIL: Is that real?
> NOAH: Uh huh. [Yes] It's on—it's a cartoon.
> ZEPHENIA: I saw that cartoon before.

It is time for lunch, so Rita stops the conversation and directs the children to put their materials away and get in line.

Noah did "saw a Godzilla"—on television. It was a "real" cartoon, as he explained to April and as Zephenia affirmed. But Noah did not necessarily write "I saw" with the deliberate intention of reporting his viewing of a Godzilla cartoon. As already discussed, Noah wrote "I saw" or "I went" routinely in his writing book. (Recall, for example, his seeing dinosaurs at the zoo.)

The first indicator during writing workshop time that Noah was deliberately writing a personal experience statement with some specific audience communication in mind involved, in fact, the frame "I saw." Twice, after drawing elaborate scenes involving shooting, he wrote variants of *I saw a good boy*. In each case, the drawn boy was good because he was "just having a water gun," as Noah explained. (Guns, including pretend ones, were not allowed in school.) Thus, his texts included deliberate semantic choices evidencing sensitivity to Rita's opinions and classroom rules.

Soon, Noah began to use personal experience frames for reporting actual, if somewhat embellished, playground events. Noah initially clung rather awkwardly to his old text frames, as in *I was a bsc bool pay* ["I was a basket ball player"], a piece about playing basketball with peers at recess (see Figure 5.3). The use of "I was" may have resulted from his frequent confusion of "was" and "saw" during both reading and writing.

"I was a basketball player" texts became more complex, as Noah began to add peers' names to his written reports, rather than only drawing their pictures, as in: *Me and Rg [Reggie] and Zephenia and dall [?] pald [played] Basti Boll*. These texts accompanied arrangements of him and his peers near a hoop, dribbling or making a basket (something I saw happen only once on the playground—and Noah made that basket). Noah worked to deliberately maintain compatibility between the textually represented and the actually experienced world. He named his fellow basketball players accurately (at least so suggested my own observations of recess play); and once he even crossed out a name he felt he had wrongly included. Such accuracy was important, as mistakes might be noted in the public sharing time.

As Noah's stiff sentences gave way to conversational ones, his syntactic structures became more varied and his word choices indexed non-academic experiences in academically appropriate ways, given the personal experience genre. After the series of basketball texts, Noah appropriated the playing of games as a canonical event to be reported and, moreover, as a context for other narrated events. In the following example, about the video game *Donkey Kong Country 2*, Noah provides increasingly more specific information about the play of "me and my brother."

Noah's Reading
I have a family and I—
[skips]
my Donkey Kong Country 2
Me and my brother play
with my favorite game
And one day my brother
broke my favorite game.

Text as Written
I have a famoin nad I
play Nicousid at my fav rom
nad play my DK*e K Cotree 2
Me and My Bother Play
Wheth My Frey Gamy
And onn Day My Bother
Bok My Fwta GAMY the End

Figure 5.3. "I was a basketball player."

Despite this evident change in Noah's classroom production events, his "I went"s and "I saw"s neither smoothly nor uniformly underwent a conversational turn from a stiff voice meeting official expectations to a conversational one narrating personal experience. His most awkward texts remained those in which Noah, with his eye for visual fiction (and a deft hand, too) and his ear for language (including official language), seemed textually adrift after a drawn fictional adventure. And this was evident in classroom events beyond the writing workshop ones.

Jumping (the written) ship for playful (drawn) waters. As illustrated first in Chapter 3, Noah's tendency to construct visually dramatic adventures could happen in any curricular event. A blank paper, a can of markers, and Noah was off. Consider, for example, the space unit Rita introduced in January. In response to Rita's first assignment to report "what I learned" (the assignment in which Marcel listed planet names), Noah did write—at least at first. But, as I listened to him, I could hear the pull of the communicative practice of visual storytelling. That pull was evident in his speech, as the slowly paced language of a child just learning to "draw speech" (Vygotsky, 1978, p. 115) gave way to sound effects, and it was exceedingly evident in his graphics, as awkward written forms gave way to finely drawn details.

As Noah sat on the rug by Marcel, Vanessa, and Denise, he began his assigned text by writing *Space case*. He copied that phrase from a book Marcel had retrieved (*Space Case* [Marshall, 1980]) to help him with spelling. But the title seemed to remind Noah of a television adventure similarly named, in which multispecies children, lost on a renegade space ship, confront varied evil others and solve near-disasters.

Noah began by writing: "Space [pause] case [pause] ses [pause] there was." But he only wrote as far as *the* (of *there*), and then he drew (not wrote) a spaceship.

"There was some stars," he next intoned, and he drew those stars.

And then, in an animated voice that soon erupted in a burst of sound effects, the spaceship "blast[ed] off" unexpectedly and went "all the way into space." The person at the controls threw TNT, and there was a burst of fire power: "BLEW::::!"

As Noah became more deeply involved in his drawn space adventure, Vanessa loudly reread her writing: "I learned that the movie *Star Wars* was made—"

"20 [years ago]," piped up Noah, sure of the next word in this oft-repeated fact.

"A long time ago," said Vanessa firmly, letting him know he was wrong.

Still, that fact, or its rhythm, seemed to stay in Noah's mind, because when he finished his drawing, he wrote that the "space [ship] come from 2 years." (Later he changed the 2 to 20).

"Is this your fact?" I asked.

"Uh huh," said Noah affirmatively. "It's on *Space Cases* [David & Mumy, 1996]. . . . They're supposed to fight bad guys."

Noah, the visual dramatist, hung on to his adapted written fact, as he had earlier to *I went* and *I saw*. Those words were not so much mediators of his efforts to recall facts as they were place holders or, more metaphorically, lifelines that connected him to the official world, whose purposes sometimes eluded him. And yet those lifelines seemed no more secure than Nintendo's dangling eyeballs. For Noah, assuming an informative voice that told "what I learned" was not a recurrent, routine way of composing—that is, it was not a practice that (at that point, in that event) engaged and sustained his composing decisions.

Noah's disjointed fictional events—his dramatic visual adventures with their dangling factual or experiential written texts—did give way to more coherent efforts. But achieving this coherence did not involve abandoning his knowledge about fictional animation and visual adventures. Not at all. It involved recontextualizing—that is, it involved both drawing upon and differentiating the symbolic and social complexities of this cultural stuff so central to Noah's sense of competent agency as a composer. Just as Noah was differentiating a written conversational voice from an all-purpose place holder (like "I saw" or "I was") and coordinating symbolic media within the personal experience practice, he also began to differentiate fictional and informative voices.

The most vivid portrayal of the developmental work entailed in recontextualization came in late January, when unofficial creatures rooted in animation and an official one rooted in print media all tried to climb aboard Noah's textual ark, as I illustrate below. I begin by introducing the media characters who figured into this textual confrontation: Little Bear and Donkey Kong.

Encountering Little Bear and Donkey Kong on Noah's textual ark. From Noah's point of view, Little Bear was a creature of the official school world and a character in a series of children's books. In these books, Little Bear is portrayed as a sweet bear cub who lives in the woods with his parents. His stories consist mainly of dialogues written in short declarative sentences, often enacting a mild conflict. In the following excerpt, Little Bear explains his future plans to his patient mother, plans that would figure into Noah's own textual adventures:

"I'm going to fly to the moon," said Little Bear.
    "Fly!" said Mother Bear. "You can't fly."
    "Birds fly," said Little Bear.
    "Oh yes," said Mother Bear. "Birds fly, but they don't fly to the moon.
And you are not a bird." (Minarik, 1957, pp. 36–37)

In the last chapter in the book, Little Bear explicitly says, "'I wish that I could sit on a cloud and fly all around,'" and his mother explicitly says "'You can't have that wish'" (p. 52). Little Bear does receive one wish—a "surprise" birthday cake (p. 35).

Donkey Kong, a big uncouth gorilla, was not of the school world. He belonged to the play world of Noah and his fraternal twin Ned. Donkey Kong lives in a video-game jungle land with his friends, the chimps Diddy and Dixie. (Dixie, a chimpette with a prehensile ponytail, is Diddy's girlfriend.) The Donkey Kong characters engage in melodramatic quest stories, as they aim to retrieve stolen items, rescue kidnaped persons, or just jump up and get a banana to energize themselves. The emphasis is on action, unlike the character emphasis of the Little Bear stories. Moreover, Donkey Kong characters do not talk. As Noah himself confirmed: "They just play. . . . They run and be happy."

Nonetheless, there *are* written graphics in the video experience: In game materials, the initials "D.K." (plus a star) appear on a wooden sign (indicating Donkey Kong Country), and words containing *O*s typically sport a star inside those *O*s. During the game, the initials "D.K." appear on barrels, which often hide one of the Donkey Kong characters; and each of the letter icons *K*, *O*, *N*, and *G* appear in floating boxes, which the monkeys try to jump up (or, perhaps, fly up) and bump.

Despite their semiotic differences, the Donkey Kong creatures and Little Bear were all furry animals drawn in an iconic, rather than more realistic, styles, and all were embedded in stories—that is, in sequenced events situated in imagined worlds. Each had an existence beyond a single narrative—Donkey Kong in different game adventures and game versions, Little Bear in different chapters and books.[2] Their similarities seemed to strike Noah, who interrupted his reading group's engagement with *Little Bear* to announce that "I'm gonna get a little tiny baby gorilla." If one is going to get a gorilla, a tiny baby one certainly seems ideal. Noah's mother seemed to think so, too, or so he suggested: "My mommy said Friday I would get one. I gotta get some bananas. . . ." The parent volunteer kept the children on task—no one responded to Noah's unusual plan.

But Donkey Kong and Little Bear seemed to have come together in Noah's welcoming imagination. After having met Little Bear, and after having voiced his intention to get a little gorilla, Noah tried to bring both bear and gorilla onto his textual ark. He wrote a story that had "both of them inside it" and yet a story that also suggested their symbolic and social incompatibility.

As might be expected, given his developmental history, Noah drew and told a story about Donkey Kong and his friends. But, to my surprise at least, he encoded that story in textual structures and, indeed, literal voices (i.e., dialogue lines) that he had appropriated from Little Bear. In so doing, he provided the observant if perplexed me with the project's most dramatic illustration of the developmental complexities of recontextualization processes—that is, of appropriating, translating, and reframing material across the borders of symbol systems and social worlds. As I illustrate below, Noah blended the stuff of his video-game play and his school reading as he maneuvered through the currents of official and unofficial classroom worlds. The resulting text was anything but stable:

> Noah is sitting by Denise and Vanessa, who are writing about their families. He talks mainly to himself, planning, rereading, and monitoring his written efforts. (See Figure 5.4.)

> NOAH: (writing and rereading *I Klo*), "call, I call, I call"
> (writing *I waw to waw fly*) "I, wish, wish"

> Noah now pauses in his writing and draws a tiny flying monkey, commenting to no one in particular:

> NOAH: This is Donkey Kong.
> ANNE: Donkey Kong?

> Sitting slightly behind Noah, I recognized "I wish to fly" from the Little Bear books. I expected the sweet cub himself, not Donkey Kong. Noah proceeds silently to write *OK*, accompanying those letters with stars and containing them in a box. He turns to me:

> NOAH: And that says, "OK." It's a Donkey Kong monkey. . . . The monkey says he wants to fly. . . . Donkey Kong Country, deep in the jungle. (said in a deep voice)

> Zephenia, a peer writing nearby, tells Noah that he knows *Donkey Kong Country 2*. After Zephenia and Noah discuss the video game for a while, Noah turns back to his writing. Now Little Bear himself appears:

> > Litt Barair I HavoA (Little Bear I have)
> > A soep fro you (a surprise for you)

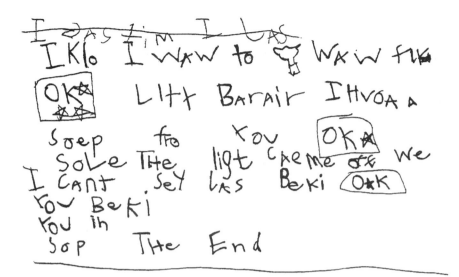

Figure 5.4. Noah's "Donkey Kong" text.

ANNE: That's not about Donkey Kong is it?

NOAH: (working to explain his text to me and, seemingly, to himself too) Oh, he he—bears live in some—no. They don't live in the jungle. It [the text] got both of them inside it. (big breath) Donkey Kong was in the video game. The monkey and the little monkey was in the video game. The little bear was playing with me and my brother. (Noah's pace picks up; he is telling a story now.) I—me and Ned had a bear, a little tiny bear. . . . The bear don't want Ned to sleep with him, cause I have a better pillow.

Noah continues writing, adding sentences about "suddenly" the lights going off (apparently because of the impending "surprise") and, then, someone saying, "I can't see." Noah's intense concentration is interrupted by Denise, who has a story to tell:

DENISE: Last night I spilled some Skittles [a candy] on my homework. I was crying.

NOAH: I was too! I was too!

DENISE: I messed up my homework all up.

NOAH: I was crying too because my mommy yelled at ME:: because I, DID IT, WRONG·· And my daddy came mad at me. And I said, "O K::, Daddy, O K::, Daddy." My Daddy is so crazy sometimes.

Noah returns to his writing. He continues the generic structure of a
Little Bear story, but his evaluative tone is strikingly different. He
includes another boxed and starred *OK*, but he does not silently
write it, as before. This *OK* is not primarily a visual icon; it is orally
expressive, like the *OK*s of his homework story.

NOAH: "Jus' be quiet, O K::?" (writing *Jas BeKi O*K*)

When I ask who is talking, Noah says that the little girl monkey is
telling the little boy monkey to "Just be quiet, O K::?" He gives her
words a tone of exasperation (her words come right after those in
which the male monkey apparently complains about not being able
to see). Noah then returns to his story dialogue:

NOAH: "YOU be quiet." (writing *You Be Ki*)
"You, YOU in, shut up!" (writing *you in sop*)

Noah's unfolding and enacted story seemed to consist of two related
but not completely integrated utterances, one rooted in visual animation
and oral play, the other in written form. His written text contains indices
of its hybridity: the starred and boxed "OK's," the small drawn figure, and
that blunt "shut up," which the gentle Little Bear would never say (although the uncouth Donkey Kong characters might and Noah, upset by
his daddy, might want to; in any case, Noah attributed the rude words to
two little monkeys).

Despite these symbolic and social complexities, within the official
world's sharing time, Noah's orally read words filtered the unruly Donkey Kong characters from public consideration. The instructional practice
was about *reading* one's *writing*. His writing, as his teacher Rita explicitly
commented, was about Little Bear. Still, Noah's peers did react to the most
audible of his unruly symbols, as illustrated below:

Noah is standing in front of his class, which is sitting on a large,
rectangular rug. He reads his piece. A few children gasp after
Noah's last sentence. Rita does not allow children to say "shut up."
After the gasps, there is general amusement and laughing. Rita
does not attend to this laughing but comments:

RITA: He didn't have any time for a picture because he was so busy
writing a Little Bear story, right? (apparently not noticing the
tiny drawing)

Rita has responded respectfully to Noah as a writer and expects the
class to do so as well. She next comments on the striking structural

feature of Noah's text, the use of dialogue: "Noah and Zephenia wrote dialogue, because both of them have writing where somebody is talking." But the children remain focused on what exactly somebody said in Noah's text and, especially, on that irritated voice that told another to "shut up"—right in front of the teacher! After Rita's comment, Vanessa comments:

VANESSA: I love the end.

There is much child mumbling and then Lakeisha's strong voice:

LAKEISHA: Can you read that end again?

And Noah, grinning, rereads the whole story.

Thus, Noah had engaged in a story-writing practice by adapting material from diverse sources. That adapting required negotiating the symbolic conventions of different media, as those icons O and K from a video game were reframed in a written text, where they were blended with the expressive "O K::" of a conversational story. Noah's adapting also highlighted social differences in the expectations and values of different worlds. A blunt "shut up" was not allowed among members of the official classroom family, but framed in a written story, it was acceptable (although, when orally rendered, it was still giggle-worthy among peers). Moreover, even though not explicitly commented on by Rita or the children, that curt command was odd coming from Little Bear (although, actually, it came from a little chimpette).

Noah's very next story contained a similar juxtaposition of Little Bear and Donkey Kong material and, moreover, a simple illustration of the complex processes involved in his recontextualization efforts. When talking with Zephenia in the above event, Noah had explained that "Donkey Kong Country 2" meant that the game had two little monkeys. In the next production event, Noah rethought the meaning of "Donkey Kong 2," as if "suddenly the light came on," inspired by a chapter book convention. After writing 2 on the top of his page, Noah commented that he was writing "Chapter 2," another Donkey Kong story. Then he turned back to the previous story and dubbed it "Chapter 1." Finally, he explicitly equated the title conventions of visual and print media: Chapter 1 "was Donkey Kong Country 1," he said, and Chapter 2 was "Donkey Kong Country 2."

On the day Noah wrote that Chapter 2, he once again voiced his intention of having his own gorilla. He told his entire fake family (with whom he was sitting) that "today I can get a baby gorilla." "Gonna bring him to school when I when I get a baby gorilla," he said. "Gonna bring him to school." Although Noah never did get that baby gorilla, he did continue to bring unexpected creatures to school, as I detail in the last section of this case.

Channeling the Waters: Looney Tunes and Silkworms

Throughout the remainder of the school year, Noah crafted stories using the structural features of a Little Bear chapter—dialogues composed of brief statements, often conflicting in nature (e.g., "You do," "You don't," "You can," "You can't"). But he also more conventionally coordinated the visual conventions and icons of animated media with print media and, moreover, he continued to explore a variety of written voices.

For example, soon after his Donkey Kong events, Noah ended a "scary story," written in the dialogue style of a Little Bear text, with a written "The End," around which were draped cartoon characters—a Looney Tunes cartoon convention (see Figure 5.5). He provided oral commentary as he drew these characters, as was his style when drawing animated adventures. One of his critters was a spider, whose web reached down from the "T" of *The* to the "E" of *End*, where it met a small mouse. The animals used that web as a slide: "Pwee! Pwee!" they said as they slid down.

Noah even used multimodal animation to enact a self-initiated "I learned that" genre during a class study of silkworms. Right before writing time one Monday, Rita read with the class the following morning message on the whiteboard:

> The silkworms grew a lot on the weekend.
> They ate a lot of mulberry leaves.
> Watch them as they chew. Listen to them.
> They eat, sleep, and poop [a popular line, repeated with enthusiasm by the children].

Noah listened intently as Rita discussed the silkworms' growth, his neck craned toward the containers of worms on the rug. Soon, it was writing time. Rita did not suggest that the children write "what they had learned about silkworms," but she did spread the containers of worms around the room, placing them here and there in the center of work tables. Noah sat down and continued to study the worms. Perhaps he had an "I learned that" event in the back of his mind because, the Friday before this event, Noah had been the only child in the room not to write such a text about a field trip to the bay. (He had missed the trip because of his asthma.)

In any case, Noah began writing with the school-appropriated frame, "I learned that." He learned, he wrote, "that silkworms can't eat hard leaves like regular leaves because they will die," a revoicing of Rita's oral cau-

Figure 5.5. "The End," Looney Tunes style. The written text itself reads: "I was in a house. Just going inside the house. / 'I think is a ghost.' / 'No ghost in that,' I said. / 'You want to eat?' I said. / 'They do not got food.' / 'Let's go home,' I said."

tion, reinforced by her written message that the worms would eat only mulberry leaves (so there was no reason to stick other kinds of leaves in the container).

Noah's text was not a place holder, nor an awkwardly placed anchor. It *was* a nod to the official world, but a communicative one, in which he seemed to reassure Rita that, yes, he knew about mulberry leaves. In fact, when she circulated by his work area, Noah told her that true story about how he was "fixing to get some" mulberry leaves for her, despite the uncooperative lady who shooed him away from her mulberry tree.

At one point, Noah stopped writing and put his ear close to the silkworm container. "I want to hear them crunch," he said, conceivably inspired by the written direction to "Listen" to the worms. But Noah could hear nothing: "They can't crunch."

When Rita came by, Noah talked with her about the mulberry leaves and about those silent silkworms. "They're scared in there," he said. "They do like this," and he lifted his head up and looked stiffly around. Implicit in his talk was a characterization of silk worms as fellow creatures whose emotions and intelligence are expressed through bodily features and movement (the qualities exploited in visual media, particularly animation).

Later, after Rita left, Noah began an animated visual adventure at the bottom of his paper. He drew a silkworm on a large leaf. Then, to convey movement, he drew zigzagging lines, all the while making "munching" noises. Finally, he added wings, commenting that the worm had turned into a moth. (See Figure 5.6.)

Noah thus crafted his first coherent, multimedia informative text. In Noah's journey to, and enactment of, this event, his engagement with Rita mattered, as did his participation in recurrent, official practices (e.g., his experience with, or at least witnessing of, the "I learned that" practice). But also important was his sense of agency and of the relevance of his knowledge and know-how. Noah coordinated visual, print, and oral material to enact what he had learned, and, in so doing, he also coordinated narrative, or storytelling, and informative voices. He was more deliberately, more skillfully, acclimating himself, and adapting his resources, to official school waters.

Just as Noah was coordinating visual and print material, he was also manipulating different kinds of written voices. As already noted, there were clear genre (or voice type) differences between Noah's written fictional stories and his personal experience narratives. But, for a text about Mother's Day, Noah used a Little Bear story voice to narrate a personal experience:

How was Mom Day, Noah? Oh fun.
Did you see a deer? Yes I did John [Noah's cousin].
You saw a black dog. Yes I did. It was runned down the hill.
My dog. (Growls)

(On Denise's advice, though, Noah did begin to write an additional text, a more conversational one telling what he did with his mom, like the one he had told during the morning rug time.)

Figure 5.6. What Noah learned about silkworms.

Late in the year, Noah even deliberately recontextualized family members' utterances in Little Bear-like conversations that were themselves part of personal experience texts. One such piece was about an occasion when his sister was "bad" and he was "mad." The family tension is played out in the familiar style of brief statements centered around a conflict:

Lats [last] night I was playing with Ned and Lee Lee [his sister] was bad. I. said dt [don't] do that. He said go in the haos [house] I was so I was mad. I newd [?] that my head off The news came on the tv. Came on. Off. I wnat [went] in my room. I od [?] All That

> [a television show] it came on. On Nickolen [Nickelodeon] came
> on. When befor I was [saw?] Lee was mad She was mad. Ned.
> The Tv. Yes. I weit [went to] my yord [yard] to Coprpr [Chopper,
> his dog].

The story was ambitious, hard to follow, but impressive, as Rita told the
class. Noah had put in "the details and the feelings," and she had responded
to those, even though she couldn't quite follow the action.

Noah's longest and most successful piece (in terms of peer response)
was composed of a startling array of voices, of ways of speaking. It was the
product of a verbally performative Noah, attentive to the voices around him.
Influenced by friends' decisions to write about the movie *Space Jam*, Noah
did so, too, recontextualizing a diversity of particular and typified voices.
Among the former, were particular utterances from the *Space Jam* script and
song. Among the latter were informational (e.g., "I know that . . ."), evaluative (c.g., "I like . . ."), and personal experience (e.g., "I saw . . .) voice types,
all of which had themselves begun as particular if partial utterances—that
is, as frames that guided Noah's transformation of unofficial and nonprint
symbols into official and written ones. Through playing with and through
those voices, Noah seemed to explore stances and positions toward others
and toward meanings themselves.

Below is Noah's reading of the *Space Jam* text to his appreciative class
(without his own periodic giggles):

> I know that Michael Jordan is a superstar. And he know that he
> goes on Space Jam. And I like when Bugs Bunny and Lola Bunny
> knows what to do. And she got the moves. And I know that
> Michael Jordan he is a ★ and he gots the moves baby. And my
> favorite character is Taz. It's a terrible just Taz. Michael Jordan is
> one of my favorite men. I'm ready to jam. I saw him and his
> underpants. Is a Taz. And Lola Bunny needs to kiss Bugs. And
> Michael Jordan.

The text is disjointed and fragmentary, like Noah's multimodal storytelling. It is also exuberant and funny, in a 6-year-old sense. Noah translated the movie's visual plot segments about underwear and kissing into
verbal prose. Moreover, he included the visual icon of a star, which was
not a direct index of a character (as in its Donkey Kong use) but a repre-
sentation of a meaning: a celebrated person, a star. And so ends the developmental history of one of my own stars, the engaging, exuberant, if
textually untidy Noah.

YOUNG CHILDREN'S WRITING
AS TESTING THE (SOCIAL) WATERS

> After supper, Katie read the babies to sleep. She read a page of the introduc-
> tion to Shakespeare and a page of begats from the Bible. That was as far as
> she had gotten to date. Neither the babies nor Katie understood what it was
> all about. The reading made Katie very drowsy but doggedly she finished
> the two pages. She covered the babies carefully, then she and Johnny went
> to bed too. (Smith, 1943, p. 82)

In *A Tree Grows in Brooklyn*, set in the early 20th century, Katie Nolan's
mother tells her the "secret" for raising children who will have a life economically better than her own. That secret is to read to them from the
great books—Shakespeare and the Bible. It does not matter, her mother
explains, if Katie herself does not understand the words; her children
will.

Of course Katie's children, Francie and Neeley, do not understand the
words, either. But they are young children, surrounded by much they do
not understand. And sometimes, words and phrases that they have heard
repeatedly come to them in emotionally, if not literally, apt situations, as
they did when Francie accused a neighborhood child of being "full of soun'
'n' furry." Unfortunately, using those words in the social waters of the
neighborhood seemed to put off, rather than engage, other children.

Like Francie, Noah and the other brothers and sisters were contemporary children surrounded by appealing voices, heard in the company of
friends, family members, and neighborhood kids, including those voices
offered by the popular media. These voices were woven into the fabric of
their everyday lives through the childhood practices they engaged in both
inside and outside the school's physical spaces. The children brought these
voices into the intertextual universe of Rita's classroom family, where their
precise ramifications could never have been predicted.

Who, for example, could have anticipated that Marcel's engagement
with the Dallas Cowboys would somehow be linked to his entry into official informative genres, to his understanding of states and cities, to his
combining of varied kinds of textual voices to compose a thank-you letter to the school librarian? Who would have thought that Noah's engagement with animated creatures would converge with and diverge
from his engagement with written ones and, indeed, with real ones, and
somehow be implicated in his early efforts to deliberately construct fic
tional stories?

The children's journeys into school literacy were not linear. Moreover, their journeys make no sense if one imagines learning written lan-

guage as neatly bounded from learning other symbolic systems, nor if one assumes that children are dedicated apprentices, hovering exclusively around designated experts.

But the children's journeys are sensible, if they are seen within the contexts of their own childhood practices, if literacy is imagined as a potentially satisfying tool for children's present lives as children, and if development is seen as involving children's recontextualization and reorganization of their everyday textual stuff. Moreover, to be seen as sensible—as sense making—children themselves must be literally seen within classrooms in which authorial decision making is a requirement, as it was in Rita's classroom. Indeed, Noah was conscious of this requirement, or so suggests the opening vignette, in which he scaffolds Wenona's decision making (and, in responding, *she* recontextualizes the cultural stuff of Coach Bombay's world).

As the opening vignette also illustrates, Noah could, with great ease, collaboratively construct elaborate scenes through words in the unofficial world, and he had done so since early in the school year. In the brothers' and sisters' world, he could skillfully "remember" invented details and enact mild conflicts, as he had an implicit understanding of the pleasures, the interactive routines, and the cultural stuff (including the textual toys) required. Noah could also, with evident ease, build such scenes through visual dramas in overlapping official and unofficial worlds. But Noah had not initially deliberately constructed involving worlds through the written medium.

Like Marcel, Noah's initial written composing was guided primarily by the desire to make proper contact with, not communicate within, the official world. As he was drawn into the textual culture of the school—its practices and values, Noah also found reason to pause, to reconsider, to rationalize a choice. The particularities of his blended and differentiated practices were different than Marcel's: Marcel was drawn to informative reporting of sports results, Noah to enacting visual dramas. But, for both children, developmental challenges consisted of differentiating and coordinating the social and symbolic complexities of production events, with their precariously positioned written texts.

By the end of his first-grade year, Noah could cover much more communicative space than he had with his initial all-purpose "I went"s and "I saw"s, written to appease Caesar. He certainly had not mastered textual structures. But he had expanded his symbolic and social possibilities by juxtaposing, differentiating, and blending textual practices and cultural resources that came from in and out of school. Like Marcel, he had moved from a place of general accommodation to an expectation to write, to the differentiation of varied genre voices and particular voiced utterances rooted in unofficial and official worlds, to a deliberate attempt to try out varied stances and to combine them in particular ways.

In Noah's case, as in any developmental history of writing, there was no smooth sailing; rather, there was becoming more aware and better able to negotiate situated decision making through writing. Tensions between different kinds of symbolic media and different social practices were in abundance in Noah's case, but ideological tensions were not so blatant. Unlike in Marcel's case, there were no public discussions of Noah's decisions, and no border skirmishes across peer social worlds in which his texts had different social meanings (as had happened between Denny and Marcel). In part this may have been because Noah was physically a smaller child who attracted less attention (both positively and negatively) and who interacted across unofficial social borders only when officially organized to do so by Rita.

Still, those issues were there. They were audible and visible in many of the composing choices that Noah made (e.g., to construct superhero scenes, to write about *Space Jam*). These choices positioned him in gendered and racialized official and unofficial worlds, as did the songs he sung, the television shows he discussed, and the kids he hung around with. Ideological tensions were also just under the surface of children's giggles and gasps in whole-class sharing time events. In Chapter 7, I will recall those giggles and gasps, noting their potential pedagogical role in making issues audible and publically negotiable.

But first, there is one more child waiting in the wings for her moment in the composing spotlight—Denise, a loyal fake sister, a pretend singing star, and a child wide awake to many ideological complexities. So I now leave Noah amid his puppies, gorillas, and silkworms and move on to Denise, with her caps, raps, and high heels.

6

Singing Stars: Denise's Musical Voices

The smooth and easy melody of "I believe I can fly" (Kelly, 1996) swoops up brothers and sisters and friends as they sit scattered among the tables in Rita's room. They are all working on their ME projects, in a most literal sense. Today they are to write their three wishes and, also, finish their portraits of themselves as grownups.

Denise is sitting by her best fake sister Vanessa at the pushed-together desks near the front of the room. As she sings about flying and "touching the sky," she draws herself as a star, a singing star. Tina Turner, to be exact. And, in Denise's picture, Ms. Turner is singing a more aggressive song. She has a dialogue bubble coming out of her mouth, in which Denise plans to write "What's Love Got To Do With It?" (Turner, 1983). Denise's Ms. Turner self is quite glamorous. She is wearing a long, slinky gown and a lot of lipstick (see Figure 6.1).

As the portrait suggests, Denise, like Vanessa, wants to be a singer when she grows up (among many other ambitions). "Good singers" are loved and cheered and, moreover, they can make "a whole bunch of money"—so much money that they "can buy all the mansions in the whole world."

Part of the ideology of stardom is wealth, and this puts Denise, at this moment, in some conflict with the official school world. Rita and the class have just read and discussed the book *Mama Do You Love Me?* (Joosse, 1991), and Rita has just told the class that she is "proud of them" because, in the discussion, they hadn't equated love with somebody buying them things (see the opening to Chapter 3). Indeed, Zephenia had told the class that "people used to say 'can't buy love.'" (The Beatles and others used to sing this too . . . and made a lot of money doing so.)

Figure 6.1. Denise as Tina Turner. She inadvertently wrote "you" for "it," which she found amusing and did not correct.

Now, as Denise works on her "Me" project drawing, she and Vanessa play with the official emphasis on the limits of money as a cause of love and happiness—and with whether or not the desire for money can be written:

As she draws, Denise jokes that she is going to make a 10,000-dollar bill coming out of Tina Turner's head (which she does *not* do). Vanessa then reads her completed three wishes to Denise:

VANESSA: Listen. (reading) "I wish that Denise will stay my friend. I wish the earth clean, and I wish my granny gets better."

Denise now abandons her drawing and starts to write her own three wishes. "I wish," she says to herself as she begins. Vanessa starts singing:

VANESSA: (singing) Got no money/ All I got is you baby/ Don't need nothing else/ I got you baby. . . ,

  DENISE: (has just reread "I wish" and now says loudly) I MADE A LOT OF MON EY!

VANESSA: (singing) Ain't got no money/Ain't got no thing but you now/I got lo::ve. . . .

Denise does not write that she wishes she had money. She returns to her portrait, adding the audience and commenting:

DENISE: And there's the audience saying, "I love you baby." Except the girls. They're saying, "Go girl. It's your birthday" [verse from Luke, 1994]. (Vanessa joins in and recites with her) "Go girl. It's your birthday."

Denise, like all the brothers and sisters, could maneuver between official and unofficial worlds, sometimes aided by a shift in modes, as the above vignette illustrates: "I wish" was written, but "I made a lot of money" was dramatically shouted out for her sister's amusement. Also like her siblings, Denise appropriated textual material from the voices surrounding her, especially from emotion-filled, musical voices.

As discussed in Chapter 2, the children used the textual toys of music for pleasure, performance, and dramatic, often collaborative, play. The later use was akin to many forms of dress-up play, in that it allowed children to slip into varied persona. Through singing, Denise, like other children, could be bouncy and upbeat, aggressive and firm, or contemplative and soulful, depending on the genre. Moreover, she could step back from the song and become the "real" singer (or the deejay). "What's love got to do with it?" queries the world-weary Tina Turner. Although Denise undoubtedly did not understand that title's literal sense, her voice captured its cynical mood (as sung by a singer whose drawn adornments and adoring audience suggested she was anything but down on her luck).

As also discussed in Chapter 2, most textual toys from popular music were not viewed by parents, teacher or, indeed, children themselves as belonging to 6-year-olds. These songs were part of children's anticipated futures as teenagers and the singers of those songs were part of their imagined futures as glamorous people, with plenty of love, plenty of money, and plenty of opportunities to sing. It was appropriate, then, that Denise drew a singer in an official version of dress-up play—imagining herself as a grown-up worker. And it was also appropriate, given the nature of the public discussion of love and money, that she kept the singer's wealth in the more playful venues of talk and drawing—and out of the official writing.

The opening anecdote featuring Denise and Vanessa unfolded in May, relatively late in the year, and it underscores the ideological dimension of writing development outcomes and, more particularly, of recontextualization processes. As Marcel and Noah's cases also illustrated, the meaningfulness of school literacy practices is constructed in the interplay of child and adult-governed worlds and of "the solid and day-to-day and the fantastic and poetic" (Jones & Hawes, 1972, p. 191). But recontextualizating the "fantastic and poetic" stuff of unofficial worlds in official ones inevitably entails ideological as well as symbolic and social learning. Children learn what aspects of their worlds should not be written in particular places as well as what can be—and, of course, they learn new ways of challenging notions of acceptability. Readers may recall, for example, Marcel's evident pleasure when his out-of-bounds Hey Arnold came to public attention, or Noah's joy in publicly reading about Michael Jordan's underwear.

In this chapter, I construct Denise's case history by tracing the intertextual threads of her performative use of rhythmic and emotion-filled language. Her case, like the cases of her fake brothers, documents the recontextualization processes through which a child blended and untangled practices and social worlds. Unlike her brothers, though, Denise took no evident pleasure in public transgressions of literate behavior. To a greater extent than did they, Denise came to clearly demarcate written language practices that belonged to the unofficial, rather than the official, world. Her case thus highlights how recontextualization processes may contribute to the split, anticipated by the children themselves, between the expressive practices of school culture and of youth culture (see Chapter 2; also, Amut-Talia, 1995; Caputo, 1995; James, 1995).

Below, I preface Denise's case with a brief overview of the potential resources of music media and, moreover, of the collaborative, expressive practices within which music texts played a role in the children's culture. Then I open Denise's developmental story in the fall of the year, as she, like all the brothers and sisters, began to construct written texts in Rita's room. Her story will be interwoven with theirs and, most particularly, with her best fake sister Vanessa.

THE CULTURAL RESOURCES OF MUSIC MEDIA

My brother, Rocky, kept a transistor radio by his bed, and he'd listen to it all night, for all I knew, long after I'd fallen asleep. In 1956 [when Henry Louis Gates, the narrator, was 6], black music hadn't yet broken down into its many subgenres, except for large divisions such as jazz, blues, gospel, rhythm and blues. On [the late night radio show] *Randy's*, you were as likely to hear . . . Clyde McPhatter doing "Treasure of Love" as you were to hear Howlin' Wolf do "Smokestack Lightning." . . . My own favorite that year was the slow deliberate sound of Jesse Belvin's "Goodnight, My Love." I used to fall asleep singing it in my mind to my Uncle Earkie's girlfriend Ula. . . . Not even in your dreams, he had said to me one day, as I watched her red dress slink down our front stairs. It was my first brush with the sublime. (Gates, 1994, pp. 21–22)

In his memoir, literary scholar and distinguished writer Henry Louis Gates, Jr., remembers the voices interwoven in his childhood in a small "colored" community in West Virginia. The strong voices of family and village members provided the rhythms and melodies of his childhood recollections. And, as the excerpt above suggests, those voices themselves sounded against the backdrop of media voices. Through radio voices especially, the young author-to-be experienced a range of musical genres and a diversity of singers and songs. Moreover, like the brothers and sisters, he seemed to use those voices as textual toys, exploring the roles, relations, and feelings a song could evoke (including those sexual and gendered ones belonging to the older kids). When he was a bit older himself, a teacher gave him literary classics to read, and he was surprised to find that literary voices could also evoke powerful emotional responses.

There is, in fact, an intimate connection between literary and musical experiences, since stories are constructed with the sound and rhythm of words. This connection is especially seen in poetry, a "making [of] music out of words" (Koch, 1998, p. 21), and it will also be abundantly clear in Denise's case, as she was drawn to the musical and expressive possibilities of words in varied media.

Nonetheless, literally transforming the textual stuff of musical texts into written words was relatively less common in Rita's room than was transforming the stuff of other media forms. Only 7 of Rita's 20 children did so (compared, for example, to 17 who so transformed film texts). Certainly, special skills are required to record music. But there are other potential reasons for this more limited use. Unlike talk about watching movies or sports shows, singing was primarily an accompaniment to other activity. When it was foregrounded, it was primarily in the social context of unofficial play, of singing games and imaginary "star" turns. And, as already noted, such singing typically was not shared with *adults*; it was constitutive of the "mimicry and mockery" of *peer* culture (Sutton-Smith, 1995, p. 7). Moreover, unofficial play with songs involved the manipulation not only of sounds but also of voices in dialogues, joint chants, and lead and backup singing arrangements. This experience would lend itself better to dialogues, plays, and choral readings than to the kinds of textual forms typically associated with beginning writing.

Still, an analysis of children's oral as well as written composing did reveal varied kinds of musical appropriations. First, children appropriated conceptual content, including the names of singers and songs, along with recurrent themes, like wanting to be with a desirable person or rebuking an irritating one. Second, they appropriated communicative practices; among the ones named by the children were "interviews," "raps," and "love songs." The collaborative singing of Denise and her sisters Vanessa, Wenona, and Lakeisha made use of certain textual features of varied genres, including voice arrangements involving lead and backup singers; remix processes, in which one does not "make up" a song but uses "words [from] another song," in Denise's words; and rhythmic and melodic styles, among them those of rap and gospel. Indeed, as illustrated in Chapter 2, the children's sense of musical genres and their features allowed them to collaboratively "make up" songs and, moreover, to manipulate complex layers of symbolic material (syllables, words, phrases, and voices or vocal parts).

Third, the children also borrowed technological conventions, like symbols (e.g., use of letters and numbers to designate radio stations) and individual control of the radio dial (e.g., references of child deejay to audience need to "turn on their radio," and to "stay tuned"). Fourth, they revoiced the words spoken or sung by singers, deejays, fans, including actual or variants of lines, verses, and choruses.

Finally, as illustrated by Denise's comment that male fans would say "I love you baby," the children appropriated from musical media ideologies of gender, fame, and love, in addition to those of race and power. These ideologies were implicit in the content of their productions, including in their visual images (e.g., in drawings of female singers in slinky gowns and high heels, males in backwards baseball caps, T-shirts, and athletic shoes, and fans who say "You go girl").

The following case history of Denise illustrates the breadth of social and textual resources embedded in childhood practices involving music. Moreover, it documents a child's distinctive travels through recontextualization processes onto—and just outside the boundaries of—the official literate landscape of school. Denise's easy slippage from officially appropriate production to performative actions for her own and others' amusement will be evident in the pages ahead, as will be her alertness to musical, emotion-filled language.

DENISE AND THE WRITTEN WORD

Six years and 2 months old when school began, Denise had gotten her first radio from her father when she was 5 years old. Denise loved to sing, and she often sang along with the radio on car rides with her mother and older brother, with whom she lived. Moreover, Denise enjoyed emotion-filled and rhythmic voices wherever she found them. Outside official whole-class events (in which she herself said she was "shy"), she often slipped into a dramatic, playful role. Once, complaining to Vanessa about being teased on the school bus, she dropped to the floor, raised her hands to the heavens, and moaned, "Why me? Why me?" (which was quite amusing, we three thought).

Denise's tendency to playfully perform for small, comfortable audiences could be misleading, however. She could adopt strong social stands against what she viewed as abuse of herself or her fake siblings. She was a loyal, responsible member of the brothers and sisters family. Once Zephenia, her secret boyfriend, teased Lakeisha, calling her a crybaby. Denise reacted firmly:

> DENISE: Stop calling her a crybaby.
> ZEPHENIA: (to Lakeisha, who makes a move toward him) Get away from me.
> VANESSA: All she was was sitting down, and she was laying her head down.
> DENISE: (to Lakeisha) Just ignore him. He ain't gonna do nothing to you. I got your back. . . .

On another occasion, Rita had sent Elizabeth to sit with Denise and Marcel during an art project. Elizabeth had social tensions with many children in the class, because, as John said, she "bossed people around," including her friends, the children from the immediate middle-class neighborhood (see Chapter 3). Elizabeth began mocking Marcel, repeating every sentence he said. He then returned the action. Elizabeth stood up, announcing that she was going to tell on Marcel to Rita. This silenced Marcel, who did not want Rita to call his mother. As Elizabeth strode across the room to Rita's location, Denise said loudly and firmly, "You did it first." Elizabeth froze. She looked toward Rita and back at Denise. Denise stared at her, unsmiling. Elizabeth sat back down. There was no more mocking from anyone.

This capacity for social responsiveness and responsibility could extend to the whole class, as mediated by Ms. Rita and, more particularly, by the whole-class sharing practice. Once, in the spring, when Rita was out of the room, the class had literally ignored a student teacher; they sat, drew, and talked about whatever they wished during writing workshop time. Later that day, Denise wrote:

> I was so mad at the class today
> becaes it was like it is a mess.

During the next class sharing time, Denise read this piece, and Rita asked her to explain what happened:

DENISE: When [the student teacher] was teaching, the class was making a lot of noise.

RITA: And you felt so strongly about it that you wrote it down. (Denise nods.) Sometimes when I get mad at people [I write] instead of going to them and getting mad and saying things I might not be happy with afterward. Sometimes I give [the writing] to them and sometimes I don't. But you know what happens to that anger? It kinda goes like phew!

NOAH: Fly away!

JOHN: Like a airplane!

ELIZ.: To somebody else!

RITA: Well, no. Just away. Not to somebody else. I don't want them to have my anger.

NOAH: Out the window to heaven.

RITA: To heaven. (thoughtfully) Did anybody have something they wanted to say or ask about that?

LAKEISHA: . . . Why did you [Denise] get mad at the class? Because you lucky you didn't get in trouble.

DENISE: I just was mad. (And then, seemingly echoing Rita's concern for others) I don't want anybody to get in trouble.

Both Denise's sense of social responsiveness and her playfulness with the dramatic, poetic possibilities of language helped shape a unique passage into official and unofficial literacy practices, as I illustrate below.

Freewheeling Conversations and Written Monotones

Denise produced the writing workshop entry in Figure 6.2 in September of the school year, drawing herself and Vanessa all dressed up for a party. Denise's companionship with her best fake sister, and their imagined outings together as little girls and glamorous teenagers provided a comfortable relational context for her entry into writing workshop time. And, as Figure 6.2 suggests, this relational context was evident very early in the year. Denise wrote a brief caption for her picture, "My [Me] and Vanessa," and used their first initials to label their respective portraits.

Although Denise learned to encode and decode faster than most of her classmates, she, like them, began with names, labels, and drawings,

Figure 6.2. "Me [My] and Vanessa." (Vanessa's name was spelled out; I blocked out the remainder of the actual name.)

especially of herself and Vanessa—and Vanessa did the same. As they drew, they checked on each other's preferences for hair baubles and outfits. Also like her classmates, Denise began writing brief prose entries by appropriating sentence frames from the class-generated "things to write about" list. During the fall of the year (from September through December), Denise inserted family members' names and, even more so, Vanessa's name into these framing devices (e.g., "I like _____" or "I went _____"). "I want [went] to Vanessa has [house] today," Denise wrote one day and, on another day, "Vanessa wit [went] to my party."

Denise's textual declarations of affection and experience seemed written in a straightforward, singular voice. But the brothers and sisters' "game" of pretending to visit each other's homes framed Denise's early texts. They were actually bits of fiction, since the girls' relationship was confined to school. Like Marcel's apparent sports reports, and Noah's awkward personal experience texts, Denise's orderly written statements could function as filters: they prevented the fake family's fictional and playful meanings from slipping through to the public sphere of the official classroom family. Nonetheless, unofficial play permeated the boundaries of official writing time, as illustrated below.

Voice play around print. As in other children's early production events, oral language, more so than written, revealed the interplay of official and unofficial worlds. That language revealed Denise's freewheeling use of varied childhood practices, among them, singing and collaborative play with dramatic, often rhythmic voices. Such voices are on display in the following vignette:

> Vanessa has just made what she regards as a drawing error and comments to Denise, sitting beside her:
>
> VANESSA: Darn it! (pause) I said "Gosh darn it"! (With bemused alarm, Vanessa is noting that she cussed.)
> DENISE: You said it again [when you admitted it]! (giggles)
> VANESSA: Oh God, plea:se take that away. I: really really really don't wanna go there [hell]. I want to come up there with Joyce [one of her grandmothers]. Plea:se let me come up there. Plea:se. There's no such as hell. There's no such as hell. There's no such thing. [She said the three lines with a repetitive rhythm that reminded me of Dorothy's "There's no place like home" in *The Wizard of Oz.*] I LOVE God. Please! Gosh.
> DENISE: She's cussing. Don't you HATE people that cuss God? I mean—

VANESSA: O::h! You said it.

DENISE: There's no such thing as the devil. There's no such thing as the devil. There's no such thing as the devil. I want to come up there with all the people who died. Great Grandma, my Grandpa—all the people that died.

VANESSA: Grandma Joyce. And Lord thank you! (urgent voice) I want to come up there with Joyce. I feel like crying. I do.

DENISE: I feel like dying. (Denise is rhyming with crying.)

VANESSA: Girl! You got the rest of your life.

As in the above event, children's playful language was an ongoing accompaniment to their writing efforts—and that pleasant playfulness could ameliorate the displeasure of a perceived error. Moreover, although the children's play could temporarily distract them from the official world, it could also sustain their participation in that world. In the following extended example, Vanessa works to provide spelling support for her friend, as Denise models the self-regulating language through which child writers may plan, encode, and monitor written text. Denise's talk is intertextually linked both to the official world (to Rita's multiple spelling strategies, her modeling of the monitoring process, and her suggested writing topic [Thanksgiving experiences]) and to the unofficial world (to child organized collaboration, affiliation, and social play).

> As Vanessa writes that she "mt go to the MOVWS" [might go to the movies] to see *Space Jam*, Denise writes about a fictional Thanksgiving Day, in which she saw Vanessa at Chuck E. Cheese (a pizza place). Vanessa resists, in a playful tone, telling Denise to say she saw somebody else. (Maybe pizza on Thanksgiving is not so appealing.) Denise continues to write, but she is struggling with spelling *Thanksgiving*. Vanessa revoices in her own vernacular Rita's frequent advice:

> VANESSA: You don't gotta spell the whole thing, just sound it out like you can, girl. . . . Cause that word . . . is long.

> Denise, however, finds the word displayed in the classroom. She then orally rereads, monitors, and plans her words, in the manner modeled by Rita.

> DENISE: "For Thanksgiving" (reading), I (writing) had, went (planning)—How do you spell *went*?

> VANESSA: W—(Vanessa now looks around the room for the word and, from a pocket chart of word cards, she retrieves *want* for her friend.)

DENISE: Read the back [of the card].
VANESSA: "I want a red pencil" (reading)—oh, that's *want*. (goes and retrieves another card) This has got to be it.
DENISE: That's *with*.
VANESSA: Where is *went*?
DENISE: I just got to sound it out! I just got to sound it out!

Denise does so, listening to the sounds as she pronounces the word slowly. She continues on, writing "for Thanksgiving I wet [went] to Hace hez [Chuck E. Cheese]," sounding out the name of that pizza place with Vanessa's help, and then she adds "and I sow [saw]."

DENISE: I just gotta put one thing and you know what it's gonna be!
VANESSA: My name, or your name, [and] I love you.

After a bit of talk and soul singing—and Rita in the background directing children to not "forget what Noah was telling us about spaces between words," the children return to their writing. Denise hands Vanessa her writing book so that Vanessa can write her name in the appropriate place in her text.

DENISE: If you sign *Wenona* I'm gonna be mad at you. (Recall that Vanessa had suggested somebody else be at Chuck E. Cheese for Thanksgiving dinner.)
VANESSA: OK. (writes her name)

Soon both children are drawing little girls on the bottom of their papers.

DENISE: I look like I'm fixing to go to church or some where fancy. (commenting on her drawing)
VANESSA: Man, I couldn't make the mouth right. Know who this is?
DENISE: Me. [Va: Nuh uh] You. [Va: Nuh uh] Wenona.
VANESSA: Nope. That's Lakeisha. . . . I'm about to make Wenona.

Rita is announcing the end of writing time, and the girls close their books and head to the rug. Sharing time is brief today—only people with "yellow" journal covers share, which does not include Denise or Vanessa.

In the above event, Denise's written declaration of at least seemingly personal experience is linked to Rita's official expectations as, indeed, are both girls' ways of participating in, and talking about, the encoding aspects of writing. Their official actions are also informed by the unofficial world's particular relations and by its collaborative practices of invented shared experiences and of guessing games. For example, Vanessa's expectation that Denise would write "I love you" is certainly not an official expectation of Rita's but very much an unofficial expectation of the "fake sisters."

Voice play in, and on, print. There were some early suggestions in written prose that Denise was attuning her ear to musical language and to official music, just as Marcel gravitated toward maps and Noah toward a cartoon-like literary bear. In the following workshop entry, written in November, the playful language so central to Denise's relationship with Vanessa occurred in print (see Figure 6.3):

> Me and Vanessa was playegeg and
> We fell down and we
> sot [started] to laf and that is a
> rum-tum-tum

In another entry, also from November, Denise appropriated official musical content. Her text refers to the Mbuti women, whose art and music had been featured in a local art museum exhibit studied by the class. Indeed, Rita had been playing the tape of Mbuti Women songs in the background. (Parenthetically, this text was also Denise's first explicit fictional story—note the title and the "once-upon-a-time" frame, which casts Vanessa and herself as characters and their playing as part of a narrative plot.)

> The Two Little Grs
> Once a panatam it was
> a grl name is Vanessa and a grl
> name is Denise and. They pley
> and play then they hrd sahag [heard singing]
> They loot and loot [looked and looked]
> They did not see it bat
> it was the MBT WaN ["Mbuti Women"]

Denise's first clear use of *un*official musical appropriations in an official event came not in writing but in reading. One day she and Vanessa responded to a written text as if it were a hymnal. This allowed them to recontextualize the discourse features of a particular kind of song, of particular voices—"the voices" of "church," in their words. Moreover, because

Figure 6.3 Denise, Vanessa, and a rum tum tum.

they shared an understanding of the genre or practice organizing those voices, they could *collaboratively* improvise within its stylistic requirements, just as they did in their radio play.

In the example below, the girls are appropriating from church music as they sit together during the morning reading period; they try to explain their performance and to encourage me to join in:

> Vanessa and Denise partner read "Lazy Mary Will You Get Up?" (a verse in their reader). The children sing the text as if they were "in church," using quiet but vibrating voices that crescendo through each page (i.e., each stanza). A syllable like *day* may become two syllables, as it is drawn out and accentuated for dramatic effect—

> DENISE: (singing) Laz-y Mary/will you get up/Will you get up?/ Will you get up?
> Yes Mo-ther/I will get up/I will I will/I will get up. Yes Mother/I will get up/I will get up to-day-ay.

Vanessa "hates [the] day ay" part. When Denise's turn comes up again, she sings:

> DENISE: . . . to day:
> VANESSA: Whew. (with relief)

Denise soon tells me it's my turn, and I reply that I can't carry a tune. The girls respond as good teachers. First, Denise makes the task easier for me:

> DENISE: You can just try to say it like this, try to say it like this.

Denise sings the text with the same syncopated swing, but slower. Vanessa interrupts and has another suggestion.

> VANESSA: Or just try to sing it like this. Just try to sing it like a pretty—like a pretty one.

Vanessa then sings the song with a simple, on-the-beat rhythm, completely changing the emotional tone of the work—and the way one might picture the girl reluctant to get out of bed, the frustrated mother. Vanessa uses no vibrato. No swing. "Like in kindergarten," says Denise, teasing me.

This breaking up, elongating, and otherwise playing with sounds and this stylistic evoking of different moods are essential aspects of literacy— the deliberate manipulation of language, and of literariness—the deliberate linking of form and emotion (Vygotsky, 1987). Moreover, the girls' "experimenting and discriminating" play with voices is evidence of their developing socioideological consciousness (so on display in that opening Tina Turner vignette) (Bakhtin, 1981, p. 345). That is, their play suggests that they are differentiating social worlds and their ways with words, and they are also actively exploiting differences for their own communicative ends. The seemingly same words can sound against the backdrop of voices found in church, in kindergarten, in a first-grade reading group, and the echoes of those differing voices matter for the present encounter. Offering a "kindergarten" voice to a "fake mama" old enough to be your grandma is an insult, however affectionately done.

Lifted and Juxtaposed Voices

During the winter months, Denise's personal experience texts, like Noah's, sounded more comfortably in the official classroom world, as she too left the routine "I wents" behind. Her personal texts could evidence a more conversational tone and a more conventional truthfulness. These newly elaborated personal texts sometimes sported words that had rhythm or drama that seemed to appeal to her. My "god dad is moving because he wants to see his whole generation," she wrote [spelling corrected]—and she couldn't suppress a grin when she read that phrase "whole generation" to her class.

Denise's genre-appropriate conversational stance was certainly due in part to her participation in the official sharing time practice, with its enacted assumptions of the veracity of "personal experience." Further, it was also supported by a new form of official guidance. In an effort to help Denise, and other children, "stick with one piece of writing," Rita sometimes wrote conversational questions in response to workshop entries; those questions asked for extensions or clarifications of reported experiences.

One day, for example, Denise responded through her writing to a tearful Vanessa, who was worried that her mama would "whup her butt" because Zephenia had gotten her new shirt dirty. With gleeful giggles, she recontextualized Vanessa's uttered worry into a theatrical "butt whupping" of her own, during which her bottom went "flying in the air." When Rita came by the table, she read Denise's text and wrote, "What did you do to get a whupping?"

Denise responded by writing: "I gat my now srt brde [new shirt dirty]." Denise may or may not have gotten her new shirt dirty and her butt whupped, but she certainly made Vanessa smile.

As written language became a more comfortable tool, Denise's texts did not become uniform and orderly. Not at all. Rather her playful responsiveness could pull her attention (and intention) in varied communicative directions, especially when participating in new, unfamiliar official practices. Indeed, her resulting texts could seem almost as socially free-wheeling as did her conversational play. Moreover, just as Denise used the new medium of writing to play in familiar ways with dramatic, some-times rhythmic voices, she also found some new textual toys in official literacy places. Both old ways of playing and new textual toys are illus-trated in the following sections.

Shifting roles and contingent voices. Denise sometimes slip-slided from one dramatic voice to another in her writing, as she responded to the social moment. In so doing, she did not necessarily treat a page as a space for a singular communicative unit (or part of such a unit). Her social and tex-tual fluidity was especially evident during the "I learned that" event con-cluding the space unit in January.

For this event, Denise initially sat on the rug by Noah, Marcel, and Vanessa. But everyone in the class finished before she and Vanessa did. So, as the rest of the class gathered on the rug for a class spelling game, the two girls moved over to a table to finish their work (as did I).

By this time, Vanessa had written two variants of the space facts that Rita had listed on the class facts chart. But Denise had wanted to do "some-thing on my own." That something began with the appropriated official opening ("I learned that") and two statements that were on topic, if slightly contradictory (see Figure 6.4).

I learned that space is a good place to be.
If I lovd [lived] in that place I would died [die].

"You can't be using that word [died]," Vanessa told her, as though *die* were a cuss word for sure. Denise then wrote an apology: Srey [Sorry] Ms. Rita. With that action, Denise oriented herself more centrally on the unofficial landscape, as the transcript excerpt below reveals:

DENISE: (to Vanessa) Better now? (in a teasing voice)

Denise now recalls, not a taught fact, but the robot child, Pre-cious—the child the two girls first drew when illustrating their "space fact" [see Chapter 3]:

DENISE: I'm gonna write, "Oh Precious." Precious, she got on my nerves. . . . "Oh Precious. You done it. You done it. Oh Precious you done it." I would say it in a mean voice. "OH PRECIOUS! YOU DONE IT! I'm GONNA (unclear) YOU! YOU DONE IT!"
VANESSA: Write it in big ol' letters!

Figure 6.4. What Denise learned about space.

DENISE: does so and then reads) "OH PRECIOUS! YOU DONE IT!"
RITA: Denise! Be quiet!

Denise looks startled, mildly embarrassed, and then smiles and writes her last line:

Sre [sorry] boys and girls (That is, "Sorry I disturbed you.")

Denise's composing actions indexed her relationship as a dutiful student recalling "what I learned," an irritated (but playful) mother whose child had "done it" now, and a polite human being, sorry for forgetting quite literally where she was. Denise's written text was not a kind of adjunct to, but rather centrally located as a mediator of her symbolic actions. With Vanessa's help, she even deliberately negotiated symbolic media, using a visual means to convey spoken meanness. Her actions, however, were quite socially freewheeling, not so much guided by a coherent text-producing practice as contingent upon emerging actions.[1]

For no child at this time in the school year was conveying deliberately studied facts a recurrent, routine way of using written language—that is, a practice that (at that point, in that event) guided and sustained child agency. Most children copied space facts, whatever their evident control over the written code. But Denise maneuvered in unofficial space, enacting varied playful encounters—apologizing, yelling, and apologizing again.

Although the "I learned that" event was her most socially unruly text, Denise, like Vanessa and Wenona too, was apt to put an "I love you," an occasional "I'm mad at you," and even a "Hi" on a page unexpectedly. Moreover, unexpected utterances could be decidedly crafted, rather than conversational in tone. Below I consider her floating bits of poetic text.

Plucked voices. Among Denise's plucked bits of appealing, liftable utterances were those from unofficial sources, including popular songs. Her written texts reflected the general classroom trend during the winter months of increased use of the textual stuff of popular media genres (see Chapter 4). In the following example, composed in March, Denise embedded a plucked voice in a personal piece about an upcoming family move. The move was actually in the works; her reference to multiple sisters, though, was true only in her fake family, and that one wasn't moving:

I am going to move
on Wednesday We
are famale I got all my
sisrs and me
sisrs and Jake [her brother] too

Those familiar lines about family and sisters were quite deliberately taken from Whoopi Goldberg in the film *Sister Act II* (Steel, Rudin, Iscovich, & Duke, 1994; originally Sister Sledge, 1979).

Denise also plucked appealing utterances from official sources, especially from poetry. Rita read poetry to the children throughout the school year, especially that of Eloise Greenfield, an African American poet who uses a range of powerful literary voices.[2] Not only did the children perform poems for various school occasions; they also spontaneously joined and recited poems along with Rita when she read to them, just as they did when she taught them groups songs.

Beginning in February, Denise, like Vanessa, began to lift bits of Greenfield's poems for her writing book. For example, the title and opening line of a poem in *Under the Sunday Tree*, the Greenfield (1988) book Rita shared first, appear in varied spots. To use Denise's spelling, the poem began, "Saucer-hat-Lady Like [Look] at that"; the extra hyphen and the misspelling of *Look* reflect Denise's reliance on her own memory of these appealing words, not on copying. Later on in the school year, Denise's favored source was the title poem in *Honey I Love* (Greenfield, 1978). The repeated lines of "I love a lot of things like . . ." and "I like the way [she/you] . . ." were easily plucked and sometimes used to frame a name or a personal statement (e.g., "I like the way you go to the bus Vanessa").

Denise's bits of uttered dialogue and poetic phrases were not always orchestrated in some clear genre or practice. And sometimes they were judged inappropriate for the task by Rita, as will be illustrated. Nonetheless, their very recontextualization—and even Rita's judgment as to their appropriateness—made them the focus of deliberate attention. It is not surprising, then, that Denise's continued journey into new written practices, official and unofficial, was constituted by a more deliberate orchestration of dramatic voices. Nor is it surprising that that orchestration was itself most evident when Denise's composing actions seemed informed and sustained by a strong sense of social place and of agency—that is, of the kind of social dialogue being enacted. Denise's more organized voices are featured in the last section of her case.

Newly Orchestrated Voices in Differentiated Worlds

In the last months of the school year, Denise evidenced new control over textual voices, even in the familiar personal experience genre. For example, she could revoice conversational utterances as dialogue in her texts, and she could carry on—but keep out of print—text-related play, as was evident in that opening vignette on wanting money and in the following one, from late May.

Denise is sitting by Wenona and Lakeisha. She is writing about a memorable visit with her dad when he had, to quote her text, *saiD he was going to tack* [take] *me to wotr world* [Water World, an amusement park]. She comments to Wenona and Lakeisha:

DENISE: Guess what? My dad said he was gonna take me to Water World and probably I'm going! (Denise sings those last two words with great enthusiasm.)

Denise now writes "And I said WHAT?!", yelling out the last word with joyous disbelief. But when Rita comes by the table, she reads Denise's last line straightforwardly, leaving the "what" hanging in the air as though there is more to come in the sentence.

RITA: What were you gonna say after that?
DENISE: "What?! You are kidding." (thereby demonstrating the symbolic tensions between oral and written communication yet to be resolved by, for example, the punctuation marks I am using)

Rita now understands. She has a brief spelling lesson with Denise, writing *take, cake,* and *lake* in a column on the side of Denise's paper. When Rita leaves, Denise appropriates those words for unofficial play:

DENISE: "Cake," or "take," or "lake." Which one do you guys like better?
WENONA: "Lake."
LAKEISHA: "Lake."
DENISE: Can't choose the same one. . . . "Take" was the best. Somebody can take "take."
LAKEISHA: "Take."
DENISE: Wenona, sorry. Lakeisha wins the surprise. Because it was "take." "Take" can take you to Santa Cruz, and that's where we're going. We might go.

As the above vignette illustrates, Denise was not only stretching her resources into official writing practices; she was also using written language to transform unofficial practices (including guessing games). In the following subsections, I highlight key official and unofficial transformations, including composing an historical drama—a variant of the "what I learned" practice; collaboratively writing an off-the-record song and a not-quite-ready-for-prime time story; and composing poems—that is, making official "music out of words."

Giving voice to history. Denise's ear for the dramatic and the poetic figured into her first semantically coherent response to a "what I learned"
task, as did an unusually voice-filled study unit. The unit was on freedom
and slavery (the one in which Marcel produced the "Hey Arnold"-like
character on the road to freedom; Noah, unfortunately, missed the whole
study unit because of his asthma).

Among the officially included voices in that unit were many non-
fictional and, often, multimedia texts, as well as fictional, artistic, and poetic
ones informed by U.S. history, a quality that Rita explicitly discussed with
the class. Among the primarily visual texts were Jacob Lawrence's paintings of Harriet Tubman's life. As Rita presented slides of these paintings,
she interwove commentary on Lawrence's distinctive artistic style with a
telling of Tubman's story as imagined by the artist. Lawrence is famous
for his drawing of hands, Rita told them, and Harriet Tubman had strong
hands. Because of her strength, she had to chop wood, haul water, plow.
But "she was not gonna give in," even though, as Rita told them, she would
be beat if she were caught running away.

Before, during, and after the study of Lawrence and his paintings,
Rita played the folk singer Pete Seeger's version of "Follow the Drinking
Gourd" (which Denise interpreted as "Follow the Drinking God," who
made the Milky Way and the North Star followed by escaping slaves).
She taught the children the words to that song and, moreover, made a
photocopy of its sheet music for the children to take home. In addition,
Rita played albums by, shared a video about, and discussed the artistic
skill of, the African American female a capella ensemble Sweet Honey
in the Rock:

"Do you want your freedom?" one of the group sings (Sweet Honey
in the Rock, 1994).

"Oh yeah," echo the others, joined by the voices of Rita and the children.

Among book media, Rita chose to read (and Denise and Vanessa chose
to reread) Faith Ringgold's *Aunt Harriet's Underground Railroad in the sky*
(1992), whose own text appropriates songs, and she also taught the class
to recite Greenfield's (1978) poem about Harriet Tubman (another text
that went home with the children):

> Harriet Tubman . . .
> Didn't come in this world to be no slave
> And wasn't going to stay one either
>
> . . . .
>
> She ran to the woods and she ran through the woods
> With the slave catchers right behind her

And she kept on going til she got to the North
Where those mean men couldn't find her

Nineteen times she went back South
To get the three hundred others
She ran for her freedom nineteen times . . . (n.p.)

As a culminating activity, Rita asked the children, once again, to write a piece to show what they had learned. They could choose to write different kinds of pieces, but they had to include facts that they had learned. Denise's response was indeed a culminating activity, intertextually linked to the many dramatic and musical voices that had constituted the unit of study, among them Ringgold, Greenfield, Seeger, and Rita.

Denise's text begins, as did many children's, with facts about Harriet Tubman. But it became a blend of fact and fiction, report and story, informative statements, dramatic dialogue, and textual repetition. Still, it is by no mean unruly, as evidenced below. (The text was collaboratively reread and edited by Rita and Denise.)

Aunt Harriet wasnt a slave
for Log. She was born a
Slave. She ran back to
saV 300 PePal. She said
We Are going To be free. But [I] w
ill [will] follow The Drinking gorD
North. We did it Said
HarrieT yes yes yes yes yes yes
But WhaT if he beats us?
HCit [Can't.] We are SafE now.

The piece reflects Denise's alertness for dramatic voices, which had so characterized her movement in unofficial realms, and it is also her first coherent piece written to display information gained from a study unit. It mediated a semantically consistent conversation, even though its words were borrowed threads from varied texts.

There were other newly organized voices surfacing in Denise's writing, but not all were officially nurtured by Rita. Among those unofficial texts were popular songs.

Transforming radio play into written verse. Transforming collaborative singing into *written* production events also involved a complex interweaving of voices. This interweaving began with the merging of a familiar official practice with a familiar unofficial one, seemingly the result, at least in part, of situational happenstance.

The brothers and sisters were all sitting together during writing workshop time. Three siblings were borrowing from the movie *Space Jam*: Marcel was making a list of character names, Noah was drawing and dramatizing the key basketball game scene, and Denise was writing a descriptive personal text, leading up to (but not actually writing) the title song: "I have the move spec Jam [movie *Space Jam*]. The song go's like this." Because there was so little time before recess, Rita asked the children to share at their work tables this day (not the usual procedure). And so, when Denise read her piece, collaborative singing of the title song followed.

Right after this event, as the class was to line up for recess, Vanessa asked Denise to "write me a song. Write me a song. . . . Make up a song. But it can't be—not a rap, OK? It has to be a song."

Denise agreed, but *both* girls took their writing books outside for recess. Denise became YoYo and Vanessa became M.C. Lyte, both female rappers who had recorded together. The girls collaboratively wrote and performed their first musical script by revoicing popular lyrics—and those written words were very different from any shared in the official world.

> DENISE: (rapping her text) "YoYo my name/Go go."
> VANESSA: (singing her text) "Don't matter what I do/Say/I can't
>   deny."
> DENISE: (singing her text) "Tell me what you want this to be./It
>   can be anything that your heart desires." (based on lyrics
>   from Ray J [1997], "Everything You Want")

This product never saw the official stage in part because, as Denise said, Rita probably wasn't "used" to this style of song. "Teen-age-er" songs were part of the children's unofficial play, even if their production involved officially valued tools and materials.

Nonetheless, the children's skill at collaboratively composing did have transformative power in the official world. As already noted, very early in the year, Denise and Vanessa smoothly collaborated during composing time, although their focus was primarily on spelling. And, late in the year, a collaborative process remarkably similar to their radio play unfolded. Readers might recall how the sisters had negotiated acceptable words for backup singers in radio play (see Chapter 2). With those negotiations in mind, consider the following vignette. Denise and Vanessa are not writing a love song but, rather, a scary story inspired by the *Goosebumps* television show (a show with which Vanessa seems more familiar).

Working in their separate writing workshop books, Denise and Vanessa divide their respective pages into 4 sections and then begin composing in different sections. In Denise's words, they are "writing a [scary] story that goes together but in different books." In her book, Denise begins in he top section of her paper with a familiar theme—playing. She writes about one boy and two girls playing together. In hers, Vanessa skips the top section and, in the second, writes:

> And a litte girl play with a litte boy but the boy was a vapyr and the boy beis [bites] her

As she writes, Vanessa seeks spelling help from Denise, who is the better speller. However, when Vanessa seeks help with a title, the expert role shifts:

VANESSA: What's the title going to be?

. . .

DENISE: "One Boy and Two Girls."
VANESSA: That's not good.
DENISE: What should it be then? "The Man and Two Women."
VANESSA: That's not good either.

Denise becomes more tentative.

DENISE: The Happy Scary Thing?
VANESSA: No. "The Thing That Make You Shiver. Things That Makes You Shiver!"
DENISE: No! (firmly)
VANESSA: "One Boy and Two Girls" don't make sense. (equally firmly)

. . .

DENISE: Well, what should it be? . . . I know what it should be called. "The Vampire."
VANESSA: Ah, whatever you want. (resigned) Wait! It should be, "Be Careful What You Wish For."

This appeals to Denise.

DENISE: And a girl could say, "I wish I was a vampire." And she could turn into a vampire.
VANESSA: And the boy was already one.

Denise writes and then reads:

DENISE: "I wish I was a vampire"—

. . .

VANESSA: "I said, to myself on a star." NO, "I wish to a star."
DENISE: Write yours! We won't have time to share!

Highlighting their unofficial practices as fake sisters and performers, Vanessa and Denise negotiated vocal parts and made decisions about what lines would sound good when. Vanessa in particular deliberately searched for the right words, given her ear for the "scary story" genre. In a dialectic fashion, the girls reframed unofficial media materials—textual toys—within their official concerns as dutiful first-grade writers; they made explicit references to "making sense" and to page arrangement (not only voice arrangement) and to text details like "titles" and "ends," just as their teacher Rita modeled. This blend of practices supported their sophisticated composing decisions, relative to their earlier spelling-related ones.

Denise, however, was worried about their elaborate collaboration and voiced worries about time to share—to perform for the group (well-founded worries, as it happened). So Vanessa returned to her own piece:

Vanessa rereads (. . . "and the boy bites her") and then adds "I yelled." She pauses when Denise reports:

DENISE: I put, "Now it is Vanessa's turn" [to read her part of our vampire story].

This deliberate translation into written form of Denise's heretofore unarticulated knowledge of radio play collaboration—her knowledge that coordination of turns is required for a collaborative performance—causes some tension:

VANESSA: You shouldn't've put that. (seriously)
DENISE: Why?
VANESSA: Now that's gonna mess up the story [i.e., the performed story].
DENISE: Nuh uh. [No it won't.] Then you gotta go [after I go].
VANESSA: I know! But you don't have to say it!
DENISE: OK. I'm not gonna say it. (begins to erase)
VANESSA: (speaking at the same time) Just—

Denise is erasing, but Vanessa seems to reconsider whether "saying" and "writing" are the same thing.

VANESSA: You're just gonna show it to me. You're gonna point to it [the line] and show it to me, right?
DENISE: (still erasing) No. I'm just gonna go [turns toward Vanessa].

VANESSA: No. Put a little [jerks head down] to it. Like this. (jerks
again) Put a little nod to it.
DENISE: OK.

What was written must be read during official sharing time—and that
would disrupt ("mess up") the performance, in Vanessa's view. There were
complex symbolic and social tensions embedded in the children's recontextualization of their nonacademic knowledge and know-how. As those
tensions surfaced, the children negotiated what was to be written, said, or
communicated through gesture.

Just as in Marcel's and Noah's most complex written productions,
Denise and Vanessa orchestrated multiple voices, supported by knowledge
embedded in diverse cultural practices and social worlds. Moreover, those
negotiations were sustained and guided by a sense of the social dialogue
they were participating in through the current collaboration; that collaboration would yield a product—a "scary story"—which itself was intended
to be recontextualized and performed for Rita's family. (Unfortunately,
although the girls worked on their story for yet another writing workshop
period, they never felt their piece was "ready" to present.)

Making music out of words. Although Denise did not bring the semantic
stuff of her radio play into the official school world, she did find some
appealing musical stuff in that world, as already noted. Perhaps supported
by her participation in official poetry performances, Denise began to write
what she explicitly identified as "poems." These were not plucked poetic
bits or dangling threads, although most were inspired by Eloise Greenfield's
"Honey I Love" poem. Among Denise's poems was:

I like apples/I like peas
I like bananas/On the trees
I like oranges/I like trees
And you all know/that I like peas
I'm not playing now/I like me.

The importance of form and, also, of rhythm and rhyme is evident in
Denise's written love of peas—a food she really did not like at all, or so
she told me.

Poets' common aspirations to select each word in the light of some
hoped for singular expression, some symbolic unity—to greatly simplify,
to like *peas* because the word goes so nicely with *trees*—led Bakhtin (1981)
to view poems as limited in their potential for orchestrating the diverse
voices of everyday life. Although he surely did not have in mind a 6-year-

old poet, he might have enjoyed how Denise slipped out of the following "I like poem" to adopt, and then to apologize for, a different (tone of) voice:

> I like to be helping my mom
> I like to be with my brother
> I do not like when Vanessa be
> like she all that and
> Mean to me and back to I like poem
> I like going to Water World with My Dad
> . . . .
> You know I said about Vanessa I am so
> so sorry

Denise shifted from the "I like poem," with its repetitive opening phrase, to a more straightforwardly personal text—an evaluation, to be specific, and an insult of Vanessa. Improvising within an understood genre, Denise acknowledged her slip textually and quickly stepped back into voice. At the very end, she apologized, apparently to Rita, who had already talked to her about writing that Wenona was fat (in an unofficial girls' club book [see Chapter 2]).

Despite her more skillful orchestration of voices, and worlds, Denise was still negotiating her journey into new practices, as were all the children (and, in a sense, as are all of us). Sometimes as she wrote, she slipped into an out-of-place voice unintentionally, as she did the day Rita asked her to redo a rhythmic but uninformative piece about Mother's Day (e.g., "I been good I been bad"; after Rita's request, Denise suggested Noah redo his Little Bear–style Mother's Day piece, so that "he didn't have to be talked to" [see Chapter 5]). And, on at least one occasion, Denise herself decided to take her written work out of official circulation.

One day the children were to come dressed as characters from favorite books. Most children instead wore T-shirts displaying characters they knew primarily from movies. Denise wore her pink Pocahontas (Pentecost, 1995) T-shirt. Rita, in contrast, wore a pink baseball cap like Nathaniel, the lead character in Greenfield's book *Nathaniel Talking* (1989).

The book opens with a rap—"Nathaniel's Rap." Its opening lines declare that "It's Nathaniel talking/and Nathaniel's me"; its repetitive hook reinforces that "I gotta rap." Nathaniel, however, has an odd rap, at least relative to the focal children's music-making. His rap has no topic beyond his need to rap, and its images of a child rapping until his "ear flaps flap" is sweet, not aggressive.

Nathaniel's rap figured that day into Denise's writing workshop entry, in which she took up Rita's suggestion to the class that they write about their chosen characters. But Denise most definitely expressed quite a different attitude than Nathaniel had—indeed, than the producers of Pocahontas had—for that matter. Denise embedded her appropriations in a not-so-sweet text, a "joke," as she described it, or a "cap,"[3] as Vanessa called it. The joke was informed by Denise's ear for snappy dialogue, and it contained textual nods not only to Greenfield's rap but also to a breath mint commercial (from which she had once plucked a line). Despite this seemingly intertextual tangle, the text is a perfectly coherent cap, as is evident below:

> Denise sits next to Vanessa during writing time. She begins to write and then tells Vanessa that her piece is "going to be funny."

> DENISE: (rereading, with a grin in her voice and on her face)
> "Pocahontas is me. [Recall "Nathaniel's me."]
> Hey, you got a problem?
> Yes I do.
> Do you?
> Yes.
> Why?
> Because you—
> Pocahontas, don't go there now.
> Oh, Denise.
> Please, stop talking,
> Because your breath is humming.
> Your breath is kicking."
> ANNE: Who's talking to you in that?
> DENISE: Mm:, Pocahontas. . . . That's a joke.
> VANESSA: She capping on you.

> I wonder if Denise is going to share this.

> DENISE: I get to take this one home! I get to take this one home!

> And Denise rips "this one" out of her writing book and puts it in her cubby (a small, box-like space for her personal things).

Denise, like the other closely studied children, drew on a wide range of voices engaged in varied textual dialogues; moreover, she made at least some deliberate decisions about where those voices might best sound, as it were. What might officially be considered a sophisticated composing effort—in terms of textual length, elaborateness, and coherence, if not in terms of adult taste—might, in the end, best stay among friends.

"ALL GOD'S CHILDREN GOT [SCHOOL] SHOES"

"If you know *how* to clap and what you're clapping *for* you can come out right with the song. . . ." (Mrs. Bessie Jones, quoted in Jones & Hawes, 1972, p. 19)

In her comments on her childhood song traditions, Mrs. Jones emphasizes that children did not just learn the music (the clapping) and the plays it accompanied (the dramas, sung or chanted, and their movements). Children learned what they were clapping or playing *for*. And, suggests Mrs. Hawes, what they were clapping or playing for was "the creation of a rhythmic bond, the fusion of the group into a single internally cooperative unit" (Jones & Hawes, 1972, p. 20).

"The only time I ever saw Mrs. Jones stop a game," writes Mrs. Hawes, was when "a player . . . simply walked in [the center of a] ring at a normal pace. [Mrs. Jones said,] 'You got to *dance* it, you got to play *on time*, you got be *be* on time. . . . Move your feet!'" (Jones & Hawes, 1972, p. 20; emphasis in original). If a player does not "get with the rhythm," she or he just can't be "'with'" somebody, "respond to them . . . complement and support their silences . . . fill in their statements (musical, physical, and verbal) with little showers of comment" (p. 24).

This negotiating of a rhythmic bond, a shared context, is different from the notion of a static context that determines the steps. A shared rhythm requires active constructing, active stepping, from engaged participants. And those participants always improvise to fit the situation. "Change the order of the verses—or add new ones from your own imagination—as the spirit of the game *as it is being played* dictates," admonishes Mrs. Hawes. "These are for *play*" (pp. x–xxi; emphasis in original).

The negotiating of a shared context is the essence of the recontextualization processes undergirding this chapter and, indeed, this book. Children negotiated their activities, both official and unofficial, responding to each other, to Rita, and to the task at hand, making use of what they regarded as relevant resources. As illustrated first in Chapter 2, in the unofficial world, the children used musical appropriations especially to assume varied stances and roles and to express varied emotions and moods through, for example, raps, love songs, cheerful "preschool" songs, and feisty crowd punchers. Their shared social sense of these varied practices, or voices, did not dictate their actions. Rather, it allowed them to be playful with each other.

In this chapter, Denise was featured as she responded to official literacy activities, seeking rhythmic bonding with Rita's classroom family and her fake family as well, especially her best fake sister Vanessa. Like her "siblings," as a writer Denise stayed close initially to Rita's suggested words, with minimal revoicing. She "liked" and "went." It was an effort to match voice and word, to coordinate mouth and hand, to monitor the unfolding text—not to mention to just figure out what was *went*, what was *want*, and what was *with* (or *what*). And yet, even in these early efforts to get something acceptable on the page, Denise could find support in comfortable collegial interactions with Vanessa.

Denise moved beyond the notion of writing as representing a pregiven world (real or otherwise) to that of writing as mediating a communicative space. She, like her classroom family, experienced this space in official and unofficial talk about written texts. But Denise did not necessarily understand what all official writing was "for."

A vivid example of familiar play in unfamiliar territory was provided by her response to the "what I learned" event during the space unit. In that event, Denise interacted fluidly in writing with Rita, Vanessa and, so it seemed, the "boys and girls," in the manner of her conversational play—not in the manner of an informational practice. Indeed, in this same event, Noah drew a cartoon space adventure and Marcel made a list of planet names (after Rita explicitly told him not to write about Dallas).

Like all the focal children, then, Denise responded to school writing in ways that reflected understood forms of agency, familiar communicative practices, and favored textual toys. And also like her fake siblings, Denise faced challenges in negotiating boundaries of symbol systems, social relations, and ideologies. Developmentally, her case history is not about mastering static textual structures (a "story," a "report") but about entering and participating in new social dialogues through a new medium. Denise ventured out into the official world, trying on, combining, and even deliberately steering clear of appropriating certain kinds of textual voices in certain kinds of social scenes. As I did with the other closely observed children, I followed the textual threads of her composing efforts. Those threads linked the actions of Denise as an aggressive singer, who nonetheless was sorry for "her words," through a range of aggressive written deeds and sweet apologies, including the poetic sharing of Denise as a history student knowledgeable about a famed figure "who didn't take no stuff" (Greenfield, 1978, n.p.).

To end Denise's case, and the book's set of cases, I refer here to an old spiritual that Rita often played: "All God's children got shoes." As a metaphor for voices, for communicative ways to get around, children do not have one perfectly fitting pair. Rather, children slip into appealing shoes taken from diverse locations and, with experience and guidance, they become more skillful and more mindful of where they're going. The children's discourse flexibility and sociocultural intelligence counter the un-

sound, misleadingly linear depictions of child literacy dominating public and professional discourse. This discourse constructs an imaginary world for adults, assuming they have sole control of the learning dial, adults who do not seem to hear the wealth of ways that children gain experience manipulating the sound, form, and meaning of language—which is, in large part, what literacy is.

In the next chapter, the brothers and sisters move to the background as I focus on the developmental theory that has evolved through this project, and its pedagogical ramifications. In spirit of Mrs. Jones and Mrs. Hawes, in so doing, I aim to further educators' efforts to "be 'with'" their children by staying tuned to the sounds of their worlds.

7

A Writing Development Remix

The world whispers to those who listen. Secrets collide in the air with visions of truth and particles of fancy. *Listen*. . . . Any boy can hear. If he only listens. (Kenan, 1994, p. 14)

In Randall Kenan's short story, 6-year-old Malcolm's parents are from "different worlds," and that's why they squabble, or so his grandmother tells him. But Malcolm has a different world, too, populated by all manner of creature borrowed from this story or that one. Malcolm wraps the words of his magical world around the "real" one. His mother is an empress of the Land of New Jersey; his father is a prince, longing for the principality of Jamaica. And Malcolm himself has a part-time job as Lord of the Sea, in which he does a lot of stints as superhero. Strip Malcolm of his transforming words, and he is a little child, whose grandma fills his bathtub and tucks him into his sheets, and whose parents fight about what's best for him and themselves.

The brothers and sisters had their world also, complete with part-time jobs involving train trips to Dallas and star turns on the local hip-hop radio station. Their world was also constructed with transforming words borrowed from appealing voices, which allowed them social places of power and pleasure (although, to be sure, plenty of squabbles).

In such imagined worlds, Vygotsky said, children can be a "head taller than themselves" (1978, p. 102). But surely they can be a whole lot taller than that. They can fly, if need be! Vygotksy had in mind the cognitive feats furthered through play. Playing children can rename the mundane and organize their behavior according to a pretend situation that they have willed into existence. Thus begins the human capacity for abstract thought and for making conscious choices, for exercising agency within (or against) the perceived rules of the game—the rules, for example, of taking a star turn on a radio show, of being on a championship football team . . . of escaping from a vampire in a horror story.

As that latter example implies, the symbolic capacities that undergird play also undergird children's ability to willfully craft a "web of meaning" out of written language, a particularly abstract symbol system (Dyson, 1989; Vygotsky, 1962, p. 100). Written language looks like linear bits of graphics; it has no perceptual echo of human voices in its colorless and flat demeanor. Thus, working early in the last century, Vygotsky viewed children's essential developmental challenge as discovering that they could "draw not only objects but also *speech*" (1978, p. 118; emphasis added).

But children's first written messages do not come from thin air, nor do they emerge directly from a "budding personality" (Vygotsky, 1978, p. 118). Their themes and forms—their very words—come from others; they are improvised revoicings. Thus, in this project, children's essential challenge is viewed as learning that they can craft *voices*, or "speaking personalities" (Bakhtin, 1981, p. 434). And essential resources for this learning are found in their everyday lives, which are filled with particular voices and prototypical ones (or genres), themselves constellations of expected themes, structures, and styles (Bakhtin, 1986).

In the preceding cases, I have tried to disentangle the children's multimodal production events and the voices of truth and fantasy that blended, collided, or simply coexisted as they sang, drew, talked, and wrote. As the children officially wrote, they could, unofficially, be playing the game of "talking about going to [each other's] houses," of "playing for Dallas," of enacting a superhero show, or of "just playing around." By unraveling the intertextual threads woven into their efforts, I have furthered, or so I hope, a developmental theory of written language that can envelope children's *varied* entry points into school literacy practices and highlight children's discourse flexibility and sociocultural adaptiveness.

In constructing the cases, then, I did not strip the children of their accumulated resources, the way Malcolm lathered himself with secret soap to turn back into a little boy (as opposed to Lord of the Sea) before his grandma fetched him from the tub. Rather, I emphasized that, as with Kenan's Malcolm, the textual doors to the brothers' and sisters' world was wide open, and they themselves listened attentively to the world whispering, shouting, and singing around them. Their school progress was marked by an expanded borrowing of textual material from outside, as well as inside, classroom doors.

In this chapter, I take my lead from the children, as I consider the study's theoretical and pedagogical implications. In the first section to follow, I wrap the project in some key words from hip-hop culture and from rap in particular, one source of the children's textual toys. I appropriate the notions of "sampling" and "remix," using them metaphorically, not as an expert. Their essence allows me some new tools for explaining the dialogic rhythm I aim to bring to an old developmental song about children building on what they know. In this new version of the old song, theoretical and instructional frames of reference assume and, moreover, logically depend on variations in any child's, and in any classroom community's, communicative and symbolic repertoire.

In the second section to follow, I elaborate on this new rhythm, using as a basic beat Clay's (1975, 1991) description of literacy development as children's "construction of inner control" over a complex, multidimensional language system. I draw on project data, revisiting a key event, to articulate in a more fine-grained way the contribution of an emphasis on recontextualization processes, and on childhood practices, to an understanding of literacy development.

Finally, in the third section, I highlight the implications of this dialogic rhythm for teachers' work in diverse local communities. To so stretch the project's usefulness, I bring to the foreground the language variation embedded in this project. For teachers in diverse settings, the project's implications underscore the importance of elementary school teachers' traditional sensitivity to children, not just as students, but as people with intertwined lives as friends, peers, and community members in a culturally and socially complex world (Dyson, with Bennett et al., 1997).

So, first up, some new voices, whose human counterparts would probably be surprised to find their words had traveled smack dab into a book about children and literacy development.

HOW THE PRESENT BUILDS ON THE PAST: IT'S A RAP

> Recontextualizing someone else's sounds [or sampling] is, after all, how hiphop started. (George, 1998, p. 92)

It is not only hip-hop's rap music that began with the recontextualization of sounds. In the Bakhtinian-informed frame of this book, so began and begins the language learning of individuals. Their unique voices can only be understood by listening to them interact with others against the backdrop of their cultural landscapes; those landscapes provide the communicative practices from which they draw. This is the essence of Bakhtin's dialogic theory—any individual utterance can "only be understood as part of a greater whole" (Bakhtin, 1981, p. 426).

Below I exploit the compatibility of Bakhtin's dialogic theory with cultural theorists' and commentators' analysis of rap. I emphasize sampling's integral link to a constellation of cultural practices, remixing's link to the technological and symbolic complexities of contemporary times, and the way both of these recontextualization processes function as a means through which young participants learn the workings of their (musical) heritages. I use these connections to rearticulate this project's approach to child writing.

Sampling the Constellation of Communicative Practices

> For the most part, sampling . . . is about paying homage, an invocation of another's voice to help you say what you want to say. It is also a means of archival research, a process of musical and cultural archeology. (Rose, 1994, p. 79)

Sampling is a means of borrowing and manipulating sounds to construct new mixes, new pieces. In rap's earliest days, Black deejays in the Bronx improvised rhymes over the beat of instrumental or percussion segments—samples—from popular songs (Cook [Davey D], 1985; Rose, 1994). They took their samples from previously recorded songs and used them as a background beat for an improvised street poetry. The samples came from break beats, the sections in a song when the melody stops and the rhythm section comes to the fore. These bass lines, guitar sections, drum riffs were put in the mix, so to speak, and they were reconfigured and extended, as deejays played their turntables as instruments.

As rap progressed, the deejays handled the sampling of "found music," and MCs manipulated and reinvented the "found" language (Yerba Buena Center for the Arts, 2001, p. 5). Individual rap songs were thus quite literally built by borrowing the sounds and rhythms of others. Moreover, as an emerging musical genre, rap was a unique blending of musical and performance practices with deep roots in the African American tradition. Among those practices were musical storytelling, like playground rhymes, "talking blues, spoken passages in gospel, and call and response" (Maultsby, 1995; Shuker, 1998, p. 247). Further, rap's adaptiveness and flexibility—its strategic intertextuality—have allowed rappers all over the world to differentiate related practices (e.g., reggae rap, female rap, gangsta rap, multicultural rap, and on and on [Osumare, 1999; Shuker, 1998]). Some rap genres are more partylike in spirit (favorites of the brothers and sisters); others are more political or theatrical.

Because of its intertextual essence, Rose (1994) sees sampling as a kind of archeology, a way in which rap artists reformulate the voices and practices that are their musical heritage. The reference to archeology implies a study of material artifacts—old records—that yield insight into the practices and system of practices into which those objects figure. Any rap, like any textual utterance, is part of a greater whole—an ongoing situation, a practice, a sphere of human activity, a society.

Sampling and child composing. In this project, the children were sampling symbolic material from the communicative practices—the varied kinds of voices—that filled the landscape of their everyday lives. Analogous to rap artists, the children appropriated and adapted thematic content, textual features, technological conventions, actual lines, and whole practices themselves as they constructed their unofficial and playful practices. Moreover, they used that same material as they moved into the print-drenched practices of official school spaces. In the process, they juxtaposed, blended, and differentiated both communicative practices and social worlds. No single multimedia production, and no written text, could be understood in isolation from the constellation of communicative practices that comprised the children's worlds.

Fine-grained studies of child composing, however, can do just that— that is, they can isolate individual children's productions from children's lives. Indeed, in certain constructivist approaches, child composing may even be reduced to "stages" of spelling (for a review of this work, see Richgels, 2001). Certain sociocultural approaches may confine children's agency to that of the expert's apprentice, making inaudible children's potential to transform unfamiliar practices into ones in which they are anything but "peripheral" (Lave & Wenger, 1991) to the goings on. Moreover, they may focus on individual practices already differentiated and defined by those in charge (the adults) and, in this way, make invisible the key human strengths of social and symbolic flexibility and adaptiveness (Gould, 1998; Sutton-Smith, 1997).

And yet, it is precisely these qualities that undergird, and are in turn furthered by, children's growth as skillful composers in varied media. Indeed, Bateson (1956, pp. 148–149) argues that "what [children] are learning when [they] play [or write or rap] is a kind of flexibility of action that is related to a frame" or communicative practice. Children learn "the fact of stylistic flexibility" (p. 149) and the "conceptual structuring of the universe" (p. 151).

Consider, for example, Denise's play with the textual toys of popular music. In *playing* the role of a singer (as opposed to simply singing), Denise deliberately appropriated and organized her verbal material within an imagined situation—that of herself being a professional singer, a conceptualization that foregrounded one career possibility against a backdrop of possibilities. Moreover, she also enacted a particular kind of singer and, indeed, could situate that singer in relationship to others (e.g., deejays, audience members) and to varied interrelated practices (e.g., song announcing, radio interviews).

Among Denise's appropriated practices were varied song genres. Denise's aggressive "Why You in My Business," the smooth line of her collaborative accompaniment to "Baby Boy" both involved choosing and manipulating words, phrasing, intonation, and turn arrangements against a backdrop of genre possibilities. Indeed, although the texts were "made up," they also used the "shared phrases and slang words" of the musical practices in which she was participating (Rose, 1989, p. 42), among them "in my business," "homey," and variants of "baby." Like all speakers, Denise selected—or negotiated the selection of—words, not for their inherent meaning as words, but for how they figured into both the practice she was enacting and the particular situation at hand (Bakhtin, 1986; Hanks, 1996). Her appropriation or sampling of musical and cultural material was a kind of archeology, in Rose's sense, a way of analyzing, paying homage to, and participating in her dynamic musical heritages.

As Denise's play illustrates, there is "no figure without a ground," to use the words of the Bakhtinian scholar Holquist (1990, p. 22). Thus, in school, children make sense of a foregrounded school literacy activity (e.g., an "I learned that" event) in the context of their experiences with other communicative practices. In borrowing and revoicing symbolic material from their landscape of possibilities, children reorganize and rearticulate their resources in school contexts. In the process, they come to understand possible "options, limits, and blends" of school literacy practices (Miller & Goodnow, 1995, p. 12). Ideally, they are not moving forward on some kind of imaginary pathway to literacy, but maneuvering with more control, more flexibility, on expanding landscapes. Their progress is evident in their deliberate composing of a voice against a backdrop of possibilities—be it that of a sports caster, a Little Bear author, or a dramatic persona (e.g., a mad mother, a contrite child).

When Denise and all the brothers and sisters began writing in school, they moved cautiously into written language events. Like many children, they used this new graphic medium for a familiar function; they wrote to represent or symbolize important people and things in their lives, especially through writing names (Clay, 1975; Dyson, 1982). By appropriating brief official text frames, they composed at least ostensibly personal statements about what they liked or where they went. But, influenced by their engagement with each other as well as with Rita, the children began to situate writing events within childhood practices and to sample the textual stuff of those practices as they tried on, combined, and avoided using certain kinds of voices in certain kinds of social scenes.

A modest but vivid example of a shift into appropriating a particular written voice is found in Wenona's case. As readers may recall, Wenona regularly appropriated the official frame "I like" and inserted the word "cats" as a place holder, even though she had no particular love of cats and did not even own one (as she explained to me 4 years later in an informal visit). One day she, Marcel, and Noah were irritated at Jamal, who had growled at them (quite literally) when he was on his way to his seat during writing time.

The three children began by putting Jamal's name in a "kindergarten" chant, "Who stole the cookie from the cookie jar?" Then Marcel decided to make a sign that said "No Jamal allowed" for the "club tent." (There was no actual tent; the club designed to exclude one child may have been a sample from a talked-about movie, *Harriet the Spy* [Beece & Hughes, 1996].) As Noah bent over Marcel's shoulder, joining in on the spelling, Wenona had another idea for a written text. "Ja mal, is a cat!" she exclaimed. She laughed as though this was exceedingly devious and so did her brothers.

Both "Jamal is a cat" and "I like cats" are simple sentences. But in terms of the mediational function, they are quite different. One is a place holder, written without any evident purpose other than to fulfill the requirement to write. The other reframes a used word from an official if constrained personal text within an unofficial practice of peer insulting (which was, in this situation, at least, a kind of imaginary play). Aiming to participate in the written fun, Wenona samples the name-calling syntax of "so-and-so is a such-and-such." A minute later, she reconsiders her utterance, switching the words around to "A cat is Jamal," which, if one had a specific cat in mind, might work better. In any case, Wenona's name-calling utterance was completed with the desired response from her siblings, something "I like cats" never received. Indeed, Wenona herself seldom gave "I like cats" any evident thought at all.

In composing a rap, writes Rose (1994, p. 80), producers manipulate their sampled sounds, paying attention to rhythm, volume, repetition, and musical breaks. They do this, not randomly, but guided by the desire to create a pleasing whole. That whole is a musical text whose meaning is intertextually bound up with a whole constellation of musical practices. So, too, when guided by some sense of a communicative frame, child composers of written text adapted, stretched, and appropriated new resources. In the process, they manipulated the elements of the written system (e.g., letters, words, syntax) in order to have a voice themselves and, thereby, participate in the social scenes of their worlds.

Remixing in Response to Contemporary Times

> [In] the reworking of an entire composition . . . the *referenced* version takes on *alternative lives and alternative meanings* in a fresh context. (Rose, 1989, p. 42; emphasis in original)

When Denise and Vanessa sang their various versions of the "Lazy Mary" text, neither child shouted out "Remix!" But in reformulating their articulation and intonation of this old song in the light of different kinds of voices (a church voice, a kindergarten voice), the girls, however inadvertently, were changing the meaning of the verse, at least for me. I had never before so experienced the frustration of the verse's long-suffering mother who could not get that child up.

The children's revising of "Lazy Mary" was in the spirit of a "remix," even if less technologically sophisticated. Remixing is a production process that exploits technological possibilities for electronically taking apart and putting back together—for reworking—entire compositions (Watney, 1994). In remixing songs, producers can reconstruct rhythms and lyrics, adapting old songs to the beats found on contemporary dance floors. Remixes can be seen as lacking in originality, or as fresh interpretations, a giving of new life.

As a process, remixing highlights the role of technology as a "colleague in creation" (Rose, 1994, p. 93). In remixing, or "versioning" (Rose, 1989, p. 42), producers respond to contemporary times by using available technology to deliberately deconstruct and reconstruct the complexity of music, its texture, timbre, and rhythm, its instrumentation and lyrics.

Remixing, as metaphor, resonates with Bakhtin's dialogic theory. In his view, utterances are one-time, concrete affairs. They can never be repeated. New speakers of those utterances are always engaging in responsive remixing to some extent. They enter into "one kind of relation or another" with the utterances, expressing agreement or disagreement, sympathy or anger, polemicizing with them, "or simply presum[ing] that they are already known to the listener" (Bakhtin, 1986, p. 69).

Both remixing and sampling make it impossible to reduce rap to an oral or written communication form. Although rap clearly builds on African American oral traditions, its production is highly technological and fundamentally literate. Authorship is important, as rappers and producers deliberately reformulate recorded sound and oral rhymes. The rhymes may be labored over—written and rewritten, learned, and orally performed. But to "simply recite or to read the lyrics to a rap song is not to understand them. . . . The music, its rhythmic patterns and the idiosyncratic articulation by the rapper are essential to the meaning of the song" (Rose, 1989, p. 40).

In Bakhtin's theory, too, the critical distinction in kinds of utterances or genres is not between "oral" and "written." A complex genre—a rap, a novel, a scientific exposition—may usually be written, but in the process of its formation, it recontextualizes or "digests" simpler, usually oral utterances, be they conversational exchanges, personal and formal letters, lists and chronicles, instructions and contracts, and on and on (Bakhtin, 1986, p. 62). To write a novel set in a certain time and space, authors' ears must be attuned to the varied kinds of voices one might hear in such a time and space. To interest new audiences, the original versions of novels may be remixed with more up-to-date voices or transformed to a new medium (such as film) where the voices embedded in a novel can be rendered more concretely, as it were.

In any Bakhtinian remix, the reworking is always in the context of some utterance type (i.e., genre) or a hybrid of types. Speakers, writers, rappers, authors of all kinds do not speak words and sentences. They respond to and construct utterances, guided by a sense of how voices should sound—that is, by communicative practices. Without them, there would be nothing to say. Individual self-expression must exploit "communal artifacts" and "communal history" (Rose, 1989, p. 43).

Remixing and child composing. One day Denise sat and watched as Wenona inventoried words she could write. The latter child had begun to match word and voice in a one-to-one correspondence and was now, in the winter months, figuring out the usefulness of sound/symbol connections. Wenona wrote these words that she "knew": *was, you, r* [*are*], *km* [*coming*] and, on the bottom of her page, *to* ("in case I need it"). After Wenona reread her words, Denise sang a melodious version, alternating *was* and *are* in a pattern of repetition and variation: "Was you coming too? Are you coming? Was you coming too?" Denise thereby took Wenona's written list and, using the familiar possibilities of the human voice, rendered that list in a new rhythm, one strikingly different from the straightforward cadence of Wenona's rendition. It was a remix.

In this project, most of the children's remixes were the other way round. They drew on familiar communicative practices and their symbolic stuff to enter into official school composing. These practices were intertextually linked with varied symbolic media and technological sources (e.g., radio, television, film, paper and pencil). Thus, the children's writing development involved, to varied extent and in varied ways, remixing semiotic material to suit the possibilities and constraints of new social practices with new expectations for the use of technological and symbolic means.

For example, Marcel remixed sports media reports into written entries in his writing book. This seems sensible, given the dominance of informational genres in both sports media and school contexts. Noah composed stories based on movies, cartoons, and video games, another reasonable genre approach. Denise and Vanessa collaboratively wrote songs and, after sampling lines and phrases, began "making music out of words" (Koch, 1998, p. 21); Denise even remixed an official text (a Greenfield poem) for her own purposes.

The children's remixing of a particular text or text type (e.g., a commercial, a movie, a song, cartoon, a television sports report) involved recontextualization processes—differentiating and appropriating aspects of a text judged encodable, translating the text into new mediational form(s), and reframing it with the expected metamessage (e.g., "I learned that . . . ," to prepare the way for studied information, "I went . . . ," to suggest a personal experience). As a result of these processes, practices themselves were juxtaposed, blended, and differentiated.

The challenges posed by this remixing consisted of differentiating and coordinating the social and symbolic complexities of production events. The original symbolic form of the source material influenced these challenges, since that form posed varied translation challenges and lent itself differentially well to school-preferred practices. Readers may recall, for example, Marcel's sports reports with the vertically arranged team names and scores, which resembled a television news display more than a prose entry. Or recall Denise's confident-sounding "The [*Space Jam*] song go's like this," although the song was to be sung, not written. Or, my personal favorite, consider "Chapter 1" of Noah's Donkey Kong pieces, with its flying monkey image and its accompanying oral narration and dramatization; despite all that symbolic activity, only "OK" was differentiated out for written form. (Four years later, Noah told me, with some irritation at his younger self, that he had made a mistake. He should have put *DK* for Donkey Kong, not *OK*.)

In remixing symbolic material, conceptual and textual knowledge could become salient and the focus of explicit attention. For example, Marcel tried to write a sports report and wondered why Oakland (home of the Raiders) was not on the class map, although Minnesota (home of the Vikings) was. Noah attempted to explain his Donkey Kong story and found himself considering what a bear would be doing in the jungle with monkeys. Vanessa and Denise clashed over a title for a "scary story" inspired by a TV series, with Denise's sounding (at least to me) a bit too much like a popular song ("Two Men and a Woman"), and then the girls clashed again over how to indicate turn taking in their yet-to-be-performed story.

The tensions generated by remixing material across symbolic borders were themselves tied to new kinds of social experiences; that is, to participating in recurring official practices with new social expectations and newly emphasized cultural tools (e.g., maps, lists, charts, easy-to-read books and song lyrics). Analogous to rap productions, some ideological tensions were raised only when the children's productions were played out in the full public of Rita's classroom family (cf. Dyson, 1997). Were texts "true" or not? Were they judged appropriate or not, given the assigned topic? Who was objecting? Peers? Rita? Certainly not a brother or sister.

At the same time that remixing from the unofficial to the official sphere was going on, unofficial text types were themselves being reconfigured. New versions of the children's practices—like guessing games, collaborative singing, even insulting—were also occurring, as were new extensions of old play. Marcel's recollections of championship games could be bolstered by written game reports (with Dallas always winning, of course). Playful plans for visiting each other's homes could be fictionally accomplished through personal experience texts.

In the quote at the opening of this section, Rose (1989) argued that reworking a composition was a means of reformulating, and thereby giving an alternative meaning to an old song in a "fresh context" (p. 42). I want to put my own accent on that last idea—a fresh context. In using these metaphors of rap, I want to support theoretical and pedagogical visions that allow children to bring their cultural and textual stuff into the classroom context and thereby make it fresh, and intellectually lively, for children and teachers (e.g., Comber, Thomson, & Wells, 2001; Genishi, Stires, & Yung-Chan, 2001; Lee, 2001; Marsh & Millard, 2000).

Summary: Key Concepts in a Developmental Remix

So what does it mean to consider written language development, particularly in school contexts, as a process of text appropriation and recontextualization, rather than solely one of children reinventing the written system or acting purely as apprentices to neatly defined practices? Certainly key concepts remain. There is still the assumption that *active children matter*: children actively respond to and make sense of the situations in which they find themselves. As in most sociocultural approaches, *active adults matter*: to realize their potential, children require interaction with knowing others. And, basic to all developmental approaches, *time matters*: children's ways of participating in written language activities change over time.

But, in the developmental remix, *active children* are regarded as just that—children, as people in a legitimate and important cultural life space, with identities, agendas, and practices informed by their cultural participation with each other and with wider institutions and communities. Their developmental pathways are never linear. Children draw upon and blend resources from varied practices (in order to make new activities meaningful), and they differentiate conventions and expectations (in order to be a more effective participant in valued social groupings).

Moreover, in this developmental remix, there is no sense in which *adults' actions* determine children's actions. As enacted events, practices are always negotiated by participants as they respond to each other. In this negotiating, participants decide what is salient about an activity and, therefore, how they should respond (i.e., what relevant resources they have). And one raison d'être for this book is to demonstrate that children may construct links between texts and contexts that adults would never anticipate (see also Dyson, 1993; Garvey, 1990; Jenkins, 1988; Opie & Opie, 1959; Paley, 1986).

Finally, in this remix, even *time* is not unilinear. The past and the future are present in children's enactment of particular social spaces. In these spaces, children sample and remix textual stuff from past experiences and generate future potential. Their capacity to make decisions about how to respond in the present social scene is dependent upon their sense of how that scene figures into a constellation of communicative possibilities.

Children may, in fact, view school writing as a mechanical activity outside their realm of control and their productive agency. Multimodal production events, in which children blend or juxtapose symbol systems, authorial stances (first, second, or third person), and official and unofficial genres or practices are probable signs that children are actively engaging with written language. These engagements may make salient the symbolic, social, and ideological features of practices, and thus they have the potential for yielding the sort of analytic talk about text constructions often celebrated by literacy development researchers (see Watson, 2001).

Studies of young children's written language typically trace changes solely in *written* processes or products, thereby presuming a linearity and continuity of symbolic form that does not exist. Vygotsky (1978) noted this lack of continuity, but he himself implied a more steady line of progress from gesture, through drawing and play, to writing. Young children's hybrids of symbolic forms and social practices suggest that Vygotsky's ideas themselves need a little remixing and a Bakhtinian bounce.

The children are not simply building from one form of symbolizing to another; they are reconfiguring, rearranging, and rearticulating concrete symbolic stuff from one situated communicative situation to another. The hoped-for outcome of all this sampling and remixing is the ability to use the written system in symbolically flexible and sociopolitically astute ways in the present world. In that present is the potential to continue to respond adaptively in an expanding and ever more multimodal world (cf. Kress, 1997).

Before I consider the implications of this developmental view for teaching, I link it in the section below to a generative and pedagogically grounded predecessor.

SITUATING CLAY'S "KALEIDOSCOPIC RESHUFFLE": A COACH BOMBAY REMIX

> [Children] initiate, construct, and actively consolidate their learning as they interact daily with their own special worlds. If we enlist their initiatives, and let them bring prior knowledge and ways of learning to new tasks, then we will have to teach less in school because they will take much of the learning load on themselves. (Clay, 1998, p. 3)

Beginning most notably with *What Did I Write?*, Clay (1975) has detailed a constructivist view of written language development. In this view, children's essential task is to take control over the written medium, to learn to direct and monitor its use in producing and receiving messages. Unlike other views of writing development emerging at that time (e.g., Chomsky, 1971; Read, 1975), Clay did not reduce early composing to spelling nor did she posit "stages" of learning.

Based on close observation of New Zealand school entrants' ways of writing, Clay analyzed how children engage with written language as a complex system, "at first in approximate, specific and what seem to be primitive ways and later with considerable skill" (1975, p. 19). Their grappling with varied levels of written language all at once "makes nonsense of stage-wise descriptions" (Clay, 1998, p. 134):

> As the child learns to write there is a rich intermingling of language learning across levels. . . . A simplification achieved by dealing firstly with letters, then with words, and finally with word groups may be easy for teachers [researchers, educational program developers, and test makers] to understand but children learn on all levels at once. . . . (1975, p. 19)

From diverse experiences with print in families and communities, young children may accumulate idiosyncratic and varied bits of knowledge—letter forms, written names, perhaps a sense of how certain kinds of print sound when read. In responding to reading and writing tasks in school, individual children orchestrate their diverse resources and develop common ways of understanding and making use of the written system. "The point of entry and the path of progress may be different for any two children. Chance experiences may produce new insights at any time which alter the entire learned pattern" (Clay, 1975, p. 7). Hence, Clay's (1998) "kaleidoscopic reshuffle" (p. 141) of written language knowledge—the reworking of children's understandings of a complex, multilayered system.

Most important for the brothers and sisters project, Clay's view emphasizes that children's learning is furthered by flexibility, so that they explore "the limits of allowable variation" (1975, p. 42). Clay emphasizes how child writers explore the allowable limits of letter formation (e.g., they may vary the formation of the letter *h*, and thereby learn when it is no longer an *h*); they may probe the potential give of directionality or page arrangement or consider the possible spellings of words. Rigid early learning may prevent needed adaptability as new writing tasks are faced. This flexibility is linked to generativeness, a willingness to manipulate controlled spelling patterns and sentence routines to generate new possibilities.

Clay's view was not only different from those of contemporaries working 30 years ago. It is still different from the dominant view. Adams (2001, p. 68) speaks the seeming common sense: "Learning must start somewhere: if not with letters and phonemes, then where?"

In asking, and answering, this question, Adams is assuming a power that, alas, she does not have. The "where" of the beginning of school learning is not in the sole hands of the curriculum developer, the test maker, the teacher. It is negotiated with children. And, as Clay suggests, it is easier to locate what children are attending to, and grappling with, in written language use if they are offered reading and writing "tasks with scope" (1998, p. 237). Such a task allows "children to enter . . . with whatever they bring to it," thereby using the task as a means of learning to solve the varied problems, or challenges, involved in taking control of this new medium. The writing workshop is an exemplar of such a task, as it aims to engage children in producing and receiving written messages.

Clay's view situates children's analytic attention to particular sounds, letters, or words in their efforts to produce messages. Tasks that isolate and highlight these elements of language most certainly can help children gain certain kinds of knowledge (Cazden, 1992). It was for this reason that Rita, like most experienced teachers, called children's attention to word sounds and to specific spelling patterns. But reading and writing acts are not collections of kinds of knowledge; they are particular orchestrations of a range of resources to achieve some end (see also Chittenden & Salinger, with Bussis, 2001). Hence the importance of "tasks with scope," in which children aim to articulate some intended meaning through manipulating symbolic forms with varied kinds of guidance (e.g., from interacting with teachers and peers and, more broadly, from classroom practices [like spelling strategies] and tools [like charts of words]).

My own developmental view is intertextually linked with Clay's. But I entered the intellectual conversation at a different time and with different conceptual tools—more sociolinguistic, sociocultural and, in this project, more folkloric than psychological. For this reason perhaps (or maybe vice versa) I have been drawn to viewing literacy from the vantage point of particular children, rather than viewing children from the vantage point of particular tasks. In my developmental remix, I have, in a sense, situated Clay's kaleidoscopic reshuffle (i.e., the transformation of children's understandings of the complex written system) within the communicative practices of particular children.

In my remix, children's orchestration of their resources for message production is energized and guided by the desire for social participation. Children's accumulation of resources is tied to their participation in the varied practices that comprise their sociocultural landscapes; in addition to the practices themselves, their resources include the thematic content, textual features, technological (including orthographic) conventions, embedded ideologies and, indeed, particularly memorable utterances from concrete enactments of those practices. Children's resources are recontextualized and transformed from one event to the next, from one practice to another, and so their developmental pathways are found in the converging and diverging trajectories of practices.

Moreover, the recontextualized symbols have their own history of use, for producers and addressees. It is a struggle to take control of symbols in particular communicative situations (Bakhtin, 1986). In Wenona's teasing play, could "a cat" be insulting words? In Noah's Donkey Kong story, was "shut up" allowed? Rude? Funny? In Marcel's freedom poster work, could Hey Arnold's bold form move beyond its cartoon origins? For all the children, what should follow the written declaration that "I learned that"? The developmental outcome of all this appropriating and recontextualizing goes beyond flexibility and adaptability with written conventions to include symbolic flexibility and sociocultural adaptability.

By sampling and recontextualizing Clay's notions herein, I am paying homage and, at the same time, articulating my own contribution to the dialogue about literacy development. And, as usual for me, I need a little help from the children. And so, I return here, one last time, to a key event—Marcel's production of a sports report about a football game between Marcel's team, the Dallas Cowboys, and the Minnesota Vikings. (See Figure 4.4.)

In that event, Marcel can be seen sampling from a score-reporting practice of televised sports shows. That practice is itself situated within the overriding frame of collaborative Coach Bombay play. During the studied event, that frame converges with the official one of the writing workshop event. This converging of different social practices, with their differing uses of symbolic media, yields varied potential challenges—potential learning and teaching opportunities, including all those discussed by Clay and more.

To begin, the converging of practices is visible and audible when Marcel translates (or remixes) the audiovisual display of sports scores to a paper and pencil display. As Clay (1975) might anticipate, Marcel's production event makes salient the complexities of sorting out the nature, and allowable variation, of varied kinds of signs, among them letters, numbers, and images. But the written conventions of Marcel's converging practices differ. In school, Marcel is expected to write using letter graphics. And yet Marcel accompanies his written "Dallas" with a star, his written "Minnesota" with a horn, just as televised sports shows typically place team emblems by their names. (The spelling of his written Minnesota, *Minne*, suggests the influence of the abbreviation on the states map, another potential point of learning.)

Further, Marcel's production event highlights concepts of directionality and page arrangement, also focuses of Clay. But Marcel's arrangement is not the result of a child engaging solely with print but rather of a child recontextualizing written language across practices. In arranging team names and their respective scores vertically, as on a TV screen, Marcel has not followed the left-to-right expectations of a straightforward prose report.

The converging of Marcel's practices is also visible and audible in the complex interplay of what is written and what is read. To hear that complex interplay, one must bear in mind that, in the official writing workshop practice, Rita emphasized, through her modeling and guiding, how the children as writers should listen to their speech and reread their writing, in part to monitor their matching of spoken and written text. And one must also bear in mind that, in the practice from which Marcel is appropriating, sports announcers read a more elaborate text than the written one that is displayed. Marcel is clearly familiar with a generic announcer's voice—its staccato rhythms, its location adjectives before team names, its proliferation of time adverbs, and its tendency to lack verbs (Hoyle, 1989).

With those practice details as background information, readers might better hear Marcel as he shifts voices, precariously positioned between practices. Consider how he initially writes *The* before he writes *Dallas*, a prose-reporting style, since he has planned the sentence, "The Dallas Cowboys beat Carolina." After a parent volunteer notes that Dallas lost, Marcel writes the screen-like display of team names and team scores, an accurate reporting of the previous week's play in which Dallas beat Minnesota. Between his columns of team names are the words *in Texas*, which would not be written on such a display, but which an announcer might read. Marcel himself now adopts an announcer voice as he rereads his accurate text to the parent volunteer: "Dallas against Minnesota. In Texas. 15 to 48." In so doing, he reads the unwritten "against," but not the written *the*.

The potential challenges extend still further beyond the sociolinguistic and textual ones. Marcel explicitly highlights his new grappling with the distinction between cities and states. "This [map] has all the states, right here," he announces. But that articulated knowledge has emerged as the geographic knowledge embedded in football team names has been re-embedded and reorganized in his efforts to consult a states map.

Moreover, there is the challenge Marcel confronts about the situated reality of "truth," since what is true in Coach Bombay's world (that Dallas always wins) is not true in the world in general—especially not the Bay Area world. Finally, there are the gender ideologies embedded in this event, which later become evident when Wenona asserts her right to play football and, again, when Rita leads a class discussion about the truth of Jamal's assertion that only boys like football.

Similar analyses could be done for all the brothers and sisters, whose cases are filled with converging and diverging practices. As the cases thus document, in developing written language, contemporary children potentially bring a lively symbolic and social flexibility to school literacy activities. And from those same activities they may garner a more deliberately controlled flexibility—the experience and skill to shift frames and to creatively adapt and craft voices for themselves in ever-widening communicative situations. Such a quality, however, is only evident when writing and writing tasks are situated within, rather than separated from, the constellation of communicative practices in children's multimodal, socioculturally complex worlds.

This developmental point of view, with its openness to children's sampling and remixing, should render anemic those views that attempt to fragment written language into a string of skills or to narrowly define those home and community experiences that can contribute to school learning. However, acting on such a view requires that teachers are able, given their own knowledge and skill and their teaching conditions, to organize curricular practices that are permeable to children's cultural stuff and to provide instructional guidance so that children can discipline, build on, and extend their resources into new realms (Weiner, 2000). Such educators need the transformative imagination of small children, so that they can see communicative agency, textual knowledge, and embedded concepts in sources other than the usual ones. I elaborate on the project's pedagogical implications in the closing section of this chapter.

TEACHERS' WORK AND THE DIALOGIC RHYTHMS
OF WRITING DEVELOPMENT

They answer each other—the child and the grown-up, the hands and the feet, the group voice and the solo voice, the words and the action, the dream world and the real world, in a continual and mutually supportive conversation . . . And it is out of this mixture, the interweaving of the solid and day-to-day and the fantastic and the poetic that the *meaning*, so important to Mrs. Jones, emerges. (Jones & Hawes, 1972, p. 190)

From the vantage point of their experiences in and out of school, the brothers and sisters negotiated their way into the official activities organized by Rita. Although she never could have anticipated (and who could have) her children's particular responses, she established the classroom conditions that made possible their entry as children with a wealth of communicative resources and social connections.

These conditions, detailed in Chapter 3, embody key pedagogical concepts that might inform other teachers' "theories of practice . . . [which guide their] curricular decisions and interactions" (Genishi, 1992, p. 197). They are an explicit acknowledgment of communicative flexibility; a dialogic arrangement of curricular activities; support for the use of, and translation across, varied symbolic tools; and an inclusive approach to cultural art forms. These concepts undergird classroom curricula that allow the "interweaving" of children's and grown-ups' voices in pursuit of meaning.

Supporting Communicative Flexibility, or, Reading Eloise Greenfield

"OH, PRECIOUS! YOU DONE IT!," loudly said (and wrote) the irritated mother Denise, before meekly writing, "Sorry boys and girls," as a chastened student. "I learned that silkworms can't eat hard leaves," wrote the informed student Noah, before the cartoon lover made a munching worm zigzagging through a large leaf. Throughout this book, the children themselves have zigzagged through varied voices, as they participated in the social scenes of their classroom lives. And those school scenes were intertextually linked with those of other scenes and other places. Like children all over the globe, the brothers and sisters appropriated diverse generic and particularized voices, which indexed particular social spheres and groups—the voices of churches, for example, or of "teen-age-ers," or of cultural communities themselves.

As detailed in Chapter 3, Rita both planned for and was alerted to a breadth of literacy voices—that is, of genres and their textual features. But she was also straightforward about the connection between variation in language use and community memberships.

Like the majority of Rita's students, the brothers' and sisters' conversations as fake siblings, their reported conversations with real family members, and their collaborative engagement in projects across the curriculum, all could echo the voices of their "mommas and kinfolk and community and black culture and the black experience" (Smitherman, 1981, p. 56). The children's heritage language was African American Vernacular English (A.A.V.E.). Thus, to use brief examples, their variation between *isn't* and *ain't* and between the presence and absence of forms of the verb *to be* (e.g., "He fine") evidenced systematic options in their language use.

(For linguistic, sociolinguistic, and pedagogical discussions of A.A.V.E., see Perry & Delpit, 1998; Scott, 1998; Smitherman, 1986, 2000; for related pedagogical discussions of bilingualism, see Hudelson, 1994; Reyes & Halcon, 2001).

Young schoolchildren's potential for play with the voices of varied others, and for communicative flexibility, is too often ignored in the public dialogue and, indeed, in the educational literature. For example, children who speak A.A.V.E. are somehow expected to simplistically divide up themselves and whole languages in dichotomous ways, like "home talk" and "school talk" (or "academic talk"), a division woefully incapable of capturing the complexity of children's official and unofficial school lives and their potential for flexibility (Vasquez, Pease-Alvarez, & Shannon, 1994). For example, young schoolchildren who speak A.A.V.E. may switch into a more standard English during formal literacy events and, also, during events in which they adopt authoritative stances relative to others (Adger, 1998; Cazden, 1999).

In the brothers' and sisters' classroom, Rita explicitly discussed variations in linguistic features of language use (i.e., in vocabulary, pronunciation, and word order) as they became relevant in spelling, decoding, or comprehension activities, just as early childhood teachers are advised to do (Piestrup, 1973). Moreover, the singers whose music she played, the authors whose prose and poetry she shared, and her own voice (as a speaker of British English) normalized language variation.

A striking illustration of pedagogical sensitivity to genre and to communicative purpose, and of children's sociolinguistic attentiveness and flexibility, occurred when the brothers and sisters first read the Greenfield (1978) poem about Harriet Tubman, which they had recited orally several times before. Vanessa and Wenona, whom I was observing, both translated certain vernacular patterns used in that poem into a more standard (or textbook-like) English; indeed, they each used a linguistic form that they had never used, nor ever did, in any official or unofficial speech, as recorded in 8 months of audiotape—a negative construction with the pronoun "anything" ("Wasn't scared of *anything*" instead of the written *nothing*). Moreover, they made exactly the same reading errors as Nanette, another member of their poetry-reading group, who spoke a variant of English considered standard.

Later, when the children performed the poem together, Rita commented on the errors that so many children had made. She noted that Eloise Greenfield is "a very good writer." And that she did not make "a mistake" when she was writing. "She's saying it in the way people would have spoken. . . . So when we're reading and writing poetry, you can break all the rules."

Rita's message was that "you" can break the perceived rules if "you" decide that another way of writing is more rhetorically effective. And, indeed, Vanessa and Wenona's errors suggest that they *were* learning to develop their ears and to be situationally flexible speakers. They had a notion of the kind of language that would be in a book and, more often than not, they would be right.

Eloise Greenfield, who writes in a diversity of voices, including different forms of English, belongs in school, as do other authors in varied media with rhetorical and artistic flexibility (see Harris, 1997). Greenfield's ability to appropriate and remix diverse everyday voices is an exemplar par excellence of the flexible crafting of voices furthered by pedagogical instruction attuned to communicative frames and to the importance of explicit acknowledgment of diverse voices.

Arranging Curricular Bookends

Rita's organization of classroom activities and her responsive style of interacting were consistent with her explicit desire for children to be thoughtful decision makers who exercise agency, some sense of willful control over their productions (cf. Nystrand & Graff, 2001). The children had decisions to make about what and with whom to write; they had to consider varied strategies for participating in writing events, be those strategies about encoding words or collaborating with others. And, by her design, they had a "little bit of tension" about being responsible to the classroom family. Every occasion for individual production was preceded and followed by public meetings in which guidance was given, progress reports delivered, and final efforts appreciated.

This design, a bookend one, in my terms, may help teachers to access more fully, and more deliberately extend, children's sociocultural resources. Children need "open-ended" composing periods, as well as more structured occasions for learning specific new writing practices. In these open-ended times, educators learn about children's cultural landscapes, and the particular voices and kinds of voices that appeal to them. By "open-ended," I do not mean loosely organized language events that entail children sitting quietly writing as teachers do likewise. Not at all. In such open-ended times, children need the opportunity to talk among themselves, just as they need to be expected to write, and teachers need the opportunity to observe and to conversationally guide individual efforts (Clay, 1998). During open-ended composing, when children interact mainly with each other, they may generate the social energy that helps initiate and guide authoring decisions at varied discourse levels (e.g., topic, discourse form, spelling). Further, particular kinds of collaborative arrangements among children may promote the recontextualization of certain kinds of resources across practice boundaries. If Denise and Vanessa had not collaborated on a horror story, for example, their turn-taking skill, and their experience with composing and critiquing genre-appropriate words and phrasings would never have surfaced in composing time (for a related argument, see Daiute, 1993).

The girls' anticipation of whole-class sharing informed and sustained their collaborative decision making. And yet, the fact that the girls did not actually share their horror story limited Rita's opportunity to name and compare their collaborative arrangement and their genre choice to other children's composing time choices. As this suggests, the "bookend" to open-ended composing—official classroom sharing and discussion—potentially provides rich instructional opportunities. Through this official practice, unexpected knowledge and unanticipated agendas gain consideration in the classroom "collective zone" (Moll & Whitmore, 1993), as children learn from each other, as well as from the teacher's "loaning of consciousness," that is, of vocabulary and analytic talk to students (Bruner, 1986, p. 175; for further examples, see Dyson, 1993).

Official sharing also allows for analytic attention to how children respond to particular composed utterances, a key aspect of critical literacy practices (Dyson, 1997; Greene, 1995). Children's giggles, laughs, scrunched-up faces, and rolled eyes are often not polite. And yet, as child responses to Noah's rude Bear suggested, in these potential disruptions are potential reflections on textual qualities and on judgments of social appropriateness and ideological worthiness. How do texts—by other children, by adult authors of the school literary canon, by media writers and producers—appeal or not? How is our pleasure, or discomfort, linked to particulars of text (plot, characters, theme, discourse features, visual images)? How is it linked to our own current location (in school) or our broader positions and histories?

Supporting the Weaving and Translating of Symbols

The brothers' and sisters' recontextualization of material across symbolic and social boundaries provides theoretical and research support for pedagogical activities too often pushed to the edge of literacy instruction—those involving the translation and transformation of meaning across medium and genre.

Each medium, each kind of constructive material, has its own semiotic limits and possibilities (Geertz, 1983; Werner & Kaplan, 1963). For example, a written word like "shot" cannot capture the arc of a ball, or a bullet, in motion the way animation can. The word "monster" is not scary, although add a roar and an image and a person screaming that word, well, then, we have some action. A written musical lyric is only a notation for a sung song; it is not the song, unlike a written novel, which is the novel (Goodman, 1968). Thus, for children to develop a place for written language in their symbolic repertoire, they must gain experience with the possibilities and limits of symbolic media, as they combine and transform— sample and remix—meanings within and across practices.

Many teachers, like Rita, know through their own experiences that children's writing, drawing, model-making, sculpting, and dramatizing on related themes allows them to make sense of learning experiences in varied ways (e.g., Gallas, 1994; Genishi, Stires, & Yung-Chan, 2001; Pahl, 1999; Paley, 1980). Moreover, these remixes may, as Rita put it, "inspire" writing, since the children have delved more deeply into their experiences. Certainly Denise's piece about Harriet Tubman was filled with the echoes of earlier singing, storytelling, drawing, and talking about freedom. Further, through augmenting their communicative reach with varied symbolic tools, children can stretch their communicative practices, even participating in social and community domains ordinarily closed to them (e.g., Comber, Thomson, & Wells, 2001; Vasquez, 2001).

Inspired by Rita and her dedication to the arts, I find myself wanting to exercise my own pedagogical imagination and consider sample instructional possibilities for the young children who have stayed 6 years old only in my mind and in this, my book. I wonder how remixing their texts across symbolic forms and social practices might help them further stretch and adapt their resources as they situate their efforts in the public of Rita's classroom.

I wonder, for example, if Noah's multimedia cartoon style would stretch itself out into particular narrative moments if he transforms a drawn and dramatized story into a multi-paged comic or picture book. I wonder, too, if his narrative liberties—and textual minimalism—might face new expectations and possibilities if the children have an Author's Theater, in which they act out their stories (Paley, 1980). Such dramatic performances may also make ideologies visible; relationships between societal categories (like race and gender) and authorial decisions may become visible, for example, in children's selections of actors for certain roles—or in their reluctance to adopt those roles (Dyson, 1997). Maybe, in this same vein, Denise and Vanessa will write a public "love song" if they consider the different kinds of love featured in classroom songs and poems. (I am thinking about this because both girls enjoy Greenfield's [1978] poem about love not meaning "all that kissing like on television.") Surely, too, they could consider the kind of musical "voice" best suited to that song.

In other classrooms, teachers will wonder about other possible ways of furthering children's communicative flexibility, given their own sensibilities and the children in their care. But, to do so, they will need an inclusive approach to cultural art forms, and that is the final implication of this project, one that has wound its way from the opening graphic, with the tippy-toed little ballerinas, through to the current chapter and its hip-hop imagery. As Marsh and Millard (2000, p. 192) write, pulling some of the threads of children's complex cultural lives, including those linked to popular culture, "will not only enrich the lives of children, it will provide teachers with potent opportunities to share in the wider discourses that are located on the margins of classroom life . . . hidden away . . . in secret childhood worlds."

Adopting an inclusive approach to the communicative arts, let alone to cultural art forms, involves more, however, than teacher agency. It involves a major ideological rethinking on the part of schools, educational agencies, and society as a whole about schooling, literacy, and the nature of contemporary childhood itself (see also Luke & Luke, 2001).

So, I now turn to these broader concerns. However, like Kenan's Malcolm, I want to avoid (metaphorically speaking) being left shivering in my textual tub without my Lord of the Sea gear. So, as I prepare to open a new chapter, I am gathering my own fortifying gear—the voices of Rita, the children's parents, and the expert adult participants who mediated my own entry into a richer, more complex world. We will all meet you, dear readers, in the next and final chapter.

8

The View from the Outside: "You've Got to Grow with Your Children"

NOAH'S DAD: What are you going to be doing with the information [from the kids]?

ANNE: I'm going to write about the kids. . . . It's going to take me a long time. But the big point is . . . I want people to value children's intelligence and to see what they have to offer, but also [another point is] what you have just said to me about [the importance of] . . . being aware of what your kids are aware of and being in touch [with their world].

This book began with an image of children who had shed their motley and many-colored threads and transformed themselves into neatly tiptoeing angel-children. Against the idyllic, pastoral scenery, they were perfect, disturbing nothing. I imagined the proud adult audience, gazing at the staged performance of children.

It was my intention to turn this gaze the other way round by situating myself, as best as I could, inside the frame of a particular childhood culture and, then, by gazing out with them at the expectations of the official, adult-guided world. As the children entered the official school frame, they did not slip off their childhood textual threads, but rather used those threads to weave themselves into the official goings on (not, of course, without more than a few dangling threads, glaring knots, and odd little shifts in weaving patterns).

In this closing chapter, I aim to situate myself outside the frame of the child culture and, instead, inside those of adults gazing at the children through the medium of my data. My guiding question is, given my analysis and crafting of the data, how did the children's parents, the cultural experts I consulted, and Rita herself respond to, extend or, indeed, reframe my stories in the world as they experienced it?

In the previous chapters, my emphasis has been on how children gain access to new experiences through appropriating, stretching, and reworking the familiar—the "big point," as I said to Noah's dad. In this chapter, there is a further message, the one emphasized by the parents: the importance of all concerned "being aware of what your children are aware of." The children's alertness came as something of a surprise for the local cultural experts not involved in media specifically directed toward children. Indeed, it was kinda "scary," said the radio deejay with a grin.

However, the children's alertness was no surprise to their parents; it reminded them of the limits of their physical reach and of the importance of helping children become thoughtful decision makers as they move among others' stories, songs, and facts. In an analogous way, that alertness reinforced for the children's teacher Rita the importance of "basic skills" ignored by the ongoing "back to basics" rhetoric—those entailed in becoming a decision-making learner.

The issues raised in the pages to come are complex and controversial and, of course, deserving of their own books, written by authors who are experts in the varied areas of popular culture. I am, however, concluding a book written as an ethnographer of children's school lives and as a researcher of child literacy. So the interest here is in the issues raised by those whose efforts, directly and indirectly, influenced the nature of the children's textual landscapes. As I move below from parents to professionals involved in the popular media to Rita, the children's actions assume new meanings as they are framed within the social units of families, communities, corporate markets, school bureaucracies, and the politics of public discourse about literacy.

PARENTS: OUR CHILDREN "ARE EXPOSED TO SO MUCH"

When I met one evening with the children's parents, I told many of the child tales told herein, as I was interested in the parents' responses and extensions. Sitting in Rita's classroom, I explained that I was interested in their children because they were such good friends and, also, because they were "wide awake children, very attentive to the world around them." I had thought, I told them, that I could "learn a lot about what it's like to be a child in school learning to write" at the turn of the 20th century by studying their children. I described how I had observed the children during assigned writing, such as when Rita asked them to write about stars, freedom, or silkworms, and during open-ended times, when they were expected to decide on their own topics and their own forms—a poem, a story, a description of something they had seen or done. I was "amazed," I said, that their composing was influenced by so many aspects of their lives— their family experiences, their play with their friends, the topics they studied in school, and by all kinds of media experiences—movies, radio songs, sports shows and, of course, books.

And then I told my tales of the children. None of the parents—indeed, no community member with whom I talked—made the mistake an academic reviewer of a funding proposal had said was "inevitable" in this project (pardon my gloating). Parents would assume, the reviewer said, that I was "promoting" popular culture instead of promoting written language, and they would be upset. On the contrary, no one thought I was promoting popular culture. The parents were more than aware that the world itself did that. To quote Marcel's mom, "They are exposed to so much."

Perhaps influenced by my own "amazement," the parents seemed amazed, too, at all that the children had gleaned from their involvement in the world around them—geography, narrative requirements, visual conventions, the complexities of song collaborations and, increasingly, their written ways of crafting stories, poems, even reports. For example, I told about Noah's production of the "silkworm" text, with its written reframing of Rita's admonishment about leaf requirements and its visual reenactment of a silkworm's life cycle, starring a cartoon-like worm. The parents were mesmerized. "That's *really* complicated for a first grader!" said Denise's mom to Noah's dad.

"Sometimes it [the paper] doesn't look like anything," Noah's dad responded. "But then when I hear the story behind it, I can see a whole lot was going on!" He said that Noah had been so into this fact about silkworms needing mulberry leaves that he had tried to get some from a neighbor lady's tree, and that neighbor had not been pleased. (This was the same story Noah had told Rita, explaining that he had been "fixing to get some, but that lady . . . said 'Don't get none of those mulberry leaves.'")

In a similar way, the parents were able to situate the textual toys of Coach Bombay's kids in everyday family pleasures. Noah's dad confirmed that Noah and his brother were big Donkey Kong fans. Marcel's mom confirmed the family's watching of football games. But she also explained that, although Marcel's interest in states had begun with football, it had expanded to involve weather. In fact, Marcel had started watching the weather report on the television every morning, checking the sky for funnel clouds, and then telling her "how everybody should be dressed."

Denise's mom explained that her daughter's interest in music was longstanding and her memory for melody and lyrics had even surprised her. She recalled that once, when the song "I'm Goin' Down ['Cuz You Ain't Around]" (Blige, 1994) came on the car radio, Denise started singing along in a perfect bluesy voice. "'What?!'" Denise's mom laughed, recalling her reaction. "'She's only [then] 5. And she's singing "I'm Goin' Down"! What does she know about it?'"

Denise's mom's question, "What does she know about it?", captured another theme in the parents' meeting. They not only situated the children's actions in their knowledge of the children as family members; they expressed their own concerns that the children's involvement with media stretched beyond their direct control as parents. There *was* recognition of the pleasure in the media, which they shared, and a feeling that children's interest could be used to teach new things. Denise's mom connected how the children used familiar materials and interests to make sense of new school tasks with how her mom taught Denise's brother the alphabet through a rap song. But the parents also had concerns about the content of some media, including what Noah's dad referred to as "the negative images," especially in "some of these rap songs." Negative images were created by the use of violent language or scenes, explicit sexual talk or actions ("when I was a little girl they didn't even show a toilet on TV," said Marcel's mom), and by the entertainment media's heavy reporting of vulgar or unethical actions of athletes, whom Marcel's mom regarded as a former source of African American role models.

All of the parents wanted their children to be decision makers about popular culture texts. They tried to monitor what their children watched on the television, the movies they saw, and—most difficult of all to control—the songs they heard. But, as Denise's mother said, "A lot of people are of the mind that if they don't hear it at home, it doesn't exist," but it does. No matter how selective parents are, she continued, "you can't control what your child hears"; you can, however, "control how you talk to your child" about what they hear. Marcel's mother felt similarly. Marcel, she said,

> is kind of bouncing back and forth between some nursery rhyme and [the rap] his brother listens to. He can sing anything, and they're [my children are] in the choir at church. And my 10-year-old is like, "This is too much church music," you know. And I was like, "You know, I don't want to say this is all you're going to listen to. . . ." If we're driving down the street and we hear something that I don't particularly find appropriate and then I hear them singing it . . . I'll ask them, "So what do you think that means? What does that word mean? . . . Do you think that everybody thinks like that? What is your opinion? Because my opinion is blah

blah blah. . . . You know what is appropriate in this house and you know what is not appropriate. You have to form your own opinion with music, with TV, with what you see in the news, with what your friends are doing."

The parents did not know where and when children would come across media texts, and they wanted to be aware of what their children were aware of. Interestingly, the popular culture experts I consulted also did not feel in total control of the media shows with which they were associated.

POPULAR CULTURE PROFESSIONALS: YOU HAVE TO "HOOK" THE AUDIENCE

The professionals from the local professional football team and the hip-hop radio station did not usually think about little children in particular as part of their concerns. Nonetheless, when I spoke with them, they viewed the brothers and sisters from their intersecting and sometimes conflicting positions as community participants, entertainment experts, and employees of corporations, as I illustrate below.

Televised Football: Children Entering Community Play with Power

Midday on a September afternoon, in a small room in my office building, Soyoung Lee, Sheila Shea, and I met with an assistant coach from the Oakland Raiders and his fiancée, whom I will name Coach and Karen. We were enormously pleased that they had taken the time to talk with us, gratis. As I did in the meeting with the parents, I began by explaining my study and by sharing project vignettes, emphasizing those involving sports media. I pointed out, and so did the coach, the textual evidence of the children's knowledge of varied sports genres, including announcing up-coming games and reporting game results and player statistics. We enjoyed together the children's use of players' numbers and of team names, symbols, and geographic locations.

Coach was surprised that children so young were so involved in the details of sports media, but he was not surprised at their choice of the Dallas team, nor even at Marcel's struggles with states and cities. He explained both these phenomena by discussing the interrelationship of sports with family life, community culture, and corporate interests.

"Football can be such an emotional game," Coach said, "and it kind of brings people together, sometimes . . . 'We're all Oakland fans . . .' and it creates a little bond." At games, he had noticed how strangers bonded in their collective yelling, "and they don't [even] know each other!" Bonding happens in homes, too, Karen pointed out, since football can become "a family thing," as it was for Marcel. "It is broadcast on Sundays when the family can all get together and watch."

Moreover, Coach added, it is not only that fans of the Oakland Raiders don't like the 49ers, but "Oakland fans don't like the 49er *fans* [emphasis added], and I'm sure [the kids] come from Oakland fan houses." (On this, he could not have been more right.) The Oakland fans are considered by the 49er fans as kind of "rough," whereas the 49er fans are considered "golf clappers" and, added Karen, "the ones that tailgate with lobster and shrimp."

"But why Dallas?" I asked.

"I'm sure they're extremely influenced by TV," said Coach. As I noted in Chapter 2, Coach's favorite team when he was a child was also Dallas, even though he was not from Texas. In his view, this was because Dallas— a team of Super Bowl fame and marquee players—is the most often televised. On the other hand, home Raiders games may not be televised if they do not sell out.

Corporate decisions, combined with geographic location, could also explain why, in football language, "Minnesota" and "Dallas" are both "the same, because they're both teams," even though one is a state and one a city. Coach elaborated:

> Nowadays, if you want to get a team in the NFL, you have to come up with . . . hundreds and millions of dollars [and that takes a big city]. . . . There's so many big cities in Texas that you are probably not going to call [your team] the Texas Cowboys. You're going to say the Dallas Cowboys. Whereas, in Minnesota, there, there's not going to be any other city [that could support a team].

In our talk, then, a small child's confusions about states and cities (e.g., why was "Minnesota" on the map but not "Oakland") became an index of intersecting family, community, and corporate media forces. Those same set of forces, thought Coach, also helped explain one potentially disturbing aspect of football talk—the violence of some of the language and the vulgarity of some of the players' displays on the goal line.

> ANNE: (showing pieces by Marcel and Noah) [The children, you notice,] don't say "won." It's usually like "whopped." . . .
>
> COACH: That's the way they talk on TV now . . . [like] John Madden making his little sounds, and saying "BANG!" and "BOOM"

and "Let's get this guy!" "They really whopped those
guys." . . . It's the same thing with [cable stations]. They
show you highlights, but they make it entertaining . . .
[and] add to the emotion of the game.

The coach asked me if the children used "rough" language in other
kinds of contexts. "Sure," I said,

but what's different about this [sports talk] is that it's . . . being
organized and presented in an academic situation [on their composing papers], so it comes more directly to a teacher's attention.

It's "impressive," I went on to say, that the children can evoke a football
game context by fashioning speech and visual graphics into written forms.
Still, the children's writing eventually is read to the first-grade class as a
whole, not all of whom are necessarily fans. Perhaps, I thought, those
contextual details are important teaching points. The coach continued the
topic of speech and its contexts:

COACH: Another thing I just thought about is that um, little kids
         especially are taught, you know, "don't do this, don't do
         that." But then in the arena of sports, it's acceptable to say
         that you are going to "kick somebody's butt." And it's
         probably an expression of, you know, not necessarily
         aggression, but that, well, "My mom said I couldn't do it
         before. I can do it now . . . in this thing called 'football.'"
ANNE: Yeah. . . . Because they're little teeny children. They got no
         power. . . . [But] they're using this big kind of language.
         This has got to be a kick.

As we talked, I remembered the parents, sensitive to the images the
media presented to their children. I wondered if people involved with sports
media considered young children as part of their audience. Coach thought
many did, noting those who monitored their end zone celebrations (i.e.,
their physical gesturing and dancing after a touchdown) beyond that required by the NFL. Football players, he noted, are greeted by all manner
of local people whom they do not know personally, including children.
And the football team has varied community outreach programs, where
players meet with young people.

In our talk together, Coach was appreciative of the positive energy
and community bonding that involvement in sports could further. In his
view, the children's affiliation with a team was a way in which they were

active members of their families and, moreover, of their geographic spot in the country, of the East Bay. He knew, too, that football could inspire play with physical power and social fame, a pleasure for small children with neither. Indeed, Karen remembered that Coach's mother talked about his own imaginary play as a child, in which he and his little brother would be particular players "going out for the pass." At the same time, Coach was straightforward and thoughtful about concerns that complemented those of the parents. Football is not just a game; it is a part of the entertainment business and thereby influenced by what corporate executives view as entertaining for a sports audience (which certainly is associated with adult men, not small children). In audiovisual media, this involves adding verbal "emotion" and a sports media personality with whom to view the game.

A similar thoughtfulness, and an analogous discussion of intersecting interests, was evident in our discussion with the radio personality who participated (unbeknownst to him) in the children's school morning routines. Hip-hop radio, however, was a source of much more concern to the parents than sports media. And, as already noted, the presence of children in the audience was a more startling topic to the radio station professionals than the presence of child football fans had been to the coach.

Hip-Hop Radio: "Tender" Children Playing with "Catchy Stuff"

Late on a summer morning, just past 11 a.m., Soyoung and I sat in the lobby of a hip-hop radio station in San Francisco. We were preparing ourselves for rejection, for the moment when the friendly young receptionist would tell us "Sorry," the deejay was too busy to see us. But no! We were escorted to a small office, in which we met with the breakfast club producer, whom I will call Kris, and the deejay himself, whom I will call DJ. (Soyoung just gushed when he walked in, saying quite sincerely how excited she was to meet him, and I think this helped get the meeting off in a warm mood. It might also account for the mugs and T-shirts we received when the interview was over!)

I began by explaining my project and by sharing vignettes of the children's recess radio play and relevant composing events. Although the children could certainly have learned songs from many sources, the vignettes clearly suggested that DJ's and Kris's radio station and, more particularly, their program was a significant source.

DJ, a personable young man, African American and from the East Bay, seemed both pleased and startled at the notion of 6-year-old fans. ("Scary!" is an exact quote.) He was "amazed" at how the children could get into "the rhythm, the rhyme, the count" of a recurrent program rap.

I commented that rhythm and rhyme are traditional parts of children's playground fare. And when I began to quote an illustrative verse, DJ joined in!

> ANNE: Mama's in the kitchen cooking rice—
> DJ: Daddy's outside, shooting dice. . . . Are [the kids] Black? [Anne affirms.] Oh. Ok. That's uh—
> KRIS: (producer, also African American) I have never heard of those.
>
> . . .
>
> DJ: You grew up in the suburbs, didn't you?
> KRIS: No I didn't. (indignantly) I grew up in Chicago.
>
> . . .
>
> DJ: We rocked the robin the whole time! (The "Mama's in the kitchen . . ." lines, as readers may recall from Chapter 2 if not from their own childhoods, are from the children's version of "Rockin' Robin".)
>
> . . .
>
> KRIS: The kids must be getting it from their parents. [Anne negates.] Then where are they getting it from?
> DJ: From their brothers and sisters. You got to know the rhyme!

Knowing the rhymes, I said, might contribute to the children's attraction to the rhythmic, rhyming poetry they heard at school and, at the same time, to the rhythmic, rhyming musical fare they heard on the radio. Nonetheless, as DJ himself said, there's something about 6-year-olds and some of that radio fare that's "scary" (even though adults might find some of that traditional playground lore pretty scary, too [Sutton-Smith, Mechling, Johnson, & McMahon, 1995]). Sometimes, I noted (silently recalling the parents' concerns), when I looked up the songs' lyrics, my hair stood "on its ends" (quite a sight to see).

Kris replied that she felt that the children did learn the songs' hooks because they easily picked up rhythmic language. Moreover, she continued, it matters that they see other kids picking up the language, too (and Kris was so right, I thought, as she continued). "It is monkey see, monkey do. And that's why they want to hear this stuff. *And* it's so catchy."

Based on his own childhood experiences, DJ felt that some songs that I might react to (like the one about "my baby's daddy" [see Chapter 2]) probably reflected harsh realities in even young children's lives. He thought that the kids probably knew older girls with babies and no mates (and I mentally flashed back to Marcel and Wenona's play lives, in which they had to babysit friends' kids, a complication of their team schedule demands). Young kids, he thought, also knew or had heard of people in jail, and they knew drugs were a common youth problem (all of which was true of the brothers and sisters).

Nonetheless, DJ and Kris both felt that some of the material, to use Vanessa's previously quoted words, was "too fast" for young children, whom they saw as "tender," precious, impressionable, and capable of picking up words from anyone and anywhere. DJ told with pleasure a vignette about his lunch date with a friend's 3-year-old daughter; that child had responded to his inquiry about her drink preference with "Actually I already brought my own drink." He loved that "actually," evoking in his voice her self-assured confidence. He used that story to connect with our theme of children "picking up"—appropriating and recontextualizing—"catchy" language from appealing others.

Perhaps because they themselves did not have children, DJ and Kris were more confident that they could control the radio dial than the children's parents had been. "If I had a 6-year-old," they each said, the child "wouldn't be listening" to their radio station. They had not yet tried to control the sounds young children hear in homes and cars, in which people of different ages share a constrained air space, a space filled with ease by radios and other music technology. They hadn't yet grappled with children participating in other private and public places where they overhear others' musical pleasures—homes of friends and relatives, public transportation, parks, laundromats—indeed, the streets themselves.

DJ and Kris stressed that their show was for teenagers and young adults (which, most certainly, the brothers and sisters understood). That target audience, like station executives, expected the "risque" to wake them up in the morning. Still, DJ and Kris were aware that people of different ages, especially "kids" (if not 6-year-olds) listened. Kids whom DJ did not even know greeted him by name on the street. And, like Coach, both he and Kris stressed that corporate desires shaped the productions they offered the public.

"The executives who own the radio stations are really into it for profit," said Kris, and "they don't think about children" at all. But she thought the breakfast club did try for some balance, and DJ agreed:

> For us on radio, you—you have to do risque things to hook the
> adult audience sometimes, because they want to laugh and they
> want to be shocked and they want to have something to talk about
> but . . . we try to offer a balance. But I don't think it's important for
> most radio stations to offer that balance.

Because we had listened to the morning show, and Soyoung had transcribed several shows (to Kris and DJ's amusement), we had documented evidence of this attempt at "balance." There were disclaimers when upcoming segments were "not for tender ears." There were public service announcements (e.g., about child vaccination needs) and community events. To balance language that made light of recreational drugs and drinking, DJ made comments about being "into living healthy and staying healthy." He commented to us about language degrading to women and its presence on certain raps hyped by record companies; like their sports media counterparts, record companies have been seen as pushing the most aggressive, and the most materialistically extravagant rappers (for an education-focused- and hip-hop-informed discussion of rap, gender, and record companies, see Adewole-Jimenez, Adewole-Jimenez, & Ucelli, 1994).

And yet, I had never heard the children replay any balancing attempts in their radio play. That play was about being a singing star and being introduced, interviewed, and generally loved. And it was about the sheer pleasure of voices in motion and of manipulating sound.

Acknowledging this, DJ's comments became similar to those of the parents. Even though he was more optimistic about parental powers to control the radio dial than were the actual parents, he would not "try to hide things from my 6-year-old. But I definitely would turn the channel if the song came on that was somehow [sexually explicit]. But then again, I don't have any children yet." Moreover, as children grew older, he felt popular music could stimulate useful talk, if parents paid attention to what their kids paid attention to:

> [Children's music listening] almost forces you to raise your child, and, you know, I think it's things [i.e., lyrics perceived as derogatory or risque] that they're going to learn on the street anyway. You'd rather your child learn it from you first, because if they talk on the street they're going to feel like they already know, and chances are they're going to misunderstand . . . You got to grow with your children, you know, you got to go through what they experience. I don't think it's good to avoid these, you know, issues, you know, but I think you got to be selective, exercise discretion.

Also like the parents, DJ and Kris discussed children's need to develop a critical consciousness. In my own study of the children's efforts, I had focused primarily on how children reframed the materials of popular culture as they became participants in school literacy. In their talk with me, the parents reframed those materials in the light of children's participation in families and family discourse about values. As media professionals, DJ and Kris reframed them in the light of children's participation as media-savvy consumers.

For example, Kris felt that children should know about how media celebrities perform even when they are not singing. She felt that, since the 1960s, production companies had abandoned efforts to educate media stars themselves in the "social graces"; neither companies nor stars seemed as adept at presenting professional images of popular artists. Moreover, she felt that many kids were not aware of the financial and business aspects of the music business, which are essential for commercial success. In her words,

> There are a lot of people who are business [people] and entrepreneurs that, because of stereotypical viewpoints, you look at them and you don't think that they understand, that they have weight in the business world . . . [K]ids don't understand. They see them with the rings and money and the clothes and the gold around the neck, but they don't understand that, "I put my money away too, I've got—I own this business here . . . my 401 [retirement plan] is already worked out."

Kris felt that teachers should invite radio station people to schools to talk with kids about the business aspects of music. DJ agreed. He thought that through information and talk about these aspects children might gain a greater "political consciousness" about the music itself. Children should know, he thought, that business interests—marketing decisions and the desire to hook a certain population segment—influence which songs one hears the most. As DJ explained, "Just because it is a hit record, it's the record that you hear the most, what they are singing is not right." (And, as he spoke, I remembered Marcel's mom's revoicing of her words to her children: "Do you think that everybody thinks like that [i.e., like that singer apparently does]? What is your opinion? Because my opinion is . . .")

DJ felt, in fact, that local heroes of all kinds, known to the children through the media, should come and talk to kids. In this way, kids might gain more realistic understandings of their longed-for careers and, also, of their heroes' opinions about language and lifestyle. As he was talking, I thought that, if DJ, Kris, and Coach were any indication, this might indeed be possible and, perhaps, it might also make more salient the presence of children in the consciousness of popular culture professionals with a sense of community responsibility. There were responsive people willing to talk about the children in their audiences, even if the children were not so visible, surrounded by the bulk and volume of adults and youth.

The parents, the coach, the radio personalities, all felt that children, in the end, cannot be separated off from family and community joys and troubles. This is a stance that, some feel, may be particularly important in the African American tradition, since the harshness of a racist world has permeated the lives of the very young (as seen in the folk art and commentary of Bessie Jones, cited throughout this book [Jones & Hawes, 1972]).

Indeed, my informants appreciated, and shared in, children's pleasures with sports and music. They felt that adults do have to "exercise discretion," as DJ said—to be selective about textual toys that seem too unwieldy, too harsh, too raw to be made sense of by young children. But the children will pick up appealing toys anyway. And then adults should not close their own ears, but listen to what children have made of the experience, providing them the security of a sense of agency and of critical consciousness. Children may appropriate adults' own strong, encouraging words to help them become more secure in their capacity to cope, to negotiate their way in a world of complicated voices.

Children's Animation: Kids Playing with Marketable Stories

Even though the sports and radio professionals did not necessarily conceive of children in their audiences, they were connected to the local community, and they saw the power of their work in the greetings they received from people on the street. The local media personnel, however, did not seem to be on the street. Indeed, they seemed to be in modern fortresses; their front-desk people referred all comers to web sites, full of just what the public needed to know. Soyoung and Sheila's efforts to secure us an interview left them feeling like spies come in from the cold (or, in the Bay Area, the cool) to make off with the latest images.

We were in luck, however. A graduate student in one of my classes had a brother who had been a professional writer for 25 years. This brother (hereafter referred to as "Pen") was currently writing scripts for children's animation. Best of all, he was quite willing to talk with us (for which willingness some thanks must go to his sister). Unlike DJ and Coach, Pen, a Jewish American, had no particular links to the African American community in the East Bay, and his specific productions were not mentioned by the brothers and sisters. Still, I was anxious to talk with a professional writer for children's animation. I wondered what a person with such expertise might see when he looked at the children's efforts.

Pen, who was based in Los Angeles, could not come to us, and vice versa. And so, late one weekday evening, Soyoung, Pen, and I used the technological wizardry of faxes and conference calls to huddle around the children's products. (We went low-tech in our own recording of the event, however, using notes rather than a tape recorder.) As in all interviews with adult informants, I explained my project and shared vignettes, especially those highlighting Noah's use of animation-based textual toys during composing time.

Unlike Coach, Kris, and DJ, Pen was not surprised that the children made use of the symbolic material of animated media; in contrast to the others, he was involved in production work that was marketed specifically to children. Nonetheless, Pen was impressed: "I think [Noah's] great." (As with the other adult informants, it is possible that my pleasure influenced his. And if this is so, it's instructive that an inquisitive but enthused stance can spread.) Situating Noah's efforts within his professional frame, Pen equated Noah's repeated drawing of objects in motion to "classic animation" production, which dominated before computer graphics become common. In the classic style, each of Noah's basketballs or bullets would be separately framed in a "cell" so as, collectively and sequentially, to convey movement. (For an example of Noah's objects-in-motion, see Figure 5.3.)

Pen's own compositional challenges in negotiating symbolic boundaries were "exactly the opposite" of Noah's, as he explained. Pen produced the script first, anticipating but not in control of the eventual and literal drawing board. Noah drew first and then sputtered out an official framed text; he was faced with the challenge of somehow transforming visual imagery into linear graphics.

Besides the symbolic challenges of multimedia composition, Noah faced some social and ideological challenges of authoring. Pen *did* identify with these challenges. Just as Noah had seemed sensitive to official appropriateness (e.g., transforming his drawn and dramatized shooting gun into a named water gun for official purposes), Pen also changed his story and renamed certain actions for his equivalent of the official world—that is, for his employers, the production companies.

Many of these changes involved budgetary concerns. For example, Pen might have written 12 alien invaders, but the company might feel that building 3-dimensional computer models for so many characters was too expensive. Other changes, however, involved the production company's sense of public sensitivities. For example, "We can't use the word 'shoot,' but instead we have to use words like 'blast'—or not 'guns' but 'laser devices' and such." As these sensitivities change, the adventure stories for children metamorphose into new versions of familiar tales (scholars of children's culture have discussed this phenomenon experienced in the particular by Pen; see Kline, 1993).

The same corporate desires for marketable products could also work against efforts for creative and critical change in children's media (another

phenomenon discussed in the literature; see Stern & Schoenhaus, 1990).
Pen had a friend who wanted to transform the typical "boy superhero"
story into one for girls. Her own husband's production company would
not make it because the board of directors felt it lacked commercial potential. Moreover, said Pen, many decisions about characters are toy-driven.
So characters might change, not to develop new kinds of media friends
for society's children, but to keep a fresh market of toys (e.g., action figures) for child consumers.

Unlike Coach, Kris, and DJ, Pen never responded to the brothers' and
sisters' composing with any particular concerns about their textual toys.
Perhaps this is because Pen was more removed than those others: he was
not a member of the local community; the children were not engaged with
any particular product linked to his own efforts. Just as likely, though, is
that Pen was a self-described "pragmatist." He viewed negotiating symbolic, social, and ideological tensions as an inevitable part of the collaborative nature of media production work. He wanted to write *good* stories
that *sold*.

Pen was pragmatic, too, when I asked about his view of media material in the classroom. He commented that any kind of text, multimedia or
otherwise, was a potential source of information. He thought humor in
particular was important: "Anything that can get the point across, anything that's ever made us laugh, we [as learners] would remember." Moreover, Pen knew of the professional skill and potential pleasure involved
in all story composing, whatever the medium. He had visited elementary
classrooms to teach children about crafting characters and about the problem solving through which characters grow.

Slipping back temporarily now to my more familiar vantage point
alongside the children, it seems to me that the brothers and sisters were
pragmatists, too. All of the children wanted to do well in school and, at the
same time, to play and enjoy themselves. They recontextualized their cultural resources as they deemed relevant within new school events. In so
doing, symbolic, social, and ideological tensions could arise as unofficial and
official practices coexisted, converged, clashed, and even were differentiated. The social and ideological matters were not add-ons to literacy learning processes; they were as inevitably a part of children's crafting of texts
in school as they were of Pen's crafting for the production companies.

Summary: On Hooking Children

Coach, DJ and Kris, and Pen were particular individuals, but there were
commonalities in their responses to my vignettes about the brothers and
sisters. They all framed their responses within their opportunities and con-

straints as employees of corporations. Although the commercial enterprises for which they worked are major influences on children's lives, those enterprises aim to entertain and to sell, not to provide intellectual, social, or emotional guidance. All cultural experts assumed the bulk of such guidance for children would come, primarily, from private households but also from public schools. (For discussions of the relationships between these institutions and childhoods, see Liljestrom, 1981; Seiter, 1993, 1999; Zipes, 2000).

Coach, DJ, and Kris were involved with entertainment media marketed to particular segments of the regional population. Thus, as members of Bay Area families and neighborhoods, the brothers and sisters participated in sports media; as daughters, sons, and siblings, they were attracted to the catchy musical stuff that brought pleasure to loved ones. Pen was involved with media marketed particularly to children. The brothers and sisters enjoyed cartoon and other media fare as "kids," but other family members could find themselves joining in on the perceived fun (which Denise's mom reported doing).

The comments of the cultural experts blend with ease into the thematic threads of this book. In using diverse cultural materials, children were indexing their generational, familial, community, and cultural memberships. These materials were constitutive of their sense of themselves and their own possibilities for joyful participation. When they were recontextualized in school literacy practices, these same materials inevitably gave rise to symbolic, social, and ideological tensions. Such tensions are, no doubt, present too for all community members who aim to figure out how to engage, protect, support, and enjoy the children in their midst. Among such community members are teachers like Rita, the last of the adult voices to be featured herein, aside from my own.

THE TEACHER: "OPENING UP" CHILDREN'S WORLDS

Rita and I had talked informally throughout the project, if just through my quick phone calls to confirm her plans, check on a field trip day, or inquire about an absent child. One day, however, after data collection had ended, I visited Rita after school for a more formal interview. As she cleaned off the board and sorted out materials, I asked about her professional history and her teaching goals; along the way, we both recalled classroom events to clarify ideas.

In fundamental ways, Rita's vision for an ideal curriculum complemented the parents' desires for their children. As they did, she put great emphasis on children as decision makers, purposefully and critically involved in the world around them. As she explained:

When I say "[the] basics" [of what school should teach] I don't
really mean just write the alphabet and the numbers. I'm talking
about the basic skills of how to be a learner. . . . I don't think
people . . . realize that the basic skills—that there are so many more
of them than that. I've got kids that I wonder how—how do they
see themselves in school? What do they think it's all about? . . .
Kids have to be helped to be involved in their own learning and
[to] make choices and decisions at least part of the time.

Unlike the parents, Rita did not stress the constraints of her physical
reach. She stressed the constraints of her place in the educational bureau-
cracy. That is, like the cultural experts, Rita situated her comments within
the possibilities and tensions of her professional life.

As a public school teacher, Rita was responsible to her students, but
also to her school, her district, the state educational bureaucracies and,
moreover, to the public. And within local and state politics (not to mention national politics) there was at the time of the project (and continuing
now) an intense focus on children perceived to be at risk of failing to become literate. The children so perceived were predominantly children of
working-class and poor families and, also, children of color. And accompanying this focus on children was a focus on public school teachers, perceived as failing to properly teach "the basics."

And by "the basics," the state curricular guidelines *did* mean "sounds,
letters, and numbers." The California Reading/Language Arts Framework
(California Department of Education, 1998) stressed that the foundational
skill for first-grade instruction was "language at the phoneme level" (p. 45),
that is, at the level of the sounds of the language. However, although
kindergartners were to form "upper and lowercase letters" and use "their
knowledge of letters and sounds to write words," first graders were to write
"sentences." By second grade, students were to write "paragraphs," and
by third, "paragraphs with topic sentences" (p. 31). (I'm not at all sure what
the framework would do with Godzilla-inspired stories, hip-hop snippets,
sports reports, Looney Tunes symbols, written insults, and fake personal
experience narratives.)

Given such a framework and, moreover, its context of public discourse
about failing schools and of state legislative action designed to mandate
"the basics" (see Asimov, 1996; Diegmueller, 1995; Gunnison, 1996; Manzo,
1997; Taylor, 1998), Rita felt uneasy. In her view, there was a feeling of
tension among the district's teachers, although less at her current school
than at others of which she knew.

As readers may recall from Chapter 3, Rita's emphasis on children
making decisions was evident in her approach to the arts. Rita's use of the

arts was a matter of professional conviction and personal energy, since the district and state's elementary arts program was a tenuous matter and had been so since 1978 when a state property tax action drastically reduced funding for the schools and thus for the arts (according to a district administrator). Moreover, Rita felt that, throughout her career, from London in the 1960s through the Bay Area in the 1990s, she had participated in conversations, debates, even arguments about how the arts related to "the basics." She did not accept the notion that, if teachers were interested in integrating the arts and themes of study (like space and freedom) throughout the curriculum, "that meant it [the curriculum] wasn't the basic skills [including sounds, letters, and numbers]."

Given the current tensions, however, children drawing, painting, talking, and writing, and moreover, engaging in imagining new planets and constructing robots; making freedom posters; examining poems, songs, and paintings; pretending to be silkworms and space invaders—all could seem, interestingly enough, to be evidence of a teacher failing to concentrate on what matters. As Rita explained, in the view of some teachers, "the reason [some kids weren't learning to read] . . . was that we [teachers interested in the arts] were the people not doing it [i.e., not helping the kids read]."

Still, Rita had supportive teacher friends and colleagues, and she had not lost her belief in the importance of the arts and of children being decision-making members of a "classroom family." Take, for example, her perspective on her student Wenona. In Rita's view, Wenona was one of those kids who is "not badly behaved" but also not connected or committed to the learning activities of the classroom. She was a child oh so active with her friends, but also one who would stare straight ahead (or lounge against a fake sibling) as Rita went through the "message of the day," a spelling or alphabet activity, or a discussion of one book or another. I had been present in the classroom when Rita, very pleased, had pointed out the eager intensity with which Wenona had participated in a series of reading and writing tasks; that participation had culminated in Wenona's loud, confident reading of the "Julie robot" piece during sharing time (see Chapter 5) and, moreover, in her attention to others' reading. In Rita's view, Wenona had invested in that robot, making decisions about its material construction, its appearance, and its qualities, even discussing her robot plans with her ("real") mother; and Wenona *wanted* to write and read about it with and for the class.

As Rita talked, I remembered my own angled vision on Wenona's involvement—how Wenona had appropriated the name of a cinematic teammate from Coach Bombay's team, how she had worked on her spelling with her fake sibling Noah before pulling him into a "Mama" game, and how both Wenona and Noah had worked to enact a dynamic and reciprocal relationship. If Rita's official activities were problematic in the light of "the basics," what about the children's responses to those activities? Their symbolic and textual resources were most definitely not sequentially ordered according to patterns of sound/symbol relations, sentence types, or selected genres, as the framework recommended. And the development evidenced in their official participation (e.g., a more deliberate planning of text beyond the usual routine phrases, the use of taught spelling strategies, the anticipation of audience response) was interrelated with their unofficial participation as fake siblings.

Recalling Wenona's robot activities with Rita, I asked her explicitly how she felt about the media texts the children brought to their school work—the movies, the cartoon characters, the songs. Like the parents, the radio personalities, and the coach, Rita respected the children's knowledge and know-how, and she voiced reservations about certain ideological content of the material. Also like the parents, she was straightforward and explicit about her views of what was inappropriate for school, particularly any images that glorified violence and any language that belittled others, individuals or groups (e.g., racist, sexist, or homophobic labels). Rita also expected the children to discuss such issues:

> If they [the children] don't know what that are saying [e.g., through song lyrics], they need to know. . . . I don't say it [my objection] wimpy. I mean, I'm *strong* about it. And then I make sure that it's [the situation, but never the named child parties involved] part of [i.e., a topic of] a discussion somewhere.

Rita also felt that part of her role was to broaden children's access to cultural art forms. Again consistent with the parents, and with my own data, Rita noted that children "are pretty open at this stage"; for example, they sing varied kinds of songs "with just as much enthusiasm." So Rita aimed to take advantage of this openness to art forms. In her view, an appreciation of, and participation in, the arts was a means for involving children as learners, for widening their involvement with artistic voices and, moreover, for deepening relationships between members of the classroom family:

> I think it makes for [a classroom family] that the kids learn to respect and like other kids because of something they've offered that's really memorable, like a song, or a poem, or an art project, or a dance.

Through allowing and, indeed, expecting children to make decisions, to communicate with others, and to craft their ideas through varied symbolic media, Rita worked toward a classroom family of committed learners, thoughtful colleagues, and responsible social actors. These ambitions were served by, not in conflict with, careful guidance and monitoring of the children's learning of the mandated, if unambitious, state basics.

THE RESEARCHER: MAKING SPACE FOR CHILDREN IN CHILDHOOD LITERACY

> If the child's modes of agency and response were simply isomorphic with or containable by *any* cultural construction of "childhood" [or "literacy," I add] real learning would never take place. What we would get instead would be stereotypic and ritualized behavior or, more likely, autistic behavior. . . . [Our theories of development] leave out . . . that most obvious feature of children—their extraordinary creativity, orneriness, and wit. (Wartofsky, 1983, p. 200)

Rita, the parents, the popular culture experts, all negotiated the possibilities and limits of their responsibilities to adult institutions, to their ideals, and to the young. Thus, the young (the brothers and sisters) constructed their childhoods within the communicative spaces, and with the technological artifacts, offered by adults in a complex of social spheres—families, economic marketplaces, and public institutions.

But, of course, a theme of this book has been that children are not so easily controlled by adults. Indeed, the very diversity of organized social spaces (e.g., families, schools, media events, not to mention those organized by the children themselves) mitigate against unilateral control. As the brothers and sisters demonstrated, on the turn of a word, or an accidental slip of the tongue, children are off into communicative and social spaces no one could quite predict, playing with textual toys no one deliberately purchased for their use, and transforming many a carefully planned curricular plot line into a collage of blending and clashing literacy practices and materials. And so it should be.

As the historian and philosopher Wartofsky suggested in the above quote, if adults were successful, and children simply did as they were told, no learning would happen (cf. Genishi, 1997). Learning, and especially learning a symbol system, requires the constructive mental action of an intentional human being anxious to take some control, to exercise some will in a world of others. In this project, children's willfulness—and their "creativity, [occasional] orneriness, and wit"—was realized in the particular ways in which the brothers and sisters engaged with the world around them, including the official school spaces.

In designing official spaces, Rita said she thought more about "uncovering the curriculum" for the children than "covering it." As Rita uncovered the curriculum through her bookend activities and spaces for the language and visual arts, the children entered those activities and communicative spaces with a diversity of symbolic and cultural materials. And I, as observer and researcher, thus gained access to the complex dialectic between official and unofficial worlds in Rita's class.

To understand that dialectic, I too had "to grow with my children," as DJ said. I learned about their worlds and stretched my own. I followed Marcel, as he linked football teams, geographic sites, and the paths of tornadoes and, thereby, home, school, and peer worlds, not to mention media experiences of varied kinds. I sat beside Denise and Vanessa, one minute inside the official study of space, the next inadvertently tapping my foot to a singing space mama with radio antennae. I watched Noah as he wrote about a little bear and drew about a little monkey, entangling himself in textual threads indexing different symbolic and social worlds. The children's lively intelligence, flexible playfulness, and sometimes exuberant inclusiveness—of cultural art forms, each other, and "everybody else" too (see Figure 8.1)—could never be contained within the staged portrayal of a pastoral childhood with which this book began.

As I now prepare to close this book, I consider again my own authorial intentions. I have wanted to place center stage in literacy research childhoods themselves and children's localized symbols and practices—in the present case, those of a small group of Bay Area kids. I have aimed to write against accounts of literacy learning that associate school success with a narrow range of social and textual experiences.

But I, of course, am aware of the limits of my own agency, no less than were the other adult participants in the children's lives. I am privileged to give voice herein to my intentions, but any utterance can fail to sound if it has no communicative space within which to reverberate. Lately the limits of available space have been much in my thoughts, as it is yet again a new school year and the familiar neighborhood tales of school success are finding their way into local papers and radio talk shows.

In these familiar tales, that achievement gap that Rita mentioned assumes center stage, dichotomizing children according to the geography of the local terrain. The tales locate successful children primarily in the Eastside area of the city, where relatively affluent European American families dominate; they locate unsuccessful children primarily in the Westside, where less affluent families of color dominate. Eastside children, as school statistics document, have headed for the private schools, severely

Figure 8.1. "I love every [ave] body [btty]."

affecting the state funding available to the schools (since state funding is distributed according to number of children that the district serves).

This year, as in others, human interest stories in the local papers feature an Eastside mother agonizing over the decision to do the "right thing" as a citizen and support the local schools and the "right thing" as a parent and find a private school filled with children deemed like her own; in the latter school, children who are "eager to soar" will not be grounded as teachers and resources accrue to the "at-risk" children (quotations from a local paper).

As this discourse spreads its way through newsprint and airwaves, I think about the city's alert children, eavesdropping on adult voices. Although children have some basis for categorizing the textual stuff of entertainment (e.g., a sense of what is "just play" or "too fast" for 6-year-olds), I do not know what children are to make of this talk, which surely they must overhear.

Perhaps, I speculate, this discourse contributed to the competitive talk about literacy of the local neighborhood children in Rita's room (see Chapter 3). Perhaps it contributed to the resistance of such talk by the brothers and sisters and their friends. In any case, as children grow older in this city, they may more explicitly articulate racial stereotypes about school success (Rubin, 2001), and children of color may more explicitly articulate a tension between peer relations and school achievement (Christianakis, 2002; Rubin, 2001).

And yet, Rita's children had experiences to counter such discourse, and they had Rita herself, who worked against narrow conceptions of school "smartness" and stereotypes of race. The children whom Rita perceived as most in need of help with literacy details, like letters and sounds, *were* from a Westside neighborhood—but, then, so were most of the children she perceived as being the least in need. Moreover, with Rita's instruction, augmented as it was by children revoicing her literacy advice to each other, children did learn those traditional skills and *so* much more; this would not have happened if the children who had been worried about had had their literacy experiences confined to a sequence of letter, then word, then sentence skills and, thus, had no official access to experience with extended texts of varied kinds (Allington, 1983; Cazden, 1988; Dreeben & Barr, 1988). Further, in academic discussions and artful explorations of silkworms, space, and freedom, there were no evident geographic (i.e., interrelated social class, race, and culture) differences in the quality of children's participation. As Rita told the children, "Everybody's good in this class at thinking."

My own professional voice herein, then, is not a thin one, located in isolated human experience. Its very existence is dependent on experiences in Rita's classroom and, before that, in experiences with many teachers who pay attention to children's worlds, teachers who guide children's involvement in actively participating in communicative practices for producing, performing, comparing, and critiquing texts. Perhaps there is no reason to slip into melodrama, allowing so much discursive control to voices that neatly categorize children and literacy.

Moreover, as I continue in this dialogic mood, that personal voice of mine is filled with the borrowed words, not only of other authors in my parentheses, but also of those teachers, in person (e.g., Celia Genishi, Julie

Jensen, Judith Lindfors, Doug Foley) and print (e.g., Jimmy Britton, Marie Clay, Geneva Smitherman), who helped me find useful words years ago.

And most certainly it has echoes of a mother's voice to a small child not yet 6, weeping the night before her first day at school, her first day in first grade, her first venturing alone into a new town's public institution, weeks after the town's children had started school. This child's brother, my brother, had told me that in first grade one had to read. What was I going to do, he asked, since I couldn't read? Well, I was going to cry. Loudly.

My mother, hearing the commotion I was causing, found my brother and me and asked what on earth was the matter. "I can't read," I wailed. I do remember wailing. My brother, as I would like to remember this scene, looked guilty. "Oh stop it," my mother said. "That's why you're going to school. The teacher's supposed to teach you." I stopped crying. And I learned to read and to write, too.

My mother once lamented (after a spate of read-to-your-child public service announcements) that she didn't read to her kids. But my mother did *much* more important things. Most relevant to this book, she taught me that I had the right stuff to learn, and that public institutions have responsibilities to respectfully serve its citizens, including the most powerless, the young.

The brothers and sisters had the right stuff to learn, too, as their textual adventures herein attest. I hope that, as they have and continue to move on from that lovely time when I was their "fake mama," no one teaches them any different.

Conventions Used in Transcripts

(abc)   Parentheses enclosing text contain notes, usually about contextual and nonverbal information (e.g., turns to me, looks at map).

[abc]   Brackets contain explanatory information inserted into quotations by me, rather than by the speaker.

A-B-C   Capitalized letters separated by hyphens indicate that letters were spoken or words were spelled aloud by the speaker.

ABC   A capitalized word or phrase indicates increased volume.

abc   An underlined word indicates a stressed word.

/   A single slashed line inserted into a speaking turn indicates the end of a verse line (i.e., a rhythmic break), e.g.,

> VANESSA: 1, 2, 3/The devil's after me

/c/   Parallel slashed lines indicate that the speaker made the sound of the enclosed letter or letters.

//abc//   Pairs of parallel slashed lines indicate overlapping speech, for example,

> MARCEL: And my football game is at night. . . . We gotta play at Arizona, Texas, San Fran//cisco//—
> WENONA: //cisco// um Stockton. That's a long way. . . . Now, how we kids gonna do our homework?

c: A colon after a letter indicates that the sound of the letter was elongated. The more colons, the greater was the elongation.

...   An ellipsis indicates omitted data; an ellipsis between ut-
             terances indicates one or more omitted speaking turns, for
             example,

        WENONA: I'm gonna look at your CD player.

        ...

          NOAH: CD player! It got—it got bad words on it.

Conventional punctuation marks are used to indicate ends of utterances
or sentence, usually indicated by slight pauses on the audiotape. Com-
mas indicate pauses within words or phrases. Dashes indicate interrupted
utterances.

Demographic Tables

Table B.1. Sex and Ethnicity of Rita's Children

	Ethnicity
Girls (*n* = 7)	
April	Asian/European American
Denise	African American
Elizabeth	European American
Lakeisha	African American
Nanette	European American
Vanessa	African American
Wenona	African American
Boys (*n* = 13)	
Cedric	African American
Denny	European American
Don	European American
Eddie	African American
Jamal	African American
John	African American
Marcel	African American
Noah	African American
Robert	African American
Ron	European American
Samuel	African/Asian American
Tommy	European American
Zephenia	African American

Table B.2. Economic Situation of Families in Two Sample Census Tracts

	Family Mean Income ($)	*Median Value of Housing ($)*
NE tract	90,845	359,600
SW tract	33,512	156,600

Note. From 1990 Census.

Table B.3. Racial Composition of City, School District, Project School, and Two Sample Census Tracts

	White (%)	*Black (%)*	*Asian/ Pacific Islander (%)*	*Hispanic (%)*	*Native American (%)*	*Other (%)*
City	58.8	18.3	14.5	7.8	0.4	0.2
School district (K-12)	34.1	41.9	9.5	13.2	0.4	0.9
Project school	37.2	47.7	6.4	4.9	1.5	2.2
NE tract	87.3	3.1	6.5	2.7	0	0.4
SW tract	14.7	70.3	6.0	8.3	0.5	0.1

Note. City percentages are based on the 1990 Census data for California. School district and project school percentages are from the 1996-1997 school year database prepared by the California Department of Education. The criteria for these racial and ethnic categories may vary across sources.

Notes

CHAPTER 1

1. Lakeisha was pulled from the classroom throughout the day for tutoring and counseling support. Despite her recognized atypical behavior (e.g., she spent periods of time rocking and sucking her thumb), she was an accepted group member—"She's just like that," to quote Vanessa. Rita also included Lakeisha in all instructional activities whenever she was present in the room; on no occasion did Rita excuse Lakeisha from tasks or neglect to monitor her participation. By mid-second grade, Rita reported (and I subsequently observed), Lakeisha had learned to read.

CHAPTER 2

1. There is a complex relationship between childhood rhymes and youth songs, especially rap. In Cooper's (1989) discussion of the broad sweep of contemporary music, he argues that adolescents are drawn to music that incorporates childhood rhymes and tales. Perhaps recontextualizing that material in new thematic contexts marks their own distinct passage from childhood, just as youth music seemed to mark the observed children's passage from "preschooler" status.

Rap music has particularly complex relationships to childhood verse. Davey D (Cook, 1985) briefly chronicles rap's immediate roots in party emceeing in the West Bronx. In his account, deejays initially acknowledged party goers by name, and these acknowledgments evoked the crowd's own shouts of names and slogans. Deejays, to mark their distinctive skill, used rhymes in their acknowledgments and "began drawing upon outdated dozens and school yard rhymes" (p. 2).

Rapping is a verbal skill with roots in the oral traditions of African American culture. However, according to Rose (1989), rapping itself is a hybrid, part of literate as well as oral traditions. Unlike childhood's oral verse traditions, raps foreground individual authorship of complexly constructed lyrics that are written and then performed. Intertextually they recontextualize material from many African American musical traditions, among them soul and gospel, far beyond children's rhymes.

CHAPTER 4

1. Marcel based his spellings on visual memory as well as sound analysis; he read "gets" for his written *gots* and "was" for his written *were*.

CHAPTER 5

1. In the cartoon featuring Godzilla, 30 to 45 seconds may go by with no character using words, as opposed to noises, to communicate with others. Any dialogue is primarily in the service of action. For example, "That monster is headed right toward our ship!" "Call Godzilla! It's our only hope!" "There must be a fierce battle going on down there." "Ok, Godzuky. Go see." "Thanks, Godzilla!"

2. Noah associated Donkey Kong with video games, and Little Bear with books. However, Noah told me that Donkey Kong was also in books and magazines, which is true. Little Bear, on the other hand, has his own cartoon and videos. Noah made no reference to those media forms of Little Bear during his first-grade year, although he did watch the channel that carries the cartoon. Such transmedia intertextuality is common in children's media (Kinder, 1991).

CHAPTER 6

1. A communicative practice is not a rigid determiner of participants' behavior. It is a potential way of producing meaning, shaped by formal symbol systems, by the existent social situation, and by participants' strategic improvisation (Hanks, 1996). In the "What I learned about space" example, Denise's responsiveness is not sustained and guided by a shared understanding of the overriding purpose of this event, at least from Rita's point of view: to recount one's learning.

2. Eloise Greenfield consistently renders child interests, including sports and music, in literary form. Indeed, during the project year, she published a poetic book about the human spirit, featuring Michael Jordan: *For the Love of the Game: Michael Jordan and Me* (Greenfield, 1997). In her works, the themes of children's play with popular music—themes of love, money, and power—are rendered in children's presents, not their imagined futures. Moreover, she uses a remarkable range of voices. Her book *Honey, I Love* (1978) includes a poem with the powerful, aggressive voice of "Harriet Tubman," who "didn't take no stuff," the playful voice of the child narrator telling "Honey [what] I love," and that same narrator's firm voice as she recalls her father's message: "Love don't mean all that kissing like on TV."

3. In the African American verbal tradition, "capping" is putting somebody down in a verbally humorous way, either in fun or in earnest. See Smitherman (1994) for a precise definition.

Glossary

ANIMATION

Cartoon characters mentioned by the children, all found in Looney Tunes cartoons and featured in the movie *Space Jam*, include:

Bugs Bunny. A clever and charming hare, known to play tricks and get himself into trouble with other unassuming Looney Tunes characters.
Lola Bunny. A vivacious bunny who is a talented basketball player and the object of Bugs Bunny's affection.
Taz(manian) Devil. A hairy creature, particularly fond of rabbits for food; he devours boulders, shrubbery, and nearly everything in sight as he moves around like a whirling tornado.

MUSIC

Music Genres, neither sharply delineated nor mutually exclusive, that figure into this project include:

Folk. Includes folk songs and playground rhymes.
 Folk songs. Initially a label for songs reflecting a local or national feeling, passed down through oral tradition; in the 60s, "modern" folk music was composed by contemporary singer-songwriters, like Pete Seeger.
 Playground rhymes (play rhymes). Chants to accompany jumping, stomping, and clapping games; passed through the generations by children themselves.
Gospel. Christian religious music. Black gospel music, with its soulful sound and marked rhythm, draws on traditional spirituals handed down from slavery times. Rita's class was familiar with Sweet Honey in the Rock, an African American female a capella group that sings gospel as well as jazz and blues.

The glossary was prepared by Soyoung Lee and Sheila Shea. Among the sources Lee and Shea consulted were Ammer (1995), Hollander (2000), Leonard (1993), and "Coach" (see Chapter 8).

Hip-hop. A label encompassing the social and cultural bearings of the urban youth lifestyle; inclusive of rap, breakdancing, urban graffiti, and fashion.

Hymns. religious songs, expressing praise or love of God, sung in various Christian churches.

Jazz. A genre marked by improvisation and group interplay; developed in the early 1900s in the southern United States from earlier African American music, including the blues and ragtime. Rita's class was familiar with the late jazz artist Ella Fitzgerald and the current Joshua Redman, a graduate of the local public schools.

Rap. Hip-hop's musical genre; originated in New York City in the 1970s when deejays improvised lyrics over recorded dance music and broadcast the results using transportable sound systems. Now a global phenomenon, rap has varied subgenres, all associated with a percussive beat and with sampling; that is, with deconstructing sounds and songs to build new ones. Sample rap artists named by the children include MC Lyte, TLC, Tupac, and Yo Yo.

> *Gangsta rap*. A subcategory of rap music, featuring gritty themes like violence, sex, and drugs. Sometimes realistic, gangsta rap can also be a deliberate play with stereotypes and public fears.

Rock 'n' roll. Varieties of popular music that evolved in the mid 1950s from country and from rhythm and blues. It is usually characterized by strongly accented backbeats and youth-oriented lyrics.

Rhythm and blues (R & B). A style of African American popular music that combines elements of jazz and blues (which itself developed from African American work songs and calls and from protest songs). R & B began in the 1940s mainly as dance music and later became the basis for both rock 'n' roll and soul music. R & B lyrics usually reflect the complexities of urban life. It is also referred to as "race music." Among the R & B singers to whom the children referred are Mary J. Blige, R. J. Kelly, and Keith Sweat.

Soul. A label developed for rhythm and blues and gospel music in the United States in the 1960s and 70s. There were varied styles of soul rooted in varied regions of the country. In Detroit, for example, Motown music was bouncy, while Southern soul was heavier, sung in a wailing style but with marked rhythm.

Televised music show: Soul Train. A program created in 1970 targeting young African American viewers. During the project year, the program continued to offer music and dance from varied genres, among them R & B and rap.

SPORTS

Basketball. A game played by two opposing teams in which the object is to score as many points as possible by dribbling, passing, and ultimately shooting a ball down the court and into the opponent's basketball net.

> *Professional basketball teams*. Groups of professional athletes who play in the National Basketball Association (NBA). There are 29 teams in the NBA, divided among four geographical divisions: Atlantic, Central, Midwest, and Pacific Divisions. During the basketball season, which begins in October and ends in June, teams play approximately 82

games per season. The only team named by the children was the Chicago Bulls, whose star player, Michael Jordan, was featured in *Space Jam.*

Football. An American version of European soccer in which two opposing teams attempt to score points by passing, kicking, and running with a ball down the field into the opponent's goal area.

> *Professional football teams.* Groups of professional athletes play in the National Football League (NFL). There are currently 31 teams in the league. The NFL is divided into the American Football Conference (AFC) and the National Football Conference (NFC). Teams play against each other within the two separate divisions; the winner of each division plays in the Super Bowl to determine the best team in the country. Each team plays 16 games in a regular season. The professional football season begins in July and ends in January. The children named many teams. From the AFC, they named: Kansas City Chiefs; Miami Dolphins; Oakland Raiders; New York Jets; New England Patriots; and Jacksonville Jaguars. From the NFC, they named teams and selected players: Atlanta Falcons; Arizona Cardinals; Carolina Panthers; Chicago Bears; Dallas Cowboys (Emmet Smith, Michael Irvin, Dion Sanders); Green Bay Packers (Desmond Howard); Minnesota Vikings; New York Giants; Philadelphia Eagles; and San Francisco 49ers (Jerry Rice).

> *Televised football events. Monday Night Football* is a popular sports show featuring a weekly competition between two NFL teams. It is broadcast on ABC, a major television network, on Monday evenings so that viewers can watch after work. A *playoff game* is a game to help determine participants in the Super Bowl. After the regular season, the playoff season begins in December. The four best teams in each division (AFC and NFC) compete to become the division champion. The champions of each division then play one another in January in the Super Bowl.

(Ice) Hockey. A game played on ice in which two teams attempt to shoot a hockey puck into the opponent's cage. Professional athletes play in the National Hockey League (NHL), in which one team is named Mighty Ducks. However, the children's reference to Mighty Ducks indexed a cinematic team that first played in 1992. The Mighty Ducks professional team, formed in 1993, was the "first team to take its name from a movie" (Hollander, 2000, p. 188).

VIDEO

Nintendo. One version of Nintendo is a video game console that can be connected to the television while a smaller version, GameBoy, is hand-held. Both allow players to play individually or compete against one another on various Nintendo game cartridges such as Donkey Kong. Within this project, video game creatures are considered animated characters and are similar to cartoon characters.

References

Adams, M. (2001). Alphabetic anxiety and explicit, systematic phonics instruction. In S. B. Neuman & D. K. Dickinson (Eds.), *Handbook of early literacy research* (pp. 66–80). New York: Guildford.

Adewole-Jimenez, A., Adewole-Jimenez, D., & Ucelli, J. (1994). *Women, men, rap and respect: A dialogue. Rethinking Schools, 8,* 14–15.

Adger, C. T. (1998). Register shifting with dialect resources in instructional discourse. In S. Hoyle & C. T. Adger (Eds.), *Kids talk: Strategic language use in later childhood* (pp. 151–169). New York: Oxford University Press.

Allington, R. L. (1983). Teacher interruption behaviors during primary grade oral reading. *Journal of Educational psychology, 72*(3), 371–377.

Ammer, C. (1995). *The HarperCollins dictionary of music* (3rd Ed.). New York, NY: HarperPerennial.

Amut-Talia, V. (1995). Conclusion: The "multi" cultural of youth. In V. Amit-Talai & H. Wulff (Eds.), *Youth cultures: A cross-cultural perspective* (pp. 223–234). London: Routledge.

Ashton-Warner, S. (1963). *Teacher.* New York: Simon & Schuster.

Asimov, N. (1996, May 11). State approves return of phonics to schools. *The San Francisco Chronicle,* p. A1.

Bateson, G. (1956). The message "this is play." In B. Schaffner (Ed.), *Group processes.* New York: Macy.

Bakhtin, M. (1981). Discourse in the novel. In C. Emerson & M. Holquist (Eds.), *The dialogic imagination: Four essays by M. Bakhtin* (pp. 254–422). Austin: University of Texas Press.

Bakhtin, M. (1986). *Speech genres and other late essays.* Austin: University of Texas Press.

Bakhtin, M. (1990). Art and answerability. In M. Holquist & V. Liapunov (Eds.), *Art and answerability: Early philosophical essays by M. Bahktin* (pp. 1–3). Austin: University of Texas. (Original works published 1919–1986)

Barton, D. (1994). *Literacy: An introduction to the ecology of written language.* London: Blackwell.

Bauman, R. (Ed.). (1992). *Folklore, cultural performances, and popular entertainments: A communications-centered handbook.* New York: Oxford University Press.

Bauman, R., & Briggs, C. (1990). Poetics and performance as critical perspectives on language and social life. *Anthropological Review, 19,* 59–88.

Beaumont, C. J. (1999). Dilemmas of peer assistance in a bilingual full inclusion classroom. *Elementary School Journal, 99,* 233–254.

Beresin, A. R. (1995). Double dutch and double cameras: Studying the transmission of culture in an urban school yard. In B. Sutton-Smith, J. Mechling, T. W. Johnson, & F. R. McMahon (Eds.), *Children's folklore: A source book* (pp. 75–92). New York: Garland Publishing.

Bogden, R., & Biklen, S. (1998). *Qualitative research in education*, 3rd ed. Boston: Allyn & Bacon.

Borgenicht, D. (1998). *Sesame Street unpaved: Scripts, stories, secrets, and songs*. New York: Children's Television Workshop/Hyperion.

Bourdieu, P. (1977). *Outline of a theory of practice*. Cambridge: Cambridge University Press.

Bourdieu, P. (1984). *Distinction: A social critique of the judgment of taste* (R. Nice, Trans.). Cambridge, MA: Harvard University Press. (Original work published 1979)

Bramley, F. M. (1988). *Tornado alert*. New York: HarperCollins.

Bruner, J. (1986). *Actual minds, possible worlds*. Cambridge, MA: Harvard University Press.

Bruner, J. (1990). *Acts of meaning*. Cambridge, MA: Harvard University Press.

Bruner, J. (1996). *The culture of education*. Cambridge, MA: Harvard University Press.

Bruner, J., & Haste, H. (Eds.). (1987). *Making sense: The child's construction of the world*. New York: Methuen.

Buckingham, D. (1993). *Children talking television: The making of television literacy*. London: Falmer Press.

Bussis, A. M., Chittenden, E. A., Amarel, M., & Klausner, E. (1985). *Inquiry into meaning: An investigation of learning to read*. Hillsdale, NJ: Lawrence Erlbaum.

California Department of Education (1998). *Reading/language arts framework for California public schools*. Sacramento, CA: California Department of Education Press.

Caputo, V. (1995). Anthropology's silent "others": A consideration of some conceptual and methodological issues for the study of youth and children's cultures. In V. Amit-Talai & H. Wulff (Eds.), *Youth cultures: A cross-cultural perspective* (pp. 19–42). London: Routledge.

Cazden, C. (1988). *Classroom discourse: The language of teaching and learning*. Portsmouth, NH: Heinemann.

Cazden, C. (1992). *Whole language plus: Essays on literacy in the United States and Canada*. New York: Teachers College Press.

Cazden, C. (1999). The language of African American students in classroom discourse. In C. T. Adger, D. Christian, & O. Taylor (Eds.), *Making the connection: Language and academic achievement among African American students* (pp. 31–52). McHenry, IL: Center for Applied Linguistics and Delta Systems Co.

Cazden, C., John, V., & Hymes, D. (Eds.). (1972). *Functions of language in the classroom*. New York: Teachers College Press.

Chittenden, E., Salinger, T., with Bussis, A. (2001). *Inquiry into meaning: An investigation of learning to read* (Rev. ed.). New York: Teachers College Press.

Chomsky, C. (1971). Write now, read later. *Childhood Education, 47,* 296–299.

Christianakis, M. (2002). *Inside the digital divide: Children using computers to write.* Unpublished doctoral dissertation. University of California, Berkeley.

Clay, M. (1975). *What did I write?* Auckland, New Zealand: Heinemann.

Clay, M. (1979). *Reading: The patterning of complex behavior.* Auckland, New Zealand: Heinemann Educational Books.

Clay, M. (1991). *Becoming literate: the construction of inner control.* Portsmouth, NH: Heinemann.

Clay, M. (1998). *By different paths to common outcomes.* York, ME: Stenhouse.

Comber, B., Thomson, P., & Wells, M. (2001). Critical literacy finds a "place": Writing and social action in a low-income Australian grade 2/3. *Elementary School Journal, 101*, 451–464.

Cook, D. (Davey D) (1985). *The history of hip hop* [On-line]. Available: http://www.daveyd.com/whatiship.html.

Cooper, B. L. (1989). Rhythm 'N' rhymes: Character and theme images from children's literature in contemporary recordings, 1950–1985. *Popular Music and Society, 13*, 53–71.

Corsaro, W. (1985). *Friendship and peer culture in the early years.* Norwood, NJ: Ablex.

Daiute, C. (Ed.). (1993). *The development of literacy through social interaction.* San Francisco: Jossey-Bass.

Diegmueller, K. (1995, June 14). California plotting new tack on Language Arts. *Education Week*, pp. 1, 12.

Dore, J. (1989). Monologue as re-envoicement of dialogue. In K. Nelson (ed.), *Narratives from the crib* (pp. 231–262). Cambridge, MA: Harvard University Press.

Douglas, S. (1994). *Where the girls are: Growing up female with the mass media.* New York: Times Books.

Dreeben, R., & Barr, R. (1988). Classroom composition and the design of instruction. *Sociology of Education, 61*, 129–142.

Dyson, A. Haas. (1982). The emergence of visible language: Interrelationships between drawing and early writing. *Visible Language, 16*, 360–381.

Dyson, A. Haas. (1989). *Multiple worlds of child writers: Friends learning to write.* New York: Teachers College Press.

Dyson, A. Haas. (1993). *Social worlds of children learning to write in an urban primary school.* New York: Teachers College Press.

Dyson, A. Haas. (1995). Writing children: Reinventing the development of childhood literacy. *Written Communication, 12*, 3–46.

Dyson, A. Haas. (1997). *Writing superheroes: Contemporary childhood, popular culture, and classroom literacy.* New York: Teachers College Press.

Dyson, A. Haas, with A. Bennett et al. (1997). *What differences does difference make?: Teacher perspectives on diversity, literacy, and the urban primary school.* Urbana, IL: National Council of Teachers of English (NCTE).

Dyson, A. Haas. (1999). Transforming transfer: Unruly children, contrary texts, and the persistence of the pedagogical order. In A. Iran-Nejad & P. D. Pearson (Eds.), *Review of research in education: Vol. 24* (pp. 141–172). Washington, DC: American Educational Research Association (AERA).

Emerson, R., Fretz, R., & Shaw, L. (1995). *Writing ethnographic fieldnotes*. Chicago: University of Chicago Press.

Erickson, F. (1986). Qualitative methods in research on teaching. In M. Wittrock (Ed.), *Handbook of research on teaching* (3rd ed., pp. 119–161). Washington, CD: AERA.

Fillmore, L. W. (1976). *The second time around: Cognitive and social strategies in second language acquisition*. Unpublished doctoral dissertation, Stanford University, Palo Alto, California.

Fisherkeller, J. (1997). Everyday learning about identities among young adolescents in television culture. *Anthropology and Education Quarterly, 28,* 467–492.

Fisherkeller, J. (2002). *Growing up with television: Everyday life among urban adolescents*. Philadelphia: Temple University Press.

Freire, P. (1970). *Pedagogy of the oppressed*. New York: Continuum.

Gallas, K. (1994). *Languages of learning*. New York: Teachers College Press.

Garvey, C. (1990). *Play (enl. ed.)*. Cambridge, MA: Harvard University Press.

Gates, H. I. (1994). *Colored people: A memoir*. New York: Knopf.

Geertz, C. (1983). *Local knowledge*. New York: Basic Books.

Genishi, C. (1992). Looking forward: toward stories of theory and practice. In C. Genishi (Ed.), *Ways of assessing children and curriculum* (pp. 191–208). New York: Teachers College Press.

Genishi, C. (1997). *Representing children in educational research: Locating Asian-American children in and out of classrooms*. Paper presented at the annual convention of the American Educational Research Association, Chicago, IL.

Genishi, C., Stires, S., & D. Yung-Chan (2001). Writing in an integrated curriculum: Prekindergarten English language learners as symbol-makers. *Elementary School Journal,* 399–416.

George, N. (1998). *Hip hop America*. New York: Viking.

Gillmore, P. (1985). "Gimme room": School resistance, attitude and access to literacy. *Journal of Education, 167,* 111–127.

Goffman, E. (1981). *Forms of talk*. Philadelphia: University of Pennsylvania Press.

Goldman, L. R. (1998). *Child's play: Myth, mimesis, and make-believe*. London: Routledge.

Golomb, C. (1992). *The child's creation of a pictorial world*. Berkeley: University of California Press.

Goodman, N. (1968). *Languages of art: An approach to a theory of symbols*. Indianapolis, IN: Bobbs-Merrill.

Goodwin, D. K. (1997). *Wait till next year: A memoir*. New York: Simon & Schuster.

Gould, J. (1998). *Leonardo's mountain of clams and the diet of worms*. New York: Three Rivers Press.

Greene, M. (1995). *Releasing the imagination: Essays on education, the arts, and social change*. San Francisco: Jossey-Bass Publishers.

Greenfield, E. (1978). *Honey, I love*. New York: Harper & Row.

Greenfield, E. (1988). *Under the Sunday tree*. New York: Harper & Row.

Greenfield, E. (1989). *Nathaniel talking*. New York: Black Butterfly Children's Books.

Greenfield, E. (1997). *For the love of the game: Michael Jordan and Me*. New York: HarperCollins.

Greenfield, E., & Little, L. J. (1979). *Childtimes: A three-generation memoir*. New York: Crowell.

Gunnison, R. (1996, December 13). State rejects 2 texts, citing phonics law. *San Francisco Chronicle*, p. A1.

Hall, S. (1981). Notes on deconstructing the popular. In R. Samuel (Ed.), *People's history and socialist theory* (pp. 227–239). London: Routledge & Kegan Paul.

Hall, S. (1992). What is this "black" in black popular culture? In G. Dent (Ed.), *Black popular culture* (pp. 21–33). Seattle: Bay Press.

Halliday, M. A. K. (1980). Three aspects of children's language development: Learning language, learning through language, learning about language. In Y. Goodman & D. Strickland (Eds.), *Oral and written language development research: Impact on schools* (pp. 9–19). Urbana, IL: International Reading Association.

Hanks, W. F. (1996). *Language and communicative practices*. Boulder, CO: Westview Press.

Hanks, W. F. (2000). *Intertexts : Writings on language, utterance, and context*. Lanham, MD: Rowman & Littlefield.

Harris, V. (Ed.). (1992). *Teaching multicultural literature in grades K-8*. Norwood, MA: Christopher Gordon.

Harris, V. (Ed.). (1997). *Using multiethnic literature in the K-8 classroom*. Norwood, MA: Christopher Gordon.

Heath, S. B. (1983). *Ways with words: Language, life and work in communities and classrooms*. Cambridge, England: Cambridge University Press.

Hollander, Z. (Ed.). (2000). *Hockey almanac 2000: The complete guide*. Farmington, MI: Visible Ink Press.

Holquist, M. (1990). *Dialogism: Bakhtin and his world*. London: Routledge.

Hoyle, S. (1989). Forms and footings in boys' sportscasting. *Text, 9*, 153–173.

Hoyle, S. M., & Adger, C. T. (1998). *Kids talk: Strategic language use in later childhood*. New York: Oxford University Press.

Hudelson, S. (1994). Literacy development of second language children. In F. Genesee (Ed.), *Educating second language children: The whole child, the whole curriculum, and the whole community* (129–158). New York: Cambridge University Press.

Hymes, D. (1972). Models of the interaction of language and social life. In J. J. Gumperz & D. Hymes (Eds.), *Directions in sociolinguistics* (pp. 35–71). New York: Holt, Rinehart & Winston.

Hymes, D. (1975). Breakthrough into performance. In D. Ben Amos & K. Goldstein (Eds.), *Performance and communication* (pp. 11–74). The Hague: Mouton.

James, A. (1995). Talking of children and youth: language, socialization, and culture. In V. Amit-Talai & H. Wulff (Eds.), *Youth cultures: A cross-cultural perspective* (pp. 43–62). London: Routledge.

Jenkins, H. (1988). "Going Bonkers!": Children, play and Pee-wee. *Camera Obscura, 17*, 169–193.

Jenkins, H. (1992). *Textual poachers: Television fans and participatory culture.* New York: Routledge.

Jones, B., & Hawes, B. L. (1972). *Step it down: Games, plays, songs, and stories from the Afro-American heritage.* New York: Harper & Row.

Joosse, B. M. (1991). *Mama, do you love me?* San Francisco, CA: Chronicle Books.

Kenan, R. (1994). Hobbits and hobgoblins. In W. H. Shore (Eds.), *Writers harvest* (pp. 13–23). New York: Harcourt Brace.

Kessen, W. (1979). The American child and other cultural inventions. *American Psychologist, 34,* 815–820.

Kinder, M. (1991). *Playing with power in movies, television, and video games: From muppet babies to teenage mutant ninja turtles.* Berkeley, CA: University of California Press.

King, M., & Rentel, V. (1981). *How children learn to write: A longitudinal study.* Report to the National Institute of Education. Columbus, OH: Ohio State University.

Kline, S. (1993). *Out of the garden: Toys, TV, and children's culture in the age of marketing.* London: Verso.

Koch, K. (1998). *Making your own days: The pleasure of reading and writing poems.* New York: Scribner.

Kress, G. (1997). *Before writing: Rethinking the paths to literacy.* London: Routledge.

Laden, N. (1994). *The night I followed the dog.* San Francisco: Chronicle Books.

Lave, J., & Wenger, E. (1991). *Situated learning: Legitimate peripheral participation.* Cambridge, England: Cambridge University Press.

Lee, C. (2001). Signifying in the zone of proximal development. In C. Lee & P. Smagorinsky (Eds.), *Vygotskian perspectives on literacy research* (pp. 191–225). Cambridge, England: Cambridge University Press.

Leonard, H. (1993). *Pocket music dictionary.* Milwaukee, WI: Hal Leonard Publishing Cooperation.

Levin, D. E. (1998). *Remote control childhood? Combating the hazards of media culture.* Washington, DC: National Association for the Education of Young Children.

Levin, S. (1988). *Highbrow/Lowbrow: The emergence of cultural hierarchy in America.* Cambridge, MA: Harvard University Press.

Levinson, B., & Holland, D. (1996). The cultural production of the educated person: An introduction. In B. A. Levinson, D. E. Foley, & D. C. Holland (Eds.), *The cultural production of the educated person: Critical ethnographies of schooling and local practice* (pp. 1–56). Albany, NY: State University of New York Press.

Liljestrom, R. (1981). The public child, the commercial child, and our child. In F. S. Kessel & A. W. Siegal (Eds.), *The child and other cultural inventions* (pp. 124–152). New York: Praeger.

Luke, A., & Luke, C. (2001). Adolescents lost/childhood regained: On early intervention and the emergence of the techno-subject. *Journal of Early Childhood Literacy, 1*(1), 91–120.

Manzo, K. K. (1997, January 15). California text adoption puts emphasis on phonics, *Education Week, 12.*

Marsh, J. (1999). Batman and Batwoman go to school: Popular culture in the literacy curriculum. *International Journal of Early Years Education, 7,* pp. 117–131.

Marsh, J., & Millard, E. (2000). *Literacy and popular culture.* London: Sage.

Marshall, E. (1980). *Space case.* New York: Dial Books.

Massey, D. (1998). The spatial construction of youth cultures. In T. Skelton & G. Valentine (Eds.), *Cool places: Geographies of youth cultures* (pp. 121–129). London: Routledge.

Maultsby, P. (1995). The evolution of African American music. *African American Review, 29,* 183–184.

McDowell, J. (1995). The transmission of children's folklore. In B. Sutton-Smith, J. Mechling, T. W. Johnson, & F. R. McMahon (Eds.), *Children's folklore: A source book* (pp. 293–308). New York: Garland Publishing.

Miller, P. (1982). *Amy, Wendy, and Beth: Learning language in South Baltimore.* Austin: University of Texas Press.

Miller, P., & Goodnow, J. J. (1995). Cultural practices: Toward an integration of culture and development. In J. J. Goodnow, P. J. Miller, & F. Kessel (Eds.), *Cultural practices as contexts for development, No. 67, New directions in child development* (pp. 5–16). San Francisco: Jossey-Bass.

Miller, P. J., Hoogstra, L., Mintz, J., Fung, H., & Williams, K. (1993). Troubles in the garden and how they get resolved: A young child's transformation of his favorite story. In C. A. Nelson (Eds.), *Memory and affect in development: Minnesota symposium on child psychology* (Vol. 26, pp. 87–114). Hillsdale, NJ: Erlbaum.

Miller, P., & Mehler, R. (1994). The power of personal storytelling in families and kindergartens. In A. H. Dyson & C. Genishi (Eds.), *The need for story: Cultural diversity in classroom and community* (pp. 38–56). Urbana, IL: NCTE.

Minarik, E. H. (1957). *Little Bear.* New York: Harper & Row.

Moll, L., & Whitmore, K. (1993). Vygotsky in classroom practice: Moving from individual transmission to social transaction. In E. Forman, N. Minick, & C. A. Stone (Eds.), *Contexts for learning: Sociocultural dynamics in children's development* (pp. 19–42). New York: Oxford University Press.

Mukerji, C., & Schudson, M. (1991). *Rethinking popular culture: Contemporary perspectives in cultural studies.* Berkeley, CA: University of California Press.

Narvaez, P., & Laba, M. (1986). The folklore-popular culture continuum. In P. Narvaez, & M. Laba (Eds.), *Media sense: The folklore-popular culture continuum* (pp. 1–8). Bowling Green, OH: Bowling Green State University Popular Press.

Nelson, K. (1996). *Language in cognitive development: The emergence of the mediated mind.* Cambridge, England: Cambridge University Press.

New London Group, The. (1996). A pedagogy of multiliteracies: Designing social futures. *Harvard Educational Review, 61,* 60–92.

Nieto, S. (1999). *The light in their eyes: Creating multicultural learning communities.* New York: Teachers College Press.

Nystrand, M., & Graff, N. (2001). Report in argument's clothing: Ecological perspective on writing instruction in a seventh-grade classroom. *Elementary School Journal, 101,* 479–493.

Opie, I., & Opie, P. (1959). *The lore and language of school children.* London: Oxford University Press.

Osumare, H. (1999). *African aesthetics, American culture: Hip hop in the global era.* Unpublished manuscript.

Pahl, K. (1999). *Transformations: Meaning making in nursery education.* London: Trentham.

Paley, V. (1980). *Wally's stories.* Cambridge, MA: Harvard University Press.

Paley, V. (1986). *Mollie is three: Growing up in school.* Chicago: University of Chicago Press.

Perry, T., & Delpit, L. (1998). *The real Ebonics debates: Power, language, and the education of African-American children.* Boston: Beacon Press.

Philips, S. (1972). Participant structures and communicative competence: Warm springs children in community and classroom. In C. B. Cazden, V. P. John, & D. Hymes (Eds.), *The functions of language in the classroom* (pp. 370–394). New York: Teachers College Press.

Philips, S. (1975). Literacy as a mode of communication on the Warm Springs Indian Reservation. In E. H. Lenneberg & E. Lenneberg (Eds.), *Foundations of language development* (pp. 367–381). New York: Academic Press, and Paris: UNESCO.

Piestrup, A. (1973). *Black dialect interference and accomodation of reading instruction in first grade.* Berkeley, CA: University of California, Language-Behavior Research Laboratory.

Purcell-Gates, V. (1995). *Other people's words: The cycle of low literacy.* Cambridge, MA: Harvard University Press.

Ramsey, P. (1991). *Making friends in school: Promoting peer relationships in early childhood.* New York: Teachers College Press.

Read, C. (1975). *Children's categorization of speech sounds in English.* Urbana, IL: NCTE.

Reyes, M. de la Luz, & Halcon, J. J. (Eds.). (2001). *The best for our children: Critical perspectives on literacy for Latino students.* New York: Teachers College Press.

Richgels, D. (2001). Invented spelling, phonemic awareness, and reading and writing instruction. In S. B. Neuman & D. K. Dickinson (Eds.), *Handbook of early literacy research* (pp. 142–158). New York: Guildford.

Ringgold, F. (1992). *Aunt Harriet's underground railroad in the sky.* New York: Crown.

Rizzo, T. A. (1989). *Friendship development among children in school.* Norwood, NJ: Ablex.

Rogoff, B. (1990). *Apprenticeship in thinking: Cognitive development in social context.* New York: Oxford University Press.

Rose, T. (1989). Orality and technology: Rap music and Afro-American cultural resistance. *Popular Music and Society, 13,* 35–44.

Rose, T. (1994). *Black noise: Rap music and black culture in contemporary America.* Hanover, NH: University Press of New England.

Rosen, S. (1992). *Which way to the milky way?* Minneapolis: Carolrhoda Books.

Roy, A. (1997). *The god of small things: A novel.* New York: Random House.

Rubin, B. (2001). *Detracking in practice: Students negotiating race, friendship, and competence in daily classroom life.* Unpublished doctoral dissertation, University of California, Berkeley.

Schutz, A. (1970). *On phenomenology and social relations.* Chicago: University of Chicago Press.

Scott, J. (1998). The serious side of Ebonics humor. *Journal of English Linguistics,* *26,* 137–155.

Seiter, E. (1993). *Sold separately: Children and parents in consumer culture.* New Brunswick, NJ: Rutgers University Press.

Seiter, E. (1998). *Television and new media audiences.* Oxford, England: Clarendon Press.

Shuker, R. (1998). *Key concepts in popular music.* New York: Routledge.

Sims, R. (1982). *Shadow and substance: Afro-American experience in contemporary children's fiction.* Urbana, IL: National Council of Teachers of English.

Smith, B. (1943). *A tree grows in Brooklyn.* New York: Harper & Brothers.

Smitherman, G. (1981). What go round come round: King in perspective. *Harvard Educational Review, 51,* 40–46.

Smitherman, G. (1986). *Talkin and testifyin: The language of Black America.* Detroit, MI: Wayne State University Press.

Smitherman, G. (1994). *Black talk: Words and phrases from the hood to the Amen Corner.* Boston: Houghton Mifflin.

Smitherman, G. (2000). *Talkin that talk: Language, culture, and education in African America.* New York: Routledge.

Snow, C., Burns, S., & Griffin, P. (Eds.). (1998). *Preventing reading difficulties in young children.* Washington, DC: National Academy Press.

Spigel, L. (1998). Seducing the innocent: Childhood and television in postwar America. In H. Jenkins (Ed.), *The children's culture reader* (pp. 110–135). New York: New York University Press.

Spigel, L., & Jenkins, H. (1991). Same bat channel, different bat times: Mass culture and popular memory. In R. Pearson & W. Uricchio (Eds.), *The many lives of the Batman* (pp. 117–148). New York: Routledge.

Steedman, C. (1992). *Past tenses: Essays on writing autobiography and history.* Concord, MA: Paul & Co.

Steele, C. (1992, April). Race and the schooling of Black Americans. *The Atlantic Monthly,* 68–78.

Stephens, S. (Ed.). (1995). *Children and the politics of culture.* Princeton: Princeton University Press.

Stern, S., & Schoenhaus, T. (1990). *Toyland: The high-stakes game of the toy industry.* Chicago: Contemporary Books.

Stewart, S. (1979). *Nonsense: Aspects of intertextuality in folklore and literature.* Baltimore: Johns Hopkins University Press.

Storey, J. (1998). *An introductory guide to cultural theory and popular culture* (2nd ed.). Athens: The University of Georgia Press.

Stratemeyer, E. (1930). *Nancy Drew mystery stories.* New York: Grosset & Dunlap.

Sutton-Smith, B. (1995). Introduction: What is children's folklore? In B. Sutton-Smith, J. Mechling, T. W. Johnson, & F. R. McMahon (Eds.), *Children's folklore: A source book* (pp. 3–9). New York: Garland Publishing.

Sutton-Smith, B. (1997). *The ambiguity of play.* Cambridge, MA: Harvard University Press.

Sutton-Smith, B., Mechling, J., Johnson, T. W., & McMahon, F. R. (Eds.). (1995). *Children's folklore: A source book.* New York: Garland Publishing.

Tannen, D. (1989). *Talking voices: Repetition, dialogue, and imagery in conversational discourse.* Cambridge, England: Cambridge University Press.

Taylor, D. (1998). *Beginning to read and the spin doctors of science: The political campaign to change America's mind about how children learn to read.* Urbana, IL: NCTE.

Valenzuela, A. (1999). *Subtractive schooling: U.S.-Mexican youth and the politics of caring.* Albany: State University of New York Press.

Varnedoe, K., & Gopnik, A. (1991). Introduction. In K. Varnedoe & A. Gopnik (Eds.), *Modern art and popular culture: Readings in high and low* (pp. 10–17). New York: The Museum of Modern Art & Abrams.

Vasquez, V. (2001). Constructing a critical curriculum with young children. In B. Comber & A. Simpson (Eds.), *Negotiating critical literacies in classrooms* (pp. 55–68). Mahwah, NJ: Erlbaum.

Vasquez, O., Pease-Alvarez, L., & Shannon, S. (1994). *Pushing boundaries: Language and culture in a Mexicano community.* New York: Cambridge University Press.

Vygotsky, L. S. (1962). *Thought and language.* Cambridge, MA: MIT Press.

Vygotsky, L. S. (1978). *Mind in society.* Cambridge, MA: Harvard University Press.

Vygotsky, L. S. (1987). *L. S. Vygotsky, collected works: Volume 1, Problems of general psychology.* New York: Plenum Books.

Walkerdine, V. (1997). *Daddy's girl: Young girls and popular culture.* Boston: Harvard University Press.

Walker-Moffat, W. (1995). *The other side of the Asian American success story.* San Francisco: Jossey-Bass Publishers.

Wartofsky, M. (1983). The child's construction of the world and the world's construction of the child: From historical epistemology to historical psychology. In F. S. Kessel & A. W. Siegal (Eds.), *The child and other cultural inventions* (pp. 188–215). New York: Praeger.

Watney, S. (1994). Remix generation. *Art forum International, 33,* 15–16.

Watson, R. (2001). Literacy and oral language: Implications for early literacy acquisition. In S. B. Neuman & D. K. Dickinson (Eds.), *Handbook of early literacy research* (pp. 43–53). New York: Guildford.

Watson-Gegeo, K. (1992). Thick explanation in the ethnographic study of child socialization. In W. Corsaro & P. J. Miller (Eds.), *Interpretive approaches to children's socialization, No. 58, New Directions for Child Development* (pp. 51–66). San Francisco: Jossey-Bass.

Weiner, L. (2000). Research in the 90s: Implications for urban teacher preparation. *Review of Educational Research, 70,* 369–406.

Welty, E. (1983). *One writer's beginning.* Cambridge, MA: Harvard University Press.

Werner, H., & Kaplan, B. (1963). *Symbol formation: An organismic-developmental approach to language and the expression of thought.* New York: Wiley.

Wertsch, J. V. (1989). A sociocultural approach to mind. In W. Damon (Ed.), *Child development today and tomorrow* (pp. 14–33). San Francisco: Jossey-Bass.

Whiting, B. B., & Whiting, J. W. M. (1975). *Children of six cultures: A psycho-cultural analysis.* Cambridge, MA: Harvard University Press.

Williams, R. (1965). *The long revolution.* Harmondsworth, England: Penguin.

Williams, R. (1983). *Keywords* (Rev. ed). New York: Oxford University Press.

Willis, P. (1990). *Common culture: Symbolic work at play in the everyday culture of the young*. Boulder, CO: Westview Press.

Wolf, S. A., & Heath, S. B. (1992). *The braid of literature: Children's worlds of reading*. Cambridge, MA: Harvard University Press.

Yerba Buena Center for the Arts. (2001). *Hip hop nation: A teacher's guide*. San Francisco: Yerba Buena Center for the Performing Arts.

Zipes, J. (2000). *The reconfiguration of children and children's literature in the culture industry*. Unpublished paper.

Zumwalt, R. (1995). The complexity of children's folklore. In B. Sutton-Smith, J. Mechling, 1. W. Johnson, & F. R. McMahon (Eds.), *Children's folklore: A source book* (pp. 23–47). New York: Garland Publishing.

Media Bibliography

In the following lists, movies, television programs, and video games are listed by title in that order; brief commentaries are provided for media productions that were central to classroom episodes analyzed in this book. Song references are then provided, organized by singer, as children typically named singers, not song titles.

MOVIES

101 Dalmatians. Feldman, E., Hughes, J., Mestres, R., & Rudd, R. (Producers), & Herek, S. (Director). (1996). Burbank, CA: Buena Vista Pictures.

Big Bully. Barber, G., & Sellers, D. (Executive Producers), & Miner, D. (Director). (1996). Burbank, CA: Warner Brothers.

Blank Check. Synder, B., Wayne, H. (Producers), & Wainwright, R. (Director). (1994). Burbank, CA: Buena Vista Pictures.

Booty Call. Eckert, J., Morrissey, J., & Turman, L. (Producers), & Pollock, J. (Director). (1997). Culver City, CA: Columbia Pictures.

The Buena Vista Social Club. Cooder, R. (Producer), & Wenders, W. (Director). (1999). Santa Monica, CA: Artisan Entertainment.

The Color Purple. Guber, P., Peters, J. (Producers), & Spielberg, S. (Director). (1985). Burbank, CA: Warner Brothers.

Harriet the Spy. Beece, D. (Producer), & Hughes, B. (Director). (1996). Los Angeles, CA: Paramount Pictures.

Honey, We Shrunk Ourselves. Bernardi, B. (Producer), & Cundey, D. (Director). (1997). Burbank, CA: Buena Vista Pictures.

The Hunchback of Notre Dame. Colin, R., Hahn, D. (Producers), Trousdale, G., & Wise, K. (Directors). (1996). Burbank, CA: Buena Vista Pictures.

Independence Day. Emmerich, R., Emmerich, U., Fay, W. (Executive Producers), & Emmerich, R. (Director). (1996). Burbank, CA: Twentieth Century Fox Film Cooperation.

Jurassic Park. Kennedy, K., Molen, G. R. (Producers), & Spielberg, S. (Director). (1993). Universal City, CA: Universal Pictures.

All lists were prepared by Soyoung Lee and Sheila Shea.

Kazaam. Armato, L., Cort, R., Field, T., & O'Neal, S. (Executive Producers), & Glaser, P. (Director). (1996). Burbank, CA: Buena Vista Pictures.

Little Giants. Molen, G., Parkes, W., & Schmidt, A. (Producers), & Dunham, D. (Director). (1994). Burbank, CA: Warner Brothers/Amblin Entertainment.

Lost World: The Jurassic Park. Kennedy, K., Molen, G. R., Wilson, C. (Executive Producers), & Spielberg, S. (Director). (1997). Universal City, CA: Universal Pictures.

Lion King. Hahn, D., McArthur, S., Schmidt, A. (Producers), Allelers, R., & Minkoff, R. (Directors). (1994). Burbank, CA: Walt Disney Pictures.

Mars Attacks. Burton, T., Franco, L. (Producers), & Burton, T. (Director). (1996). Burbank, CA: Warner Brothers Studios.

Matilda. Bregman, M., Peyser, M. (Producers), & De Vito, D. (Director). (1996). Burbank, CA: Sony Pictures Entertainment.

Mighty Ducks. Avnet, J., & Kerner, J. (Producers), & Herek, S. (Director). (1992). Burbank, CA: Walt Disney Pictures.

D2: The Mighty Ducks. Avnet, J., Claybourne, D., Kerner, J. (Producers), & Weisman, S. (Director). (1994). Burbank, CA: Walt Disney Pictures.

The Mighty Ducks movies were key sources of children's play material. They feature Coach Bombay, a young, White former prohockey player and lawyer. In the first movie, Coach Bombay leads a peewee hockey team in Minnesota. In the second, explicitly referenced by the children, Bombay coaches "Team USA" at the Junior Goodwill Games in Los Angeles; the team is largely the old Mighty Ducks. In addition, a local L. A. "street hockey" team is featured. In both movies, Coach and team learn lessons about cooperation and fair play. Although the Mighty Ducks are mainly [but not exclusively] male and White, Wenona identified with "Julie-the-Cat," a female team member in D2.

Pocahontas. Pentecost, J. (Producer), Gabriel, M., & Goldberg, E. (Directors). (1995). Burbank, CA: Buena Vista Pictures.

Return of the Jedi. Lucas, G. (Producer), & Marquand, R. (Director). (1983). Burbank, CA: Twentieth Century Fox Film Corporation.

Sister Act. Schwartz, T., Rudin, S. (Producers), & Ardolino, E. (Director). (1992). Burbank, CA: Buena Vista Pictures.

Sister Act 2: Back in the Habit. Steel, D., & Rudin, S., Iscovich, M., Mark, L. (Producers), & Duke, B. (Director). (1994). Burbank, CA: Buena Vista Pictures.

Space Jam. Falk, D., Ross, K. (Executive Producers), & Pytka, J. (Director). (1996). Burbank, CA: Warner Brothers.

Space Jam was the most referenced movie during the project year, perhaps because it combines animation, sports, and music, the latter two featuring African American stars. In the film, basketball great Michael Jordan winds up on the "Toon Squad," a basketball team formed by Bugs Bunny with the other Looney Tunes. They play against the unruly space aliens, Nerdlucks, the peons of the vicious tycoon Swackhammer, owner of a theme park down on its luck. The Nerdlucks, initially diminutive, steal the basketball talent of NBA stars and become the unprincipled "Monstars." If the Tune Squad loses to the Monstars in the big game, the Looney Tunes are to become Swackhammer's slaves, forced to entertain the alien masses. Of course, they do not lose, especially with Jordan's animation-enhanced powers. Accompanying the movie's action is a hip-hop and R & B score, including "I Believe I Can Fly" [Kelly, 1996], a favorite group song of the brothers and sisters.

Star Wars. Kurtz, G., Lucas, G. (Producers), & Lucas, G. (Director). (1977). Burbank, CA: Twentieth Century Fox Film Cooperation.

Toy Story. Arnold, B., Catmull, E., Guggenheim, R., Jobs, S. (Producers), & Lasseter, J. (Director). (1995). Burbank, CA: Buena Vista Pictures.

Turbo: A Power Rangers Movie. Levy, S., & Saban, H., Tzachor, J. (Producers), & Levy, S., Winning, D. (Directors). (1997). Los Angeles, CA: Twentieth Century Fox Film Corporation.

TELEVISION PROGRAMS

All That. Donatelli, N., Robbins, R., Rosen, A., Tollin, M. (Producers). (1995). Orlando, FL: Nickelodeon Studios.

Barney. Leach, S. (1988). Richardson, TX: Lyons Group.
This show was considered definite "preschool" material by the children. The show features a jolly and loving purple dinosaur named Barney; he shares a classroom with young humans who join him for songs, rhymes, and stories.

The Brady Bunch. Arnod, J., Baldwin, P. (Director), & Schwartz, S. (Executive Producer). (1969). New York: American Broadcasting Corporation.

Captain Planet and the Planeteers. Heyward, A., & London, R. (Executive Producers). (1990). Atlanta, GA: Turner Broadcasting.

Godzilla. Wildey, D. (Producer), & Patterson, R., Urbano, C., Dufau, O., & Gordon, G. (Directors). (1978). Hollywood, CA: Hanna Barbera Production.
Noah especially appropriated from this animated version of Godzilla, in which the former monster is a kindly superhero who rescues a crew of humans from varied evil beasts.

Goosebumps. Protocol Entertainment (Producer), & Stine, R. L. (Creator). (1996) Beverly Hills, CA: Fox Television.

Hey Arnold. Snee-Oosh Inc. (Producers) & Bartlett, C. (Creator). (1996). Orlando, FL: Nickelodeon Studios.

Martin. Bowman, J., Carew, T., Lawrence, M., & Williams, S. (Executive Producers). (1992). Universal City, CA: Universal Studios/You Go Boy Productions.

The Mighty Morphin' Power Rangers. Levy, S., & Saban, H. (Executive Producers). (1993). New York, NY: Saban Entertainment.

The Mighty Morphin' Power Rangers Zeo. Bronaugh, V., Florentine, I., Radler, R., & Sloan, D. (Directors). (1996). Beverly Hills, CA: Fox Television.

Moesha. Finney, S. V., & Spears, V. (Producers). (1996). Los Angeles, CA: Sunset Gower Studios/United Paramount Network (UPN).

Mortal Kombat. Kasanoff, L., & Roman, P. (Executive Producers). (1995). Los Angeles, CA: New Line Cinema.

Muppet Babies. Hanson, J. (Producer). (1984). Hollywood, CA: Jim Hanson Productions.

New Tom and Jerry Show, The. Barbera, J., & Hanna, W. (Executive Producers). (1975). New York, NY: American Broadcasting Corporation.

Ninja Turtles. Wolf, F. (Producer). (1987). Los Angeles, CA: Eyemark Entertainment.
Sesame Street. Singer, D. (Producer), & Stone, J. (Director). (1969). Alexandria, VA: Public Broadcasting Service.

> *Like* Barney, *this is a show directed at preschoolers; it features varied puppets who sing, dance, and negotiate daily life on Sesame Street with varied human neighbors. The songs associated with this show, like the character Ernie's "Rubber Ducky"* [Moss, 1970], *could be sung without ridicule by the children, unlike those of* Barney.

Sky King. Jack Chertok Productions. (1951). Burbank, CA: National Broadcasting Corporation Studios.

> *This was my childhood pleasure, not that of the brothers and sisters.*

Soul Train. Cornelius, D. (Producer & Creator). (1970). Chicago: WCIU-TV.

> *See music section of glossary.*

Space Cases. David, P., & Mumy, B. (Creators), & Bell, J., Blyth, J., & Hanus, O. (Directors). (1996). Orlando, FL: Nickelodeon Television.
Superman. Burnett, A., Dini, P., & Timm, B. (Producers). (1996). Burbank, CA: The WB Network.
Two Stupid Dogs. Potamkin, B. (Producer). (1993). Hollywood, CA: Hanna-Barbera Productions.

VIDEO GAMES

Donkey Kong Country, Donkey Kong Country 2, Donkey Kong Country 3. Stamper, T. (Creator). (1986). Redmond, WA: Nintendo of America Inc.

> *See Chapter 5 for description.*

SONGS

Barney. (1993). Lee Bernstein. (Writer). I love you. On *Barney's favorites Vol. 1* [CD]. Richardson, TX: Lyons Partnership.
Blackstreet. (1996). Fix. On *Another level* [CD]. Los Angeles: Interscope Records.
Blackstreet. (1996). I wanna be your man. On *Another level* [CD]. Los Angeles: Interscope Records.
Blige, Mary J. (1994). I'm goin' down. On *My life.* [CD]. London: Uptown Records.
Blige, Mary J. (1992). My love. On *What's the 411?* [CD]. Universal City, CA: Uni/MCA Records.
Brandy. (1994). Best friend. On *Brandy* [CD]. New York: Atlantic Records.
B Rock and the Biz. (1997). My baby daddy. On *My baby daddy* [CD]. New York: Bad Boy Entertainment.
Brown, James. (1971). I got you (I feel good). On *Love, power, peace: Live at the Olympia, Paris, 1971* [Record]. New York, NY: Polygram Records Inc. (Original work published 1965)
Coolio. (1995). Gangsta's paradise. On *Gangsta's paradise* [CD]. New York: Tommy Boy Music Inc.

Day, B. (1958). Rock-in robin. On *Rock-in robin* [Record]. Los Angeles: Class Records.

Goldberg, W. (1994). If you want to be somebody. On soundtrack for D. Steel et al. *Sister Act 2* [film].

Hill, Dru. (1996). In my bed. On *Dru Hill* [CD]. New York: Island Records.

Hyland, Brian. (1994). Itsy bitsy teenie weenie yellow polka dot bikini. On *Brian Hyland's big hits* [CD]. Universal City, CA: MCA Records. (Original work published 1960)

Jackson 5, The. (1971a). ABC. On *Greatest hits, Jackson Five* [Record]. New York, NY: Motown Record Company.

Jackson 5, The. (1971b). Rockin robin. On *Greatest hits, Jackson Five*. [Record]. New York, NY: Motown Record Company.

Kelly, R. (1995). Step in my room. On *R Kelly* [CD]. Chicago, IL: Jive Records.

Kelly, R. (1996). I believe I can fly. On *Space jam* [CD]. New York: Atlantic Records.

Luke. (1994). It's your birthday. On *Freak for life* [CD]. Liberty City, FL: Luke Records, Inc.

Makaveli. (1996). Hail Mary. On *The 7 day theory* [CD]. Beverly Hills, CA: Death Row/Interscope Records.

Mase. (1997). Lookin' at me. On *Lookin' at me* [CD]. New York: Arista Records.

MC Lyte. (1998). In my business. On *Seven & seven*. [CD]. New York: Elecktra Entertainment.

MC Lyte. (1996). Cold rock a party. On *Bad as I wanna b* [CD]. New York: Elecktra Entertainment.

MJG. (1992). That girl. On *No more glory* [CD]. New York, NY: Universal Music and Video Distribution, Inc.

Moss, J. (1970). Rubber duckie. New York: Festival Attractions/American Society of Composers, Authors and Publishers.
Children heard on Sesame St.

Notorious B. I. G. (1997a). Going back to Cali. On *Life after death* [CD]. New York: Artista Records.

Notorious B. I. G. (1997b). Hypnotize. On *Life after death* [CD]. New York, NY: Artista Records.

Pointer Sisters. (1982). I'm so excited. On *So excited* [album]. New York: Planet Records.

Quad City DJs. (1996). Space jam. On *Space jam* [CD]. New York: Atlantic Records.

Queen. (1986). We are the champions. On *Queen: Live at Wembley 86* [record]. Burbank, CA: Hollywood Records.

Raposo, J. (1973). C is for cookie. Milwaukee, WI: Jonnico Music Inc./Hal Leonard Cooperation.
Children heard on Sesame St.

Ray, J. (1997). Everything you want. On *Everything you want* [CD]. New York: WE/Elecktra Entertainment.

Rose, Betsy. (1990). Mother earth. On *Sacred ground* [CD]. El Cerrito, CA: Kaleidoscope Records.

Sister Sledge. (1979). We are family. On *We are family* [CD]. Los Angeles: Rhino Records.
The children associated this song with Whoopi Goldberg from the movie Sister Act 2.
Sweat, Keith. (1996). Nobody. On *Keith Sweat* [CD]. New York: Elecktra Entertainment Group.
Sweet Honey in the Rock. (1994). *Freedom lives.* On *I got shoes* [CD]. Redway, CA: Music for Little People.
SWV. (1997). Can we? In *Release some tension* [CD]. New York: RCA Records.
Turner, Tina. (1983). What's love got to do with it. On *Private Dancer* [CD]. Hollywood, CA: Capitol Records.
Westside Connection. (1996). (Ice Cube, WC, and Mack 10: Artists) Gangsters make the world go round. On *Bow down.* [CD]. Los Angeles: Priority Records.
Xscape. (1995). Who can I run to. On *Off the hook* [CD]. New York: Columbia Records.
Yoyo (and MC Lyte). (1996). One for the cuties. On *Total control* [CD]. Beverley Hills, CA: Elecktra Entertainment.

Index

About the Author

Anne Haas Dyson is a professor in the literacy program of the College of Education at Michigan State University. During the writing of this book, she was a professor of language, literacy, and culture in the School of Education at the University of California, Berkeley, where she received Berkeley's Distinguished Teaching Award. A former teacher of young children, she studies the social lives and literacy learning of school-children. Among her publications are *The Need for Story: Cultural Diversity in Classroom and Community* (coedited with Celia Genishi), *Multiple Worlds of Child Writers: Friends Learning to Write, Social Worlds of Children Learning to Write in an Urban Primary School* (which was awarded NCTE's David Russell Award for Distinguished Research), and *Writing Superheroes: Contemporary Childhood, Popular Culture, and Classroom Literacy.*